Ethnic Americans

Ethnic Americans

A History of Immigration

FIFTH EDITION

LEONARD DINNERSTEIN

AND

DAVID M. REIMERS

Columbia University Press   *New York*

Columbia University Press
Publishers Since 1893
New York   Chichester, West Sussex
Copyright © 2009 Columbia University Press

Library of Congress Cataloging-in-Publication Data
Dinnerstein, Leonard.
Ethnic Americans : a history of immigration /
Leonard Dinnerstein and David M. Reimers. — 5th ed.
p.   cm.
Includes bibliographical references and index.
ISBN 978–0–231–14336–3 (cloth : alk. paper) —
ISBN 978–0–231–14337–0 (pbk. : alk. paper) — ISBN 978–0–231–51270–1 (ebook)
1. United States—Ethnic relations. 2. Ethnology—United States.
3. United States—Emigration and immigration. 4. Americanization. 5. Immigrants—
United States—History. 6. United States—Emigration and immigration—
Social aspects. 7. Nativism. I. Reimers, David M. II. Title.

E184.A1D48 2009
305.800973—dc22
2008033694

∞

Columbia University Press books are printed on permanent and durable acid-free paper.
This book is printed on paper with recycled content.
Printed in the United States of America

References to Internet Web sites (URLs) were accurate at the time of writing.
Neither the author nor Columbia University Press is responsible for URLs that may
have expired or changed since the manuscript was prepared.

For
Mackenzie Drew Dinnerstein
and
Samuel Bowie-Reimers

Contents

Contents

List of Tables

Preface

The original impetus for writing this book was Americans' heightened concern with, and glorification of, ethnicity and ethnic values at the end of the 1960s and early 1970s. Both of us were brought up in the 1930s and 1940s, when one learned that becoming a "good American" meant shedding foreign ties, culture, and religion, and adapting to what now might be called the values and beliefs of white, Anglo-Saxon, Protestant America. By the 1970s, however, ethnicity had become chic. People wore buttons announcing that they were proud to be Polish or Italian, reporters wrote favorably on the virtues and values of ethnic working-class neighborhoods in cities like Baltimore and Pittsburgh; and people of a variety of backgrounds, instead of Anglicizing their names, "ethnicized" them. In such a context we prepared the first edition, confident that Americans were showing renewed interest in the experiences of their immigrant forebears.

Since that time the peoples of European ancestry have mixed with one another in a manner that their grandparents did not dream of, and much of the assertion of ethnicity of the 1970s has proved to be superficial. Yet the interest in ethnicity is stronger, and scholars of immigration and social history have published a remarkable number of books and articles exploring the nation's immigrant past. The new scholarship has greatly enhanced our understanding of several peoples, and particularly of the women of those cultures. We now know so much more than we did only a few years ago of the Huguenots and Scots of colonial America, of the Irish and Germans throughout the nineteenth and twentieth centuries, of Italians and Jews in a wider variety of American cities and of their unique experiences. There are also a plethora of works on Hispanics and Asians, written by members of those groups, that simply did not exist thirty-five years ago. As a result of this explosion of knowledge, we have attempted to revise this volume, incorporating as much of the recent scholarship as possible while adjusting and enhancing earlier interpretations.

As in the earlier editions, we have focused on those non-English people who came to the New World after 1607. By limiting the topic in this fashion we have obviously excluded Native Americans. Their history is in many respects unique and requires separate treatment. In *Ethnic Americans* we have, of course, discussed blacks who came to the United States, both involuntarily and voluntarily, from Africa and the West Indies. Indeed, more black immigrants have come to the United States in the last fifty years than in the entire period of slavery.

Two years after the publication of the third edition of *Ethnic Americans* in 1988, Congress passed a law that increased yearly immigration allowances by 35 percent; in 1996 Congress made other significant changes. We have incorporated the impact of the provisions of those laws in this text. When the third edition was being written in the middle 1980s, new trends in the history of immigration became visible, and these trends have continued. The last years have witnessed the greatest wave of immigration in American history, and it appears that immigration will remain high for at least the foreseeable future. An overwhelming majority, probably 85 to 90 percent, of newcomers hail from Latin America and Asia rather than from Europe. In 1960 the leading country of origin for immigrants in this country was Germany, with nearly one million Germans in the United States. Next was Canada, followed by Poland and the Soviet Union. In 2005 Mexico, the Philippines, India, China (excluding Taiwan and Hong Kong), headed the list. Just at a time when members of older European groups have been undergoing rapid change, and in some cases virtually disappearing as separate cultures, whole new ethnic communities have emerged. In the last decade of the twentieth century totals for immigration approached ten million people, more than the sum in any previous 10-year period in American history. During the first decade of the 21st century, immigrants have kept coming and their continued arrival of individuals without appropriate documents has caused consternation among millions of Americans.

We offer this fifth edition in the hope that it continues to be not only a brief summary of the immigrant experience but also a reflection of the most recent scholarship and public policies.

Leonard Dinnerstein
David M. Reimers

Ethnic Americans

Introduction

Since the end of the sixteenth century the greatest migration of people in the history of the world occurred. Sparked by the expansion of Europe, the quest for gold and silver to enrich the new modern nations, and the Industrial and Agricultural Revolutions that forced peasants off of the land and into the cities, the movement also gained momentum from many other factors in social history, including the doubling of the European population between 1750 and 1850. At the same time, intensified religious persecutions and relaxation of emigration restrictions in various nations combined with a transportation revolution to facilitate the movement of peoples who wanted to seek adventure, economic security, and/or social stability.

More than 100 million people left their native homes between 1600 and 2008. A majority of them reached first the British colonies, and later the United States. Other migrants have gone to every continent in the world. The United States, however, is the first nation to bind together a disparate group of people who eventually emerged as one indivisible nation that celebrated its multicultural past while, at the same time, trying to make all white people look like they came from the same cookie cutter. Non–Anglo-Saxon newcomers have always been expected to adapt to, and blend in with, the people already here. People of darker skin, and later those of other races, were kept in subordinate positions and shunned when they tried to blend in with the majority. Thus, along with multiculturalism, immigrants of varying stripes were made to feel inferior and less worthy as individuals until their differences no longer stood out.

Thus, along with a quasi tolerance for other people to help build the British colonies, and later the United States, into major political powers, demands were made that those who chose to live in this country absorb the major elements of the dominant culture. For those who would, or could, not do this because of race, religion, or political beliefs, acceptance would not only be withdrawn but they would be physically attacked, disparaged, and discouraged from remaining among us. At the same time, however, from the colonial period to the present, as the American economy grew, there have been varying degrees of labor shortages, and people, regardless of their backgrounds, have been encouraged to settle here—permanently or temporarily—to help meet the nation's economic needs.

Respect for the newcomers did not coincide with the economic benefits that they helped provide to the nation. There seemed no tolerance on the part of members of the dominant culture for people who worshipped differently from mainstream Protestants, who spoke a foreign language, or whose cultural values differed from those valued by Americans. Moreover, there seemed, and even seems today, that there was no understanding that newcomers felt most secure living among others like themselves, speaking the same language, and continuing with customs that nurtured them before their arrival in the United States. Thus, from the denunciation of Scots-Irish and others in colonial America, through the attacks upon the Irish, the Chinese, the Italians, the Slavs, and the Jews in the nineteenth and twentieth centuries, and the scorning of Latinos in the twentieth century, we see the ugly heads of racism and nativism coexisting with our rhetoric of welcome and tolerance.

Even in the late twentieth and early twenty-first centuries people are still disparaged for following the precepts of religious teachings that do not conform with the Judeo-Christian tradition or whose behavior mocks the values of the nation's dominant culture. Americans, for example, who have wanted to assist or "elevate" newcomers to "fit in" with the majority in the United States have, in effect, told immigrants that aspects of their cultures were less than praiseworthy and that to become real Americans they had to absorb existing values. Also, in our own day, we look down upon people who do not show high regard for educational and business accomplishment, who prefer glorification of family and group over individual achievement, and who may practice some other religions that are not fully under-stood by the Judeo-Christian tradition.

While reading this text it is important to keep these ideas in mind. Note always how immigrants are treated and how they are evaluated in terms of how closely they approach the Anglo-Saxon ideals physically, emotionally, and intellectually. And notice, as well, how scorned, how rejected, and how viciously they have been treated because they could, or would, not conform to dominant American values. These traits have always been present in the United States and have reflected themselves in different ways, at different times, and with different groups. Thus, racism and nativism have always been present along with acceptance and encouragement. And in every era most Americans, even those who have descended from groups previously denounced, accept the ways of the dominant culture and are threatened by others who they claim desire to undermine the pillars of society.

In spite of the hostility that many immigrants encountered, millions kept coming to America. Some sought political rights and others wanted to wor-ship as they pleased. Still others were refugees and had no hope for changes at home. Most, as is still the case today, were searching for economic oppor-tunities. The immigrants often struggled to get ahead, but for those who did not speak English, were not white, and had little education, mobility was dif-ficult. Still, they usually managed to improve their lot, if only modestly. Yet the chances they found in America prompted them to tell their families and friends that they too should come to the United States. For many, American dreams were about their children and grandchildren. For white immigrants a better life for their descendants was usually realized. For nonwhites the path upward was much more difficult. Even today these hopes are strong, and the list of those wanting to try their luck in America remains long.

1

The Beginnings

Immigration to America, 1492 to the 1820s

Nearly every school child knows that Christopher Columbus, sailing under the flag of Spain in 1492, inaugurated the European exploration, conquest, and eventual settlement of the Americas. Columbus himself completed four voyages to the New World, but he never set foot on what became the continental United States. Spain, like Columbus, looked to the Caribbean islands, Central and South America, and Mexico as the valuable regions to be explored and conquered, for there lay the treasures of gold and silver that enriched the Spanish conquistadors and monarchs.

Within thirty years after Columbus's first voyage, Hernán Cortés conquered Mexico and demonstrated the riches of the New World. In the long run Spain wasted the products of the Western Hemisphere, but the initial wealth proved immediately attractive. Cortés was quickly followed by other Spanish explorers and conquerors who also found valuable metals in South America.

While the main Spanish empire lay below the southern border of the eventual United States, the Spanish were active north of the Rio Grande River too. In the 1540s Vasquez de Coronado searched for gold in what is today Arizona and New Mexico. Some Spanish explorers went as far north as Virginia on the East Coast and what is now Colorado in the Rocky Mountain West. Iberians founded the first European colonial settlement, St. Augustine, in 1582, and later several other places in present-day Florida. The colonies in Spanish Florida, however, were never large, and when Great Britain took over Florida, many of the Iberian settlers fled. They came back when Spain resumed control of the area. The government in Madrid, however, never encouraged other Spaniards to settle in Florida, and restricted their possession to Roman Catholics and native inhabitants, whom they tried to convert to "the true faith."

Spanish settlements were also developed in the Southwest of what is now the United States. They included present-day Texas but the adventurers did not find gold or silver there. Instead they worked as ranchers and farmers. In an attempt to boost the population of its Texas lands, Spain imported Spanish-speaking Canary Islanders, but only a few thousand people came. Several thousand Canary Islanders, though, went to Louisiana when Spain took over that territory from the French in 1763. But the French dominated the culture of New Orleans and Louisiana, and in 1803 Spain returned the area to France. In turn, the French sold the entire Louisiana territory, which stretched north and west as far as present-day Montana. At the time of the transfer Louisiana contained only 40,000 persons, half of whom were black slaves.

It was in the present state of New Mexico that Spain made its major impact and where most of its colonists resided. Santa Fe, the capital of the present state, was founded in 1610, three years after the English arrived in Jamestown. Spaniards ruled harshly in the Southwest and the Pueblo Indians in New Mexico revolted in the 1680s, remaining independent until Spain resumed control after putting down the insurrection only a few years later. When the 1848 Treaty of Guadalupe Hidalgo with Mexico and the United States was signed at the end of the Mexican-American War, this country acquired the entire southwestern territory, which stretched into present-day California. However, about 60,000 of the 75,000 people residing there lived in what is now New Mexico. In 1854 the United States purchased an additional stretch of land in New Mexico and Arizona, to facilitate the building of a transcontinental railroad in the southern portion of the country.

Although Spaniards pursued gold and silver in the Western Hemisphere, the Spanish government restricted the numbers of settlers to Roman Catholics. As a result, Franciscan missions dotted areas in New Mexico, Arizona, and along the coast of California, where the towns were run by priests, soldiers, and government officials. Elite Spaniards living in the newly acquired territories had already turned to the cattle industry and had prospered before the United States took control of these lands. When the United States took over, and despite promises made in the Treaty of Guadalupe Hidalgo to respect the rights of the people already there, many of the original owners lost their property, while the others who retained control were weakened when the cattle boom ended in the 1880s.

Despite the beauty of the American Southwest, few Spaniards desired to start life anew in a distant and undeveloped continent. Eventually, only a few thousand of the 600,000 Spaniards in the New World chose to live north of the Rio Grande River. Without a substantial number of women, with or without families, willing to go to the New World, the settlements remained small. Thus intermarriage, as well as rape, occurred to satisfy men's needs. When the United States annexed much of Mexico's northern territory in 1848, it found most of the inhabitants, *mestizos,* were a product of mixed Spanish and Indian blood.

In the sixteenth century, when other European nations saw wealth arriving in Spain, British, French, and Dutch ships attacked and looted the vessels returning from the New World. Jealous of Spain's acquisitions, these other nations joined in the hunt for riches. However, the nations that began their search later founded colonies in the Caribbean and then on the North American continent. Not only were they searching for minerals but sugar produced in the Caribbean offered another form of wealth for plantation owners. So, too, did animal furs as well as several products produced on the mainland like tobacco, rice, and cotton.

The main French interest in the New World was in Canada but not many people settled there. Like the Spanish, the French government wanted only Roman Catholics in their colonies and, again like the people in Spain, most of the French preferred to remain at home. France had some influence in introducing French culture in Louisiana and especially in New Orleans, but since the area was poor, unhealthy, and dangerous, it lacked appeal to women. So the French government sent mostly male prisoners and indentured servants to labor in Louisiana, and also encouraged the slave trade. These three groups constituted the majority of newcomers in France's Louisiana territory.

In 1624, Dutch colonial efforts began with the founding of New Amsterdam (later renamed "New York" when the British assumed control of the colony in 1664). The West India Company that ran the colony from Holland cared primarily about profits, which they found to some extent in the fur trade with the American Indians. Unlike the French and Spanish governments, the Dutch, and later the English, welcomed almost anyone of European heritage to reside in the areas that they controlled. As a result of this policy not only did the colony become diverse and prosper, but it set the tone for future settlements in New York City of people from every area of the world. No other city in the United States, not even Chicago, has the diversity that continued and still exists in the nation's largest city.

Despite the liberal policy of acceptance that characterized the Dutch and English governments, as well as the chartered companies that promoted growth in the New World, both the Dutch and English settlers sought to isolate themselves from other colonists. Most of the non-Dutch and non-English regarded these groups as aloof, but that did not seem to bother those developing their own communities and celebrating their own cultures. The Dutch, who settled mainly in New York and New Jersey, are representative of immigrants to America who held on to their cultures and values for several generations. They considered their heritage too important an aspect of their lives to relinquish it easily. Unlike the English, Dutch law gave women greater property and inheritance rights. Partners in a Dutch marriage held property equally, and widows with children split inheritances. Gradually, English customs crept into Dutch practices and women found themselves receiving less of their husband's estate than they had formerly. This change, like others within the eighteenth-century Dutch community, marked the gradual loss of Dutch culture.

But other aspects of Dutch culture lived on long after the British conquered New Netherland and renamed it New York. Worship in the Dutch language continued in some parts of New York and New Jersey until the 1820s, while some future generations of farmers continued using the Dutch dialogue in these states as late as the twentieth century. Both the Dutch and the English, like most other Protestant groups, then and in subsequent generations, regarded education highly, and their children learned not only the three Rs but also enough religion to make them God-fearing Christians. Instruction was in their native tongues until approximately the eighteenth century when English became dominant, but not universal, throughout the United States. Both sexes were taught the same things in their earliest years, including careful instruction in the Bible. As the children grew, girls received instruction in sewing and other domestic arts while boys were directed toward more sophisticated learning. Among a mother's prime responsibility was the education of her children.

In the long run, English settlers came to dominate life in British America. They sent more people to the colonies from the homeland than did any other European nation before the end of the eighteenth century. These men and women, and later the Scots and Scots-Irish, set the tone of the colonies while expecting others to give up their own cultures and blend with the majority. No group was absorbed immediately, although one of the fastest to disappear, the French Huguenots (Protestants), practically passed from the scene by the second or third generation. For some newcomers, however, such as some of the Germans in Pennsylvania and South Carolina, it took two to four generations, and even longer in some cases, before acculturation and then assimilation occurred.

The first English colonists to arrive on the North American continent came directly from England to Virginia. The settlement at Jamestown in 1607 resulted from the visions of some London-based fortune hunters. These early colonists had difficulty surviving and many died within a few months. Those that lived struggled against disease, poor work habits, and hostile Indians. By 1622, famines, pestilence, and Indian wars had practically destroyed the colony, and the English crown assumed possession.

More successful were groups of Pilgrims and Puritans who journeyed to New England in the 1620s and settled in what is now Massachusetts. They left Europe to avoid the plague of a faltering European economy but their move to the New World also afforded them the opportunity to implant their own cultural values. No other groups, no matter how large, were ever as significant in the development of the United States as these two groups. Their ideologies emphasized the importance of the Protestant faith, diligent application to work, and individual accomplishment. They often paid homage to those who attained great wealth. They cherished the Anglo-Saxon legal heritage and revered the written compact. They brought the English language to the New World, along with a strong sense of the role of families. Men dominated their families and were political leaders. But women too had roles in society: they ran the households and reared the children. All of these aspects of their culture were firmly implanted in American soil and became the foundations for American society. Every succeeding immigrant group that came to the English colonies, and later to the United States, had to absorb these aspects of the dominant culture to be accepted as Americans.

After Charles I succeeded his father, James I, on the English throne in 1625, domestic concerns prevented him from giving much attention to the colonies. Nevertheless, he granted an area of land north of Virginia to George Calvert, Lord Baltimore, which was christened Maryland. Calvert, a Roman Catholic, hoped the colony would be financially profitable and serve as a haven for his coreligionists. He died before actually receiving the grant from the king, and the deed went to his son, Cecilius, who embarked on a voyage to the New World in 1634. From the beginning there were large numbers of Protestants in Maryland, and to protect Catholics in case of eventual discrimination, Lord Baltimore urged passage of the Toleration Act in 1649; it granted freedom of religion to all who believed in the divinity of Jesus Christ. Five years later, however, under the domination of a Protestant legislature, the act was repealed and Catholics were denied legal protection. The repeal signified quite strikingly how the colonists, and in later centuries other Protestants, regarded the Roman Catholic faith.

From 1649 until 1661 Oliver Cromwell governed England as a protectorate, but upon his death Charles II, son of the beheaded monarch, reinstituted the monarchy and claimed the throne as his birthright. During his reign (1661–1685) England discouraged emigration. The mercantile theory, which held sway for the next century, dictated that the wealth of nations lay in their inhabitants and their production, and that loss of population meant, in effect, loss of riches.

Many colonies therefore had to devise ways to attract immigrant laborers. Along with ship captains they sent agents ("newlanders") to Europe to promote their attractions. Newlanders often dressed in fancy attire and wore pocket watches with heavy gold chains to attest to the wealth found in the New World. They carried tales of maids who became ladies, tenants who became landlords, and apprentices who had advanced to artisans only a few years after reaching their new dwellings. But "the best advertisement for the colonies," one historian wrote, "was clearly the success of the pioneers. Messages they sent back home inevitably had the effect of removing the last psychological barrier from the minds of many already inclined to leave." "It is as good Country as any Man needs to Dwell in," one Scots-Irishman wrote home in 1767, "and it is much better than I expected it to be in every way." Going to America thus came to mean, as one scholar put it, not launching into the vast unknown "but moving to a country where one's friends and relatives had a home."

Most Europeans, especially the ones willing to try their luck in the colonies, could not afford the fare to the New World. That proved to be a minor matter, or so the would-be immigrants were led to believe. Shipping agents accepted indigents who signed indentures agreeing to work in the colonies for a period of three to seven years to pay for their passage. Immigrants who accepted these terms were often "sold" on board ship, and often members of the same family wound up with different "masters." Some parents had to "sell their children as if they were cattle," and if parents or spouses died, the remaining members of the family had to serve extra time to pay for the deceased's passage. Unaccompanied children or those whose parents had died during the journey were usually indentured until the age of 21.

Ship owners regarded their passengers as freight on which they hoped to maximize profits. The space between decks seldom exceeded five feet, and the immigrants, regardless of gender or marital relation, slept two or three to a berth; each individual rarely had an area of more than two feet by six feet to call their own. Voyages lasted six weeks to six months. Stormy days forced passengers below deck, but portholes for light and ventilation were practically nonexistent. Overcrowding, disease, pestilence, brutal shipmasters, and shortages of food and water added to the tribulations of the ocean crossing. Many children under 7 sickened and died. Older folk considered themselves lucky when they arrived in the New World. In 1752, on a ship from the Netherlands to Pennsylvania, only 21 out of 340 passengers disembarked; the others had starved to death. On another voyage from Belfast in 1741, 6 of the 46 who died "were consumed by the sixty survivors." On a fourth ship, many drank salt water and their own urine, and on another those who complained of hunger "were put in irons, lashed to the shrouds and flogged." No wonder that one immigrant German schoolteacher wrote, "The glimpse of land revives the passengers, especially those who are half dead of illness. Their spirits, however weak they had become, leap up, triumph, and rejoice within them. Such people are now willing to bear all ills patiently, if only they can disembark soon and step on land." In fact, hundreds of thousands did. In the seventeenth century, for example, roughly half of all newcomers to the Chesapeake Bay colonies of Virginia and Maryland arrived as indentured servants. Protestant males who met their contractual obligations received "freedom dues" at the end of their commitments. These gifts included money, tools, new clothes, and in some cases, land. But there can be no question that they had earned what they received. By the time of the American Revolution nearly 250,000 had paid for their passage by slaving away for a number of years.

Still another source for colonists and labor came from Africa. Many Africans may have been treated as indentured servants in the early years of their arrival, which began in 1619, but by the 1660s they constituted a to-tally different kind of servant: they were sold for indefinite periods of ser-vitude and their issue remained in the same status. In other words, while the colonists treated many, if not most, of the black Africans as indentured servants, within decades of their first arrival they increasingly became seen as slaves. After the restoration of Charles II to the thrown of England, the Royal African Slave Company received a monopoly from the crown and began importing Africans who would be sold to the colonists for lifetime indentures. In that same decade Virginia and Maryland passed their first slave codes. By the beginning of the eighteenth century slaves outnum-bered indentured servants in the southern colonies, which depended upon their labor to produce tobacco, rice, and cotton.

Like the indentured servants the black slaves lived in bondage—but theirs never ended. Both groups lived in brutal and demeaning circum-stances, and faced harsh penalties for resisting their masters, but one saw freedom at the end of their labors while hopes of the others for a better life was no more than a mirage. Children born to indentured servants, as well as the offspring of slaves, assumed their mothers' status. Laws proclaimed that conversion to Christianity did not end bondage. Not until the Ameri-can Revolution did the southern colonies make it easier for individual mas-ters to free their slaves but, of course, the institution of slavery remained until the end of the Civil War.

In some colonies, North and South Carolina for example, citizens never debated the institution of slavery. In part this may have been because early white settlers in these areas had come from the Caribbean where slavery was well entrenched and the whites knew the value of slave labor. Then, too, when the Carolinas were established during King Charles II's reign, slavery had already been established and was spreading in Virginia and Maryland. In Georgia the original intent of the organizers was to have a colony of only free white men and women, but shortly after its settle-ment in 1732 landowners successfully petitioned to allow the importation of slaves. By the time of the American Revolution, the million or so black slaves constituted 40 percent of the southern population.

Slavery was also part of the social and economic fabric of the northern colonies. The total number of slaves in the North was small (slaves com-prised only 14 percent of the population in New York City at the start of the American Revolution) compared with the numbers in Virginia and its sister southern states. Nonetheless, colonists in both regions profited from the labor of African Americans. Northern slave codes were not as brutal as those in the South, but African Americans in bondage retained that status for life.

One of the major seekers of non-English laborers for his colony, William Penn, toured western Europe in his quest. At first Penn reserved vast areas of his colonial territory for fellow Quakers, but the enormous need for people and workers in the colony led him to recruit other groups as well. About 25,000 English and Welsh members of the Society of Friends settled in the colony's Delaware Valley from 1675 to 1725; Congregationalists and Anglicans arrived too. But the Quakers set the tone for society in that half century. Like the Puritans, they were a deeply religious people persecuted in England for their religious beliefs. Quakers rejected the doctrine of predestination and held an enlightened view of humankind. They opposed taking oaths, fighting wars, and establishing a rigid religious hierarchy, and they were generally tolerant of other religions and immigrants. Although Penn condemned Jews for rejecting the New Testament, he urged them to "see the error of their ways and accept the divinity of Jesus." His intolerance of Jews, however, did not affect other Quaker concerns. Their humanitarianism led them to attack the institution of slavery and recognize the need to improve women's rights.

Penn printed hundreds of pamphlets in English, German, French, and Dutch, describing the wonders of Pennsylvania. Europeans were told over and over again that it was a land where crops never failed, where game roamed aplenty, where abundant supplies of wood stood ready for use in building houses, barns, and furniture, where religious freedom was guaranteed to all, and where no political restrictions harassed dissenters. Moreover, the colony promised universal male suffrage, a humane penal code, and no compulsory military service. As one historian later wrote, "Pennsylvania was in truth a land of milk and honey." No wonder that in the colonial era more immigrants sailed for Philadelphia than for all other ports combined.

People came to the New World for a combination of economic, religious, and political reasons. Some escaped tyrannical princes, others because of a different faith, and still more because crop failures, famines, and never-ending wars made future prospects seem bleak. The relaxation of emigration restrictions in Switzerland and the German states in the eighteenth century also stimulated them, as did glowing letters from friends and relatives who had already gone to the English colonies.

The majority of Germans were Lutherans or members of Reformed churches. Germans formed churches even in back country several hundred miles from Philadelphia. By 1760 there were 18 German communities; by 1780 the number had reached 30. Yet Germans were by no means limited to these two denominations. The radical pietistic sects also took hold in America, and made up about one fourth of the German congregations at the time of the American Revolution. Many members had experienced persecution in Europe and were eager to find the freedom to follow what they believed to be the true faith. Among them were Moravians, Mennonites, Swenkfelders, and Amish. These deeply religious immigrants tended to settle and even migrate together as distinct enclaves.

Pennsylvania received the largest number of Germans, but they spread out across most of the colonies. The English government was eager to recruit Germans to develop its land and to build ships along New York's Hudson River. By promising to pay their way to America, Queen Anne induced several thousand to head for New York. The program, however, lacked funds and was poorly planned, so shipbuilding efforts failed. But some Germans stayed on near Rhinebeck, New York, while others left for better opportunities elsewhere.

Germans also struggled to make a living in the back country of the southern colonies. In the early 1740s Moravians abandoned their Georgia settlement and began moving to Pennsylvania, the center of the largest German community in the New World. In the end colonial Germans prospered. Their concern for their property was proverbial; it was often said that a German took better care of his cows than of his children. After settling on good land the Germans built sturdy houses and barns and tilled their farms with diligence and enthusiasm. One historian has written that they "produced in their children not only the *habits* of labor but a *love* of it." They fed their stock well, exercised frugality in diet and dress, and were known for their thrift, industry, punctuality, and sense of justice.

But the colonial Germans had little desire to blend with the rest of the population. They kept to themselves, continued speaking German, attended their own churches, and rarely took the opportunity to become British citizens. They maintained their own culture and feared that the use of English and contact with other groups would completely anglicize their children. Because of their aloofness they antagonized the dominant English group in the colonies, especially in Pennsylvania, which viewed them as dangerous elements. Even Benjamin Franklin, an urbane and decent man, disliked the Germans who poured into Pennsylvania in the eighteenth century and he questioned: "Why should the *Palatine Boors* be suffered to swarm into our Settlements, and by herding together, establish their Language and Manners, to the Exclusion of ours? Why should *Pennsylvania,* founded by the *English,* become a Colony of *Aliens,* who will shortly be so numerous as to Germanize us instead of our Anglifying them?"

Another group of settlers was the Scots-Irish. They had gone to northern Ireland from Scotland as part of the British policy to control Irish Catholics, and the Scots were Presbyterians. Most of the Scots-Irish (who were usually referred to as the "Irish") had settled in Ireland in the sixteenth and seventeenth centuries and had been living there for many decades. In the late seventeenth century English mercantile laws had prohibited the exportation of Irish woolens except to England and Wales, and this nearly crippled Ulster's profitable foreign trade. Then successive increases in rents, termination of farm leases, poor harvests, curtailed supplies of flax to linen manufacturers, increased food costs, and restrictions precluding Presbyterians from holding political offices piled woe upon woe. Furthermore, the English Parliament decreed that the children of all Protestants not married in the Church of England must be declared bastards. The absurdity of this ruling also resulted in " 'many persons of undoubted reputation' [being] prosecuted in the bishops courts as fornicators for cohabitating with their own wives." But not until 1717, when the fourth successive year of droughts ruined crops, did the Scots-Irish begin serious preparations for migration to the New World. The first group to leave their homeland may have been motivated by religious as well as economic conditions, but thereafter, glowing shipping advertisements, letters from friends and relatives in the colonies, and poor economic conditions in Ireland sparked further movement. Intensive and protracted Scots-Irish emigration to the American colonies correlated with the ebb and flow of prosperity in the linen industry in Ireland.

The original Scots-Irish settlers went to Worcester, Massachusetts, and Londonderry, New Hampshire, where they met a chilly reception. Colonists who had arrived earlier regarded them as "uncleanly, unwholesome and disgusting." Pennsylvania, on the other hand, because of its tolerance, readily received whoever chose to come. Perhaps even more important, the ships carrying flaxseed went to Philadelphia, and so the Scots-Irish went there too. Most arrived as indentured servants, but once their periods of service ended they moved to the frontier, and their settlements predominated in central Pennsylvania and portions of Maryland, Virginia, and the Carolinas. Unlike the Germans, the Scots-Irish were forever on the move.

Although they were a colonial minority, the Scots-Irish left a mark on American society that remains to this day. Wherever they went, the church and the schoolhouse followed. Devoutly religious and with an intense desire for learning, they stressed the importance of an educated ministry and the dissemination of knowledge. Their stern morality pervaded the American scene. The Presbyterians frowned on dancing, card playing, the theater, breaking the Sabbath by any diversion, and engaging in frivolous pastimes. On the other hand, not all were as dour as this might suggest. One scholar tells us that many among them "also danced, fiddled, sang, reveled, raced horses, gambled, got drunk and fought, celebrated St. Patrick's Day and shot off guns on New Year's Eve."

Behind the Scots-Irish, Germans, Africans, Dutch, and English, the Scots were the largest group of Europeans to arrive in the British colonies during the colonial era. They totaled approximately 25,000 people by the time of the American Revolution. They, too, kept to themselves but they also welcomed newcomers from various regions of the old country and absorbed them into the ethnic community. They made their mark in the colonies in the organization of commerce, the development of mining, and advances in medical science. They were merchants and proprietors in a variety of businesses and, like the Dutch, valued education for their offspring. Most were overwhelmingly attached to the evangelical Presbyterian church, and family networks among Scottish settlers were an important source of religious unity.

One of their primary areas of settlement in British America began in the 1680s, when approximately 600 Scots moved into east Jersey. By 1750 one fifth of the population of New Jersey was made up of Scottish settlers and their descendants; by the middle of the eighteenth century, these people "turned central Jersey and the whole corridor from New York to Philadelphia into the center of Scottish Middle Colony life."

Although they were not as large in numbers as the Scots-Irish from Ulster and the Germans, one scholar reminds us that

In several particulars, the experience of Scottish settlers can serve as a model for that of many colonial ethnic groups. With a few striking exceptions—such as the Huguenots, who were notorious for submerging their national identity and attaching themselves to other Protestant communities—the confrontation with alien cultures in the New World helped to unify settlers from diverse and seemingly unconnected regional backgrounds under a common national banner. They often achieved that consolidation around a particular religious identity, such as Scottish Presbyterian, Dutch or German Reformed, or, in the next century, Irish Catholic. That process often created ethnic entities that seemed more Scottish, or more German, or even more English, than their European counterparts.

What this scholar really was saying, and what is common today in some parts of the United States, was that in colonial America religious and ethnic identities were often intertwined. One was not merely French, Dutch, or Scottish, but French Huguenot, Dutch Reformed, or Scottish Presbyterian. Colonists thought of one another in terms of these double identities and denounced one another more often in religious than in national terms.

Because so many diverse people came to America from 1607 to the 1770s, one should not think that all were welcome in the labor-short economy. There were definite limits to the acceptance of immigrants. Blacks were wanted but only as slaves. Another source of labor, convicts, were not wanted at all but they were thrust upon the colonies by British governmental officials. Instead of imprisoning criminals, the British banished prisoners to the colonies. It has been estimated that between 1717 and 1775, 50,000 convicts found themselves in the New World, rather than in jail. Some had been criminals in Great Britain but others had been tradesmen who had fallen on hard times and had run afoul of the law. Colonists did not want these felons dumped upon them but colonial governments could not control the traffic. Besides, laborers were needed.

While convicts were viewed with suspicion at times, no group was as hated in the British colonies as the Roman Catholics. Carrying with them their European traditions, some of which harked back to the Reformation, the Protestant settlers had tolerance for almost no deviants, but "the prospect of the arrival of Roman Catholics of any nationality" particularly, one scholar tells us, "curdled the blood of most provincials." Roman Catholics constituted less than 1 percent of all of the colonists and half of them were in Maryland, but their numbers had nothing to do with Protestant fears. Those who hated Catholicism exaggerated its potential influence. Most Pennsylvanians, for example, imagined swarms of Irish and German Catholics in their midst even though statistics belied such apprehensions. One Pennsylvanian disinherited a daughter because she married a Roman Catholic.

Catholics lived freely in the middle colonies, but in times of social crisis an inordinate amount of fear swept the towns in which they dwelled; their presence was deemed harmful to community harmony. This was especially true in the middle of the eighteenth century during the French and Indian War. In December 1760, the Catholic church in Lancaster, Pennsylvania, was completely destroyed by enraged Protestants, and Catholics were penalized in the colony in other ways as well. They were disarmed, prohibited from serving in the militia, and forced to pay double taxes. "And those residing in the colony were registered so that their every movement could be scrutinized."

The seeds of many societal prejudices had been planted in Europe and carried over to the New World. The sense of self-righteousness and other attitudes seen in the colonial period carried into the early Republic and never quite disappeared. Outsiders were welcomed for their labor and scorned because aspects of their cultures did not easily blend with those of the majority. As various white groups acculturated and assimilated, however, they joined older stocks of Americans in looking down upon the newcomers *du jour,* fearing that the then new immigrants would undermine American values and even replace what existed with whatever the foreigners brought along with them. This has never happened, although aspects of different cultures such as the German Christmas tree, Italian pizza, and Mexican tiles have been absorbed so that contemporaries now view them as "American."

In the Revolutionary era, and in subsequent periods of crisis in the United States, prejudicial commentaries have always abounded, even if those victimized had no responsibility for whatever crisis existed. Even as intelligent a man as John Adams, the second President of the United States, could write to his wife after visiting a Catholic church in Philadelphia:

This Afternoon's Entertainment was to me most awful and affecting. The poor Wretches, fingering their Beads, chanting Latin, not a Word of which they understood, their Pater Nosters and Ave Maria's. Their holy Water—their Crossing themselves perpetually—their Bowing to the Name of Jesus, whenever they hear *it*—*their* Bowing and Kneelings, and Genuflections before the Altar. The Dress of the Priest was rich with Lace—his Pulpit was Velvet and Gold. The Altar Piece was very rich—little Images and Crucifixes about—Wax Candles lighten up. But how shall

I describe the Picture of our Saviour in a Frame of Marble over the Altar at full Length upon the Cross, in the Agonies, and the Blood dropping and streaming from his Wounds . . .

Hostility toward Catholics may have been the most virulent prejudice, nevertheless ethnic tensions and disputes in colonial America, as well as in every era since, existed. Jews and Catholics rarely enjoyed the right to vote in colonial America; Jews in particular were proscribed from becoming physicians and attorneys in some colonies while New York City prohibited Jews and Quakers from testifying in court until after the American Revolution ended. During the war anti-Semitism in Pennsylvania intensified and did not begin to subside until after Thomas Jefferson assumed the presidency in 1801. At the end of the eighteenth century colonists generally regarded Jews and Quakers as clever and wealthy; Germans as fat, stupid, and drunk; Scots-Irish as violent and drunk. French, Spanish, and other Catholics were dubbed "slaves of their tyrannical rulers and the Catholic Church, although hot-blooded and amorous as individuals." Moreover, many of the colonies had an established church—Congregational in New England and usually Anglican elsewhere—and residents, regardless of faith, were taxed to support these institutions.

But community mores in most of the colonies generally were favorable to intercultural marriage as long as the non-English or non-Protestant member accepted the dominant religion of the spouse. As a result the commercially successful Huguenots and Jews, to name but two of the groups, often made alliances with the "best families" in the colonies and then raised their children as Anglicans or, later, Episcopalians. Consequently both the Huguenot and the Jewish communities practically disappeared. In the United States today the only remnants of Huguenots are their historical and genealogical societies in places like South Carolina; New Rochelle, New York, and Rhode Island. As for the colonial Jewish population, it was absorbed into the dominant culture. Today, a majority of American Jews trace their ancestries either to the great migrations from Eastern Europe in the late nineteenth and early twentieth centuries or to the movement from the German states in the 1840s and 1850s.

In contrast, numerically larger colonial minorities like the Scots-Irish and the Germans preserved and maintained their traditional ways well into the nineteenth century. Germans in places like Pennsylvania and the Carolinas continued speaking their own language, the Dutch maintained schools for their children in New York until after the Revolution, and a good deal of sectional controversy that has generally been attributed to geographical locale may in fact have had its roots in ethnic differences. The Scots-Irish on the frontier in Pennsylvania may have been angered as much by Quaker control in the Keystone State as by lack of military protection. The Regulator movement in the Carolinas, which pitted Scots-Irish in the West against English descendants in the East, may also have had ethnic overtones.

Between the end of the French and Indian War in 1763 and the beginning of the American Revolution in 1776, three times as many Europeans flocked to the British mainland colonies than had come in the previous three decades. Thousands of Germans and Scots-Irish left home and so, too, did approximately 10,000 Scots. They were drawn by the fact that the American standard of living then was equal to, and probably better than, that of Europe. And there was the good news from the colonies to persons back home about the abundant prospects for newcomers. (Rarely was the turmoil between and amongst different ethnics highlighted by colonial letter writers.) As one scholar has noted, "the forces of attraction were powerful, generated by the magnet of a labor short American economy, which grew swiftly in certain regions and in certain kinds of activities." Few immigration records exist for the colonial era, but in the 1770s the British government wanted to know which people were moving and from whence they came.

Of those who left records, most of the Scots and English were men, but many families also migrated to the New World. A considerable number possessed skills, but they had fallen on hard times or believed that America, where skilled workers were in demand, offered better prospects for them. Such family and skilled immigrants proved quite different from the early days in Virginia where so many indentured servants were young men without skills.

As the colonial period ended, a rather distinctive ethnic picture could be seen. In New England an overwhelmingly English heritage predominated; aside from some Scottish, Huguenot, and Scots-Irish elements, few other minorities could be found. In the southern colonies was a large black population of slaves who coexisted not only with the English but also with strains of all the groups such as the Germans, Scots-Irish, Scots, and Huguenots. However, it was in the middle colonies that diversity was so pronounced. Cities such as New York and Philadelphia counted all sorts of people within their environs, while the rural areas of these states, and New

Jersey as well, seemed more Scottish, or Dutch, or Scots-Irish, or German. In time, ethnic diversity was spread to the rest of the United States as millions of immigrants poured in from all over the globe. In the Southwest, not annexed until the mid-nineteenth century, Hispanic culture dominated. But, as noted, the population of that large region, from Texas to California, numbered only a few thousand compared to over two million people of European stock in the English colonies in 1776.

The war for independence from England and the formation of a new American government had a nationalizing effect on the formerly separate colonies and their inhabitants. Many of the immigrants and their children were now quite proud to regard themselves as Americans, not as transplanted Europeans. Some ethnic groups—notably the Germans who lived between the Delaware and Susquehanna rivers in Pennsylvania, and the Broad and Saluda rivers in South Carolina—resisted Americanization longer than others, but sooner or later most of them assimilated.

The pattern of minority life developed in the English colonies in the seventeenth century set the standard for future European minorities in this country. The English colonists and later Americans of the majority group appreciated the labor that the newcomers could provide, but expected them to absorb existing customs while shedding their own as quickly as possible. Minority group members were despised for their ignorance of English, their attachment to cultures and faiths prevalent in the Old World, and their lack of knowledge of the American way.

One group from the Haitian rebellion was not so welcome. These were the thousands of "free people of color." The free people of color, who were mostly of mixed race, lacked equality with the whites, but they were not slaves. When they landed on American shores, some planters thought that they would bring with them ideas of freedom for slaves. As a result several states passed laws to prevent Haitian free people of color from landing, but these laws were not enforced. By 1810, 3,102 free people of color had arrived in Louisiana. They added to the free black population of New Orleans, and many were able to find a niche as skilled artisans. However, as conditions in the Caribbean changed, their migration ended.

From 1790 to 1820 fewer than 300,000 immigrants came to the United States. The new Constitution of 1787 said virtually nothing about immigration, and after passing a few laws in the 1790s, the federal government generally allowed states to regulate immigration until 1875. Germans and Scots-Irish continued to arrive after 1790, including a few German soldiers who had fought in the Revolutionary War. But other groups were more prominent. During the upheavals of the French Revolution and the slave rebellion in Haiti, which began in 1791, thousands of French-speaking refugees arrived from France and Haiti. Most of the French exiles settled in coastal cities such as Philadelphia, Baltimore, New York, and Charleston. Occasional groups of political refugees, like the 25,000 or so French-speaking immigrants who fled their Caribbean plantations in the 1790s in the wake of slave uprisings, might be given safe havens. But these newcomers, usually middle or upper class, brought a courtliness or sophistication that allowed them to mingle with the elite in American society. As a result they assimilated rather quickly and suffered much less from minority status than did those of lesser education, wealth, or position. Many, however, returned to France after 1800, and those remaining made only a minor impact upon American society.

The arrival of French-speaking exiles helped to reinforce the French flavor of New Orleans life. They joined other French settlers, among whom were a group, the Acadians, who had originally lived in Canada. England drove the Acadians out beginning in the 1760s when the English won control of Canada. Some Acadians went to France while others settled in the Caribbean. However, several thousand Acadians were forced to find a home in Louisiana. There they comprised a new ethnic group, the Cajuns, French-speaking farmers and trappers.

English radicals, fleeing political oppression in Great Britain, also entered the United States during the 1790s, as did members of the United Irishmen. The United Irishmen were part of a movement to end English domination of Ireland, and when their movement failed in the late 1790s, some fled to America. Federalists worried about these immigrants with radical ideas, and some Jeffersonian Republicans believed that French refugees did not have a proper appreciation of American republicanism. These "wild" Irish and French "radicals" were seen as outsiders who would undermine and overthrow the new nation.

As a result, Congress gave President John Adams power to deport persons deemed dangerous, even in time of peace. Adams did not use this authority. However, a sedition act was used against Irish-born Congressman Matthew Lyons for libeling President Adams in the press. The crisis and conflict over immigration resulting from the French Revolution ended in 1800, however. In 1790 Congress passed the first naturalization act; it granted whites the right to become citizens after only two years' residence in the United States. Legislators subsequently altered the period of years required for citizenship, but in 1800, after the election of Thomas Jefferson to the presidency, Congress set the time at five years, where it has remained ever since.

The limitation of naturalization to "free white persons" indicated the underlying racism of American society. While some of the founding fathers wanted America to stand as an asylum for mankind, there were limits. It appears as if most lawmakers agreed with Benjamin Franklin when he wrote, "and while we are, as I may call it, *securing* our planet, by clearing *America* of woods, and so making this side of our globe reflect a brighter light to the eyes of inhabitants in *Mars* or *Venus*, why should we in the sight of superior beings, darken its people? Why increase the sons of *Africa* by planting them in *America*, where we have so fair an opportunity, by excluding all blacks and tawneys, of increasing the lovely white and red?"

Following the Civil War, Congress would permit persons of African descent to naturalize, but few Africans arrived during the next 100 years. The limitation of citizenship to "free white persons" and "persons of African descent" meant that Asians could not naturalize. Not until 1943 were the Chinese permitted to become citizens and not until 1952 was race finally eliminated as a bar for immigrants to become American citizens.

2

An Expanding Population

Immigration from 1830 to the 1890s

The story of immigration to the United States in the nineteenth century differs on the basis of whether one is talking of immigration to the East and Midwest or immigration to the West. From the 1830s through the early 1890s the predominant newcomers in the East arrived from Ireland and the German states in Europe. Significant numbers of Scandinavians did not really arrive until after the Civil War. All of these groups left countries during the evolution of their societies from agricultural to industrial ones and specifically during times of severe economic depressions at home and hundreds of thousands of job openings in the United States. Eventually people from all over Europe arrived in this country, with the largest single number entering through the port of New York City. In the East and Midwest growth came mostly from mining and manufacturing and depended on a stream of European immigrants willing to do the most menial of jobs as well as persons required to provide all of the services needed by large groups of people.

With the exception of the discovery of gold in California in 1849, when people thought they would get rich simply by going to that state and putting shovels in the ground, most of the West developed in the 1870s and thereafter, and its growth can be attributed primarily to the mining of a variety of minerals (gold, silver, copper), the completion of the cross-country

[TABLE 2.1]

Immigration to America, 1820–1930

DECADE	GERMANY	IRELAND	ENGLAND, SCOTLAND, WALES	SCANDINAVIA	ITALY	AUSTRO-HUNGARY	RUSSIA AND BALTIC STATES	TOTALS
1820	968	3,614	2,410	23	30	—	14	8,385
1821–1830	6,761	50,724	25,079	260	409	—	75	143,439
1831–1840	152,454	207,654	75,810	2,264	2,253	—	277	599,125
1841–1850	434,626	780,719	267,044	13,122	1,970	—	551	1,713,251
1851–1860	951,657	914,119	423,929	24,680	9,231	—	457	2,598,214
1861–1870	827,468	435,697	607,076	126,392	11,725	7,800	2,515	2,314,824
1871–1880	718,182	436,871	548,043	242,934	55,795	72,969	39,287	2,812,191
1881–1890	1,452,970	655,540	807,357	655,494	307,309	362,719	213,282	5,246,613
1891–1900	505,152	388,416	271,538	371,512	651,783	574,069	505,281	3,687,564
1901–1910	341,498	339,065	525,950	505,324	2,045,877	2,145,266	1,597,308	8,795,386
1911–1920	143,945	146,199	341,408	203,452	1,209,524	901,656	921,957	5,735,811
1921–1930	412,202	220,564	330,168	198,210	455,315	214,806	89,423	4,107,209
Totals	5,947,883	4,579,182	4,225,812	2,343,667	4,751,311	4,279,285	3,370,427	

Source: Immigration and Naturalization Service, Annual Reports.

railroad in 1869, and the aid of Congress. The territory west of the Mississippi River has received greater assistance for economic growth, per capita, from Congress than any other section in the United States. Railroads were granted hundreds of thousands of acres to stimulate their building in areas which had relatively few people. The Homestead Act of 1862 awarded 160 acres of free land to people who would work on it for five years. Most of the beneficiaries were railroad owners, but individuals also could obtain areas for farming and ranching. Then the Newlands Reclamation Act of 1902 provided funds for irrigating much of the arid lands so that they might be utilized for farming. This led to spectacular agricultural development from Texas to California.

The West depended not only on European immigrants to dig in mines, build railroads, and both plant and harvest agricultural crops, but on Asians and Mexicans as well. The Chinese came during the gold rush and the search for minerals. Most of the Mexicans in the West became Americans after the United States annexed Texas in 1845 and signed the Treaty of Guadalupe Hildalgo (1848), which resulted in the transference to the United States of most of the lands in Mexico's northernmost areas. Thus after the completion of the transcontinental railroad in 1869, the building of other lines going both north and south as well as east and west, and the discovery of a wealth of minerals in the Rocky Mountain areas, the West began to contribute substantially to the wealth of the nation.

Although the Irish and Germans stood out as the major minority groups throughout the United States (few Germans went to New England) in the nineteenth century, the Protestant Germans had a great advantage over the Catholic Irish because most others in the nation (blacks as well as whites) equated Christian with American and Catholicism with foreign. After several generations, and some social mobility, the Irish joined the Germans in moving up the socioeconomic ladder, primarily because of the whiteness of their skins. Southern and eastern Europeans who arrived at the end of the nineteenth and beginning of the twentieth centuries were mostly Catholic and Jewish, and it took longer for them to elevate their status in the eyes of their neighbors. The Asians and Mexicans in the West were considered the lowest level of immigrants (some people of European descent even considered them less than human), and it was well after the middle of the twentieth century before the civil rights movement and/or the new immigration legislation of the 1960s and thereafter allowed people from these groups to earn the respect of their neighbors and the social and economic opportunities available to Europeans and their descendants.

The Irish were the major first group of impoverished Europeans to leave their homeland in the nineteenth century. The Irish Poor Law of 1838, the enclosure movement on the land, and finally the great famine at the end of the 1840s when blight ravaged the potato crops and brought untold misery and starvation to millions, all combined to increase emigration. A French observer who had visited both America and Ireland before the Great Hunger said the condition of the Irish was worse than that of black slaves, and concluded: "There is no doubt that the most miserable of English paupers is better fed and clothed than the most prosperous of Irish laborers." As hundreds of thousands starved to death during the famine, one of the few lucrative trades left in Tipperary was the sale of coffin mountings and hinges. One man lamented, "Every day furnished victims, and the living hear, and endeavor to drive from their minds, as soon as they can, the horrifying particulars that are related. I have this day, returning to my house, witnessed more than one person lying in our district at this moment unburied. I have known of bodies here remaining in the mountainous parts, neglected for more than eight days." Many of the destitute went to England and some to South America, but more than a million came to the United States. The majority of these people remained in the port cities of New York and Boston, where they landed, because they were too poor to move any farther; but others traveled west. As conditions improved in Ireland in the middle of the 1850s, emigration subsided, but another potato rot in 1863 and still another famine in the 1880s swelled the Irish emigration statistics. Almost 4 million Irish came to the United States in the nineteenth century. Their impact in this country has far exceeded both their numbers and their percentage of the population. Within nineteenth-century immigrant groups, only among the Irish did women predominate. The famine and the shortage of land left many of them with dim prospects for marriage. Many decided not to marry or to postpone marriage, and to support themselves. They went to the cities, frequently finding jobs as domestic servants. But why stop in Dublin, many asked, when stories of America made emigration sound like a better choice? So they headed for New York and Boston and other cities, where they readily found jobs in domestic service.

For contemporary Americans such work has a low status, but this was not necessarily the case for Irish women. In contrast with grim prospects at home or jobs in sweatshops, domestic service offered food and a clean place to live. Thus the Irish women became the ubiquitous "Bridget," the domestic worker employed by each middle-class family. Some of these women eventually married and left their jobs, but others remained single. Many opened bank accounts and provided passage money to bring their brothers and sisters to the United States.

Along with the Irish came the Germans. But unlike the Irish, they continued to be the largest ethnic group arriving in all but three of the years between 1854 and 1892. Before the end of the century more than 5 million Germans reached the United States; in the twentieth century another 2 million came. The exodus, at first primarily from the rural and agricultural southern and western regions of Germany, fits the general pattern of immigration. Crop failures, high rents, high prices, and the changeover to an industrial economy stimulated the move. Conditions were not as bad as in impoverished Ireland, but they were bad enough. One observer told of the "poor wretches" on the road to Strasbourg: "There they go slowly along; their miserable tumbrils—drawn by such starved dropping beasts, that your only wonder is, how can they possibly reach Havre alive." Relatives and friends who went first to America wrote glowing letters, for the most part, and this in turn stimulated further waves. Rich farmers who saw a bleak future in Germany, poor ones who had no future, peasants and paupers whom the state paid to leave, a handful of disappointed revolutionaries after 1848, and an assortment of artisans and professionals came in the 1840s and 1850s.

In late 1854 reports circulated in the German states of large numbers of shipwrecks and cholera epidemics at sea that resulted in death rates as high as 50 percent. At about the same time, nativist agitation in the United States reached a peak and the American economy turned downward. These factors slowed immigration in the late 1850s. Then came the Civil War, which deterred people already beset with their own troubles from emigrating.

Between 1866 and 1873, however, a combination of American prosperity and European depression once again increased German emigration totals. Congressional passage of the 1862 Homestead Act granting free land to settlers, the convulsions in the German states owing to Bismarck's wars in the 1860s, the high conscription rate, and low wages at home also prompted German emigration. When the United States suffered a severe depression between 1873 and 1879, immigration figures were correspondingly depressed. But when the American economy improved, anxious Europeans once again descended on American shores. Germans who believed that prosperity would never be theirs at home left in record numbers; in 1882 more than 250,000 passed through the immigration stations here. The American depressions of the late 1880s and 1893–94 cut emigration sharply, but by then an improved industrial economy in Germany provided greater opportunities than in the past, and fewer Germans felt compelled to seek their fortunes in the New World.

Scandinavians—the largest northern European group, after the British, Germans, and Irish, to populate America in the nineteenth century—increased their numbers in the United States markedly after the Civil War. The first group of nineteenth-century Scandinavians arrived in the autumn of 1825, when about 50 Norwegians settled in Kendall, New York, about 30 miles southwest of Rochester. In 1841 a Swedish colony developed in Pine Lake, Wisconsin. During the next decades, Scandinavians continued to come, but never in the numbers that either the Irish or the Germans did. For example, Scandinavian immigration totaled only 2,830 in 1846 and not much more in 1865. After 1868, however, annual immigration from Norway, Sweden, Denmark, and Finland passed the 10,000 mark. Jacob Riis, social reformer and friend of Theodore Roosevelt, for example, left Denmark for America in 1870. Like so many other immigrants, he arrived with little but "a pair of strong hands, and stubbornness enough to do for two; [and] also a strong belief that in a free country, free from the dominion of custom, of caste, as well as of men, things would somehow come right in the end." Other Scandinavians obviously agreed, for annual immigration from Scandinavia did not fall below 10,000 until the disruptions caused by World War I. In the 1920s, when other Europeans resumed their exodus, the Scandinavians joined them.

As in the case of the Irish and the Germans, Scandinavian immigration can be correlated to a large extent with economic conditions at home and in the United States. Sweden enjoyed a period of good crop production between 1850 and 1864; the years between 1865 and 1868, however, culminated in a great famine that coincided with particularly bountiful times in the United States. During those years, the numbers of emigrants increased sharply, doubling from 1865 to 1866 and tripling from 9,000 in 1867 to 27,000 in 1868. The exodus from Norway of a large percentage of the nation's entire population at that time can be explained almost wholly by the industrial transformation and the consequent disruptions at home. Norwegian migration can be grouped into three significant periods: from

1866 to 1873, when 111,000 people came; from 1879 to 1893, when the figures went over 250,000; and from 1900 to 1910, when the numbers totaled about 200,000.

Industrialism came earlier in Denmark than in either Norway or Sweden, and the rural upheaval sent people into the cities and towns. But there were simply not enough jobs for those willing to work, and many artisans and skilled laborers sought opportunities in America. Wisconsin was the first state to attract Danes in any substantial number, but subsequently large contingents could be found in Iowa and Illinois as well. Before 1868 families generally emigrated from Denmark as units, but thereafter unmarried, young adult male immigrants exceeded married ones by an almost 3:1 margin. A plurality of these Danes were farmhands, but there was also a sprinkling of small landholders, craftsmen, and unskilled factory laborers. By 1920, U.S. census figures recorded 190,000 Danish-born.

Although economic factors overshadowed all others for the Scandinavians, it would be misleading to overlook social difficulties as motivating forces, except in the case of the Danes, who had no serious political or religious problems. In Sweden and Norway church and state were aligned, and both dissenters and nonconformists were penalized. There was no universal suffrage, and tightened conscription laws bothered many young men and their families; one scholar noted a particularly high proportion of emigrants among those eligible for military service in Sweden in the 1880s. Swedes in particular also abhorred the hierarchy of titles and the rigidly defined class system. After living in the United States, one Swede wrote home that his "cap [is not] worn out from lifting it in the presence of gentlemen. There is no class distinction between high and low, rich and poor, no make-believe, no 'title-sickness,' or artificial ceremonies. ... Everybody lives in peace and prosperity."

Another compelling, perhaps decisive, reason was something called "American fever." Just as in colonial America, after the Europeans arrived in the New World, they wrote to their compatriots and described the wonders of America, or the "land of Canaan." Nowhere did these letters have a greater impact than in the Scandinavian countries. They were passed carefully from family to family, published intact in the local newspapers, and discussed avidly from pulpits on Sundays. The influx of favorable mail inspired whole villages with the fervent desire to immigrate to America. Not all the letters from the United States glowed with praise, however, and many complained of the adjustment to the New World. But as one immigrant succinctly put it, "Norway cannot be compared to America any more than a desert can be compared to a garden in full bloom."

The Irish, the Germans, and the Scandinavians constituted the main group of non-English European immigrants before the 1890s, but others also chose to immigrate to the New World. Between 1815 and 1850 the predominantly rural Welsh endured severe agricultural discontent as the nation began industrializing. A depression hit Wales after 1815. The winter of 1814 had been the coldest in memory; and in 1816, "the year without summer," Wales began to feel the effect of a population explosion. By mid-century the region's inhabitants, like those in the rest of Europe, had doubled in number. The high birth rate, the increase in illegitimate births, and the pauperization of the peasants compounded the discontent. By comparison, the United States, to which an individual could sail for £2 or £3 from Liverpool in 1836, seemed to be a pot of gold at the end of the rainbow. The availability of land, the growth of American industry—especially in iron making and mining, where many Welshmen could use their skills—and the increasing number of "American letters" tempted those most inclined to seek a better life.

Dutch religious dissenters also considered American economic opportunities inviting. Beginning in the 1840s they founded colonies in Michigan, Wisconsin, Iowa, and what would later be South Dakota. Their departures from Europe corresponded with the potato blights and economic depression in Holland. By 1902 more than 135,000 Dutch, most of whom had arrived in the 1880s and 1890s, lived in the United States.

Several other groups, including the French from France, French Canadians, Chinese, and German Russians, also made significant impressions on the United States. Overpopulation at home and the diminishing size of agricultural plots that had been divided and subdivided for generations finally induced French Canadians to start emigrating in the 1830s, although most left Canada between 1860 and 1900. The approximately 300,000 emigrants settled for the most part in the mill villages and factory towns of New England, although scattered communities developed in New York and the upper Midwest.

The discovery of gold in California in 1849 had a great impact on the Chinese. News of the strike reached China by way of American merchant ships, but only the people of Toishan, a depressed agricultural province about 150 miles northwest of Hong Kong, responded. Toishan's agricultural output could feed its population for only about one third of the year, and floods and typhoons frequently devastated the community. As a result, many Toishanese moved into commercial activities and came in contact with Westerners in Hong Kong and Canton, the two major cities closest to their province. They were therefore receptive to the opportunity for enrichment in the United States, and a number of the more adventurous males made the long journey. Only a few women accompanied them. Perhaps half of these young men left their wives and families behind, and a good number returned home after a period of years in the United States working in the mines or on the railroads. It was not acceptable for single women to emigrate. Some who did were virtually seized from their families or sold to merchants who brought them to America to become prostitutes. In 1870, 61 percent of the 3,536 Chinese women in California had their occupation listed as prostitute. Other immigrant women ended up as prostitutes, but these Chinese women prompted some charges that the Chinese were immoral and unworthy of becoming Americans.

After the initial discovery of gold, about half of the Chinese settling in the United States came from Toishan, and a large percentage of the others came from areas surrounding that province. Lack of contact with Americans probably deterred other Chinese from going to the United States, and after 1882, when Chinese laborers were banned, few entered. The ban on Chinese immigrants did not include merchants and they and their wives continued to emigrate, though in small numbers. In 1930, 80 percent of the Chinese in America were men, largely living in bachelor societies, and about half of the women resided in San Francisco. These women were mostly confined to their prescribed roles in families.

The United States added Spanish speakers to its population when it acquired Florida in 1819, and many more following the Mexican-American War. The 1848 Treaty of Guadalupe Hidalgo permitted the U.S. to annex most of the Southwest. About 75,000 Mexicans living in this region were granted the right to become American citizens. Many did so, but a switch in loyalty did not prevent them from being overwhelmed by European Americans following the discovery of gold in California. Mexicans endured the loss of their lands, sometimes fraudulently; the loss of power; and an end to the pastoral life of Mexican California. The shabby treatment did not deter others from Mexico from immigrating to the United States. Like Europeans and Chinese, they came to work in the gold fields, along with other immigrants from Peru and Chile. Still other Mexicans, mostly men, came to work as cowboys or in agriculture. They were the forerunners of a greater migration from Mexico that occurred after 1910. Unfortunately, as historian Elliott Barkhan has written, "to subdue and control" both the earlier and later waves, Mexicans were subjected to "denigration, intimidation, subordination, exploitation, and expropriation."

German Russians, Germans who had settled in western Russia several generations earlier and who had been allowed not only to maintain their cultural heritage but also to be free from military service, began arriving in the United States in the 1870s after the Russian government abrogated earlier agreements and tried to incorporate these people into the nation's broader society. Most of these Germans traveled to what later became North and South Dakota, but others could be found in Montana, Kansas, and Nebraska. Almost all were Lutherans, Mennonites, or Hutterites, and some of their colonies today are more in tune with the values of yesteryear than they are with those of contemporary American society.

The physical and economic growth of the United States in the nineteenth century made it mandatory for Americans to turn to the new settlers for cheap labor to plow fields, build canals and railroads, dig mines, and run machinery in fledgling factories. Without the newcomers the vast riches of the nation could not have been exploited quickly. Major efforts and inducements were made to lure Europeans, French Canadians, Chinese, and, later, Latin Americans to the United States. Their strong backs and steadfast enterprise were necessary to turn American dreams into American accomplishments. At the forefront of these efforts were the state and territorial governments, the railroads, and the various emigrant-aid societies, which were buttressed by federal legislation.

Just as the Atlantic seaboard states had made efforts in the colonial period to attract settlers, so in the nineteenth century practically every state and territory of the American West, plus several others, sought to entice select groups of Europeans to their area. More people meant more schools and post offices, larger federal appropriations for internal improvements, larger markets for goods, faster economic development, "and the speedy arrival of the eagerly desired railroad."

In 1845 Michigan became the first state to provide for the appointment of an immigration agent to recruit settlers at the New York docks, and Wisconsin followed suit seven years later. After the Civil War, though, the competition among states for Europeans intensified, and efforts to attract them expanded on a vast scale. At least 33 states and territorial governments eventually set up immigration bureaus, advertised in European and American foreign-language newspapers, sent agents to northern and western Europe, and published their brochures, guidebooks, and maps in English, Welsh, German, Dutch, French, Norwegian, and Swedish. Each state elaborated upon its virtues, "the likes of which," one historian has written, "had never been known—except to other states seeking immigration." Minnesota, proud of its "beautiful lakes, forests, prairies and salubrious climate"—and quiet about its subzero winters—offered two prizes for the best essays on the state as a place for European immigrants and then published them in seven languages. Kansas specifically exempted the Mennonites from militia service, and thousands of them moved there from central and eastern Europe in the 1870s.

In 1870 the recruitment movement came to a head when several midwestern governors organized a national immigration convention at Indianapolis. Delegates from 22 states and the District of Columbia discussed how the federal government could be more helpful in encouraging foreigners to settle in the United States, and they petitioned Congress to establish a national immigration bureau. The heyday for the state bureaus ended with the depression of 1873, but several continued into the 1880s and 1890s. On the eve of World War I, Louisiana officials still distributed enticing brochures in several foreign languages to those disembarking at New Orleans, and the legislatures of Michigan, Wisconsin, and South Dakota continued to make appropriations to induce foreigners to settle in their states.

The railroads worked as hard as the states to attract immigrants and, in fact, in the words of historian Carl Wittke, were "probably the most important promotional agencies at work for some years around the turn of the century." After 1854, but especially in the 1870s and 1880s, most of the transcontinental railroads actively promoted immigration to the areas where they owned lands. The more people who settled in any given location, the more business and profits for the trains. Crops and merchandise would have to be moved. With additional markets and sources of labor, industrialists and governmental aid would surely follow. Like the states, the railroads subsidized agents in Europe, advertised and printed brochures in many languages, and played up the virtues of their respective territories. In addition, some gave free or reduced passage to prospective settlers, established immigrant receiving houses near their terminals, and built churches and schools for fledgling communities.

The first railroad to seek foreigners aggressively, the Illinois Central, inaugurated its program in 1854. The line sent special agents to the German states and the Scandinavian countries, and these men attended fairs and church services, arranged meetings, advertised in the local press, and promised fabulous inducements to prospective settlers. Not only did they help secure ocean passage, but they also provided free railroad transportation to Illinois for prospective land purchasers and their families. If the immigrants then bought land from the company, the Illinois Central allowed for long-term payments at 6 percent interest, gave discounts to the farmers for shipping their future crops on the line, and agreed to pay all land taxes until land-buying payments were completed. Immigrants preferred buying railroad lands to homesteading free governmental acreage because of these inducements, and because the railroads often offered choicer properties.

The Illinois Central had almost completed its efforts in 1870 when most other railroads were inaugurating their land and development bureaus. Some functioned as agents for states: the Burlington line, for example, represented Iowa; and the Northern Pacific line acted as Oregon's East Coast representative. Railroad companies also published monthly newsletters in various northern and western European languages, and the Northern Pacific even set up its own newspapers in Germany, Switzerland, and England. From 1882 to 1883 alone, the company printed 635,590 copies of its publications in English, Swedish, Norwegian, Danish, Dutch, and German and also distributed a monthly newsletter for immigrants, *Northwest*. The Burlington's efforts resulted in the sale of nearly 3 million acres in Iowa and Nebraska, and the Northern Pacific is credited with having more than doubled the population of Minnesota, the Dakotas, Montana, and the Pacific Northwest between 1880 and 1900.

Working together with the railroads and state agencies to encourage immigration were the various emigrant-aid societies. But unlike the state agencies and railroads, these semiphilanthropic organizations were more interested in assisting arriving Europeans and easing their travails in a foreign land by providing interpreters, clean boardinghouses, and employment bureaus in the United States than in encouraging them to come to America in the first place. This aid was clearly necessary, for as one Swedish emigration agent explained, "most of the emigrants are entirely ignorant about how to come to America."

Numerous steamship lines also promoted vigorously their own interests by seeking out immigrants. By 1882, 48 steamship companies traversed the Atlantic, each competing furiously with the others for the immigrant traffic. Fares were relatively cheap. One could go from England to the United

States, for instance, for about $12 to $15, from Copenhagen to New York for about $30, and from Odessa to Dakota Territory for $75. In many cases minor children accompanied their parents at no extra cost. Publicity and services attracted customers. The Red Star, Anchor, and Hamburg-American lines, among others, established more than 6,500 agencies in the United States to sell prepaid tickets. As early as the 1850s the Irish were sending more than a million dollars a year—about half in prepaid tickets—to their relatives and friends at home, and other immigrant groups were no less diligent. Estimates are that in the 1880s most of the Scandinavians emigrating to the United States came on prepaid tickets or purchased them with money specifically sent for that purpose. Although there are no exact statistics available, historians assume that 25 to 70 percent of all immigrants in the late nineteenth and early twentieth centuries received either prepaid tickets from the United States or money designated to facilitate the journey.

Although the companies vied for the immigrant traffic, few felt compelled to make the voyage comfortable for steerage passengers. Before the 1850s immigrants came in sailing vessels similar to those the colonists had arrived in a century or two earlier. The average journey across the Atlantic took about 44 days; voyages of four to six months were not uncommon. Like their forebears, many of those arriving in the nineteenth century, especially on English packets, which had been built for carrying cargo and not people, suffered inhumane treatment. Overcrowding, filth, stench, and poor ventilation were standard on almost all vessels, and tales of starvation and brutal assaults stand out in the accounts of the crossings. In 1846 a Dane who sailed to New York on a German ship wrote home, "Steerage became a regular brothel. We had four prostitutes and five thieves." Dysentery, cholera, typhoid fever, lice, and a disease known as "the itch" also presented problems. Those housed in the ship's bowels slept and ate on wooden bunks, which looked like dog kennels. One mid-century ship from Ireland possessed only 36 berths for 260 people; another had only 32 for 276. After one Irish ship had docked in New Orleans, customs officials found passengers and pigs lying together in "filth and feculent matter." One observer wrote that "it was a daily occurrence to see starving women and children fight for the food which was brought to the dogs and the pigs that were kept on the deck of the ship." An emigrants' guide in 1851 likened the fate of steerage travelers to that of prisoners on the African slavers; and as a surgeon who had served on six emigrant ships wrote, "The torments of hell might in some degree resemble the suffering of emigrants, but crime was punished in hell, whereas in an emigrant ship it flourished without check or retribution."

With the advent of steamships, however, conditions and amenities improved. The average crossing lasted fourteen days in 1867 and only five days in 1897. On the steamers all passengers had their own berths, women slept separately from men, and the galley provided three meals a day. Overcrowding and foul odors still existed, and the turbulence of the North Atlantic still forced many passengers to their knees to pray for divine assistance; but temporary inconveniences for two weeks or less could be endured. Moreover, between 1855 and 1875 both European and American governments established stringent rules to improve conditions for emigrants and restrict abuses by shipmasters.

Immigrant traffic followed commercial routes. Because of the Canadian timber trade and because British officials concluded that the fastest way to send mail to Canada was via Boston, a number of vessels, mostly British ships carrying the Irish, went to Massachusetts. Trade along the Mississippi River made New Orleans the major southern port; consequently it received the bulk of immigrants landing in the South. Since the journey to Louisiana took an extra two or three weeks and the climate in the lower South was muggy, most Europeans shunned that route. New York, the nation's major commercial center, also served as its chief immigration depot. After 1816 it accommodated more than 70 percent of the newcomers, and its reception centers at Castle Garden (on the southern tip of Manhattan) and later at Ellis Island became world famous.

Regulation of foreigners entering British America had been a function of the individual colonies and later, by tradition, of the states. Beginning in 1819 the federal government required the collection of vital statistics but otherwise allowed immigrants to enter unfettered until 1875, when it imposed additional regulations.

New York State, where most of the newcomers landed, passed a series of laws, beginning in 1824, requiring ship captains to post bonds indemnifying the state for any expenses incurred in connection with paupers disembarking there. Later the state required a $1 head tax on every steerage passenger to finance an immigrant hospital. In 1847 New York established the State Board of Commissioners of Immigration. The commissioners were granted the power to collect vital statistics, board and inspect incoming ships, establish and manage an immigrant hospital, and quarantine those who had communicable diseases. The commissioners, who served without pay, made every effort to assist the newly arrived foreigners. In 1855 they set up Castle Garden, a model reception center, through which everyone disembarking in New York had to pass. In this way the foreigners were counted, and their ages, occupations, religions, and the value of property they brought with them were recorded. Immigrants arriving at the center had to bathe with soap and water. Afterward they could purchase items like bread, milk, and coffee and use the extensive kitchen facilities to prepare their own food. Although officials encouraged everyone to leave the depot within hours of arrival, those who wished to remain could sleep overnight in the galleries. Beds were not provided, but a few thousand could be lodged. Immigration officials had already inspected and licensed numerous New York City boardinghouses and posted lists of suitable accommodations. Before this time many "greenhorns," as the immigrants were called, had been fleeced by boardinghouse agents and cheated by phony ticket sellers and other swindlers. To counteract this, Castle Garden also provided money exchanges and railroad and canal ticket booths for those going inland and disseminated information about the United States and employment opportunities throughout the country.

Castle Garden remained the nation's chief immigrant depot for more than 35 years. In 1876 the U.S. Supreme Court forbade New York State to collect bonds from ship captains on the ground that they were equivalent to head taxes, and for the next six years the state financed the reception center out of its general funds. In 1882 Congress levied a 50-cent head tax on newcomers and defrayed New York's expenses out of the monies collected. The federal government finally took charge of immigration in 1890. Ellis Island then replaced the abandoned Castle Garden as the gateway to America for millions of Europeans. On the West Coast, Angel Island in San Francisco Bay received newcomers from China and other nations that bordered the Pacific Ocean.

Once through Castle Garden or Ellis Island, foreigners dispersed quickly (see table 2.2). Those too poor to go anywhere else remained in New York. Others, determined to reach the wooded regions and fertile prairies of the Midwest, obtained the necessary railroad or canal tickets and proceeded on their journeys. A favorite route began with a boat ride up the Hudson River to Albany and across the Erie Canal to Buffalo, then continued by water, rail, or wagon to the ultimate destination. Most of the nineteenth-century newcomers from Germany and Scandinavia wanted their own farms; the

[TABLE 2.2]
The Urban Immigrant, 1870:
Irish, German, and English Populations in American Cities

NAME OF CITY	TOTAL POPULATION	IRISH	GERMANS	ENGLISH
1. New York, N.Y.	942,292	202,000	151,203	24,408
2. Philadelphia, Pa.	674,022	96,698	50,746	22,034
*3. Brooklyn, N.Y.	376,099	73,985	36,769	18,832
4. St. Louis, Mo.	310,864	32,239	59,040	5,366
5. Chicago, Ill.	298,977	40,000	52,316	10,026
6. Baltimore, Md.	267,354	15,223	35,276	2,138
7. Boston, Mass.	250,526	56,900	5,606	6,000
8. Cincinnati, Ohio	216,239	18,624	49,446	3,524
9. New Orleans, La.	191,418	14,693	15,224	2,005
10. San Francisco, Calif.	149,473	25,864	13,602	5,166
11. Buffalo, N.Y.	117,714	11,264	22,249	3,558
12. Washington, D.C.	109,200	6,948	4,131	1,231
13. Newark, N.J.	105,059	12,481	15,873	4,040
14. Louisville, Ky.	100,753	7,626	14,380	930
15. Cleveland, Ohio	92,829	9,964	15,855	4,530
16. Pittsburgh, Pa.	86,076	13,119	8,703	2,838
17. Jersey City, N.J.	82,546	17,665	7,151	4,005
18. Detroit, Mich.	79,577	6,970	12,647	3,282
19. Milwaukee, Wis.	71,440	3,784	22,600	1,395
20. Albany, N.Y.	69,422	13,276	5,168	1,572
21. Providence, R.I.	68,904	12,085	596	2,426
22. Rochester, N.Y.	62,386	6,078	7,730	2,530
23. Allegheny, Pa.	53,180	4,034	7,665	1,112
24. Richmond, Va.	51,038	1,239	1,621	289
25. New Haven, Conn.	50,840	9,601	2,423	1,087
26. Charleston, S.C.	48,956	2,180	1,826	234
27. Indianapolis, Ind.	48,244	3,321	5,286	697
28. Troy, N.Y.	46,465	10,877	1,174	1,575
29. Syracuse, N.Y.	43,051	172	5,062	1,345
30. Worcester, Mass.	41,105	389	325	893
31. Lowell, Mass.	40,928	103	34	1,697
32. Memphis, Tenn.	40,226	2,987	1,768	589
33. Cambridge, Mass.	39,634	7,180	482	1,043
34. Hartford, Conn.	37,180	7,438	1,458	787
35. Scranton, Pa	35,092	6,491	3,056	1,444
36. Reading, Pa.	33,930	547	2,648	305
37. Paterson, N.J.	33,600	5,124	1,429	3,347
38. Kansas City, Mo.	32,260	2,869	1,884	709
39. Mobile, Ala.	32,034	2,000	843	386
40. Toledo, Ohio	31,584	3,032	5,341	694

[TABLE 2.2] *(continued)*

The Urban Immigrant, 1870:

Irish, German, and English Populations in American Cities

NAME OF CITY	TOTAL POPULATION	IRISH	GERMANS	ENGLISH
41. Portland, Me.	31,413	3,900	82	557
42. Columbus, Ohio	31,274	1,845	3,982	504
43. Wilmington, Del.	30,841	3,503	684	613
44. Dayton, Ohio	30,473	1,326	4,962	394
45. Lawrence, Mass.	28,921	7,457	467	2,456
46. Utica, N.Y.	28,804	3,496	2,822	1,352
47. Charlestown, Mass.	28,323	4,803	216	488
48. Savannah, Ga.	28,235	2,197	787	251
49. Lynn, Mass.	28,233	3,232	17	330
50. Fall River, Mass.	26,766	5,572	37	4,042

*Brooklyn, New York, was a separate city in 1870. It did not become part of New York City until 1898.

Source: U.S. Census, 1870.

Homestead Act, invitations from the states and the railroads, and letters from relatives drew most of them to the north central plains, where land was either free or cheap. (As late as 1879 some Wisconsin land sold for 50 cents an acre.)

Those too poor to finance any trip—like many of the Irish—accepted offers from canal and railroad builders to be taken to various construction projects and mines throughout the nation. As a result, pockets of Irish could be found in every region of the country working in the most dangerous mines below ground and above it laying down railroad tracks. Strong Irish colonies existed in St. Louis, New Orleans, San Francisco, and even in Butte, Montana. Most of them, however, remained either in the port cities where they arrived or lived in the northeastern quadrant of the nation. Thus by the end of the nineteenth century the largest concentration of Irish could be found in the states of Massachusetts, New York, Pennsylvania, and Illinois.

As already noted, Germans constituted the most numerous of the nineteenth-century immigrants. Originally they hoped to plant a new Germany in America. Missouri in the 1830s, Texas in the 1840s, and Wisconsin in the 1850s were the states that they had hoped to make their own, but American expansion and ideology quickly frustrated such visions. Americans were unwilling to allow any group to carve out its own exclusive territory in the United States, and subsequent waves of immigrants showed no respect or tolerance for the wishes of those Germans who wanted to insulate their settlements. Germans toiled as farmers in rural areas and as both skilled and unskilled laborers in urban communities. Nearly half of them settled in Illinois, Michigan, Missouri, Iowa, and Wisconsin, but Texas published its laws in the German language in 1843, and Germans constituted one fifth of the white population there four years later. Many of the counties of west Texas owe their beginnings to German immigrants, and by 1900 about one third of the state's white population had German parents or grandparents. Germans also dominated the foreign-born statistics and lent a particular flavor to cities like St. Louis, Cincinnati, and Milwaukee. In New York City they outnumbered all other foreigners except the Irish in 1870. One observer described New York's German section in the 1850s: "Life in *Kleindeutchland* is almost the same as in the Old Country. ... There is not a single business which is not run by Germans. Not only the shoe-makers, tailors, barbers, physicians, grocers, and innkeepers are German, but the pastors and priests as well. ... The resident of *Kleindeutschland* need not even know English in order to make a living." One chronicler made the same observation about people in and around Fort Wayne, Indiana. Until World War I it was possible for German immigrants, and for their children, to live a German-American life—attending German-language parochial or public schools, dozing through long German sermons from the pulpit, reading Fort Wayne German newspapers, purchasing grocery, hardware, and agricultural supplies from German stores that prudently employed German-speaking clerks, attending German band and choral performances, sharing a "grawler" of locally brewed German beer and locally packed German sausages with fellow workers at one of the 170 friendly ethnic saloons, and ultimately to take final rest in an exclusive German Lutheran, Catholic, or Jewish cemetery.

Scandinavians, a third group whose presence in nineteenth-century America is frequently noted, went mostly to the wheat-growing regions of Illinois, Wisconsin, Iowa, Minnesota, the Dakotas, Kansas, and Nebraska, as well as to Utah and Washington territory in the Northwest. The rich and fertile soil, the open spaces, and the harsh winter climate reminded them of their European homes, and with each successive wave of settlement there was the added attraction of living near friends and relatives from the old country. The solicitations from the actively recruiting states and railroads steered them into the Midwest, and the boom times of the early 1880s kept them there. Minnesota's population, buttressed by heavy migration from Germany and Scandinavia, soared from 8,425 in 1860 to 101,109 in 1870 and to 1,301,826 in 1890. Wisconsin, Iowa, Illinois, and the Dakotas showed similar rises. But the bitter winter of 1886–87 and the successive years of failing wheat crops slowed the pace. Beginning in the early 1890s Scandinavians responded to the industrial opportunities in the Northeast and the Middle Atlantic states as well as in the lumber camps and sawmills of the Pacific Northwest. The influx of Scandinavians and others into what would become the state of Washington in 1889, for example, reached such proportions that the population jumped from 75,000 in 1880 to over 1 million in 1910. Every census after 1910 shows more than 60 percent of the Swedish-born and their children living in urban areas. In 1917 Chicago had the largest number of Swedes and Norwegians in the world next to Stockholm and Oslo, respectively, and 13 years later the federal census found a sizable Norwegian population comfortably established in a middle-class neighborhood of Brooklyn, New York.

Other nineteenth-century newcomers went to both urban and rural areas. The French Canadians had established communities in Winooski, Vermont, and Woonsocket, Rhode Island, as early as 1814 and 1815, and before the middle of the century they could also be found in Madawaska and Burlington, Vermont. In 1850, moreover, they constituted about half of the population of Plattsburgh, New York, and environs. By the end of the nineteenth century they constituted a major minority in New England and much smaller ones in the cities of northern New York, Michigan, Illinois, and Wisconsin. Welsh people who came to America headed for the mining camps in Pennsylvania and Ohio. The Dutch, who went to the wooded and lake regions of southwestern Michigan, northern Illinois, and southern Wisconsin, also had settlements in Iowa, New York, Wyoming, and Arizona. Czechs, on the other hand, went mostly to the prairie lands in Wisconsin, Nebraska, and Texas. Some of the mountain states in the West attracted English, Scottish, and Welsh settlers, and the Mormons in Utah were particularly successful in converting some Dutch and Scandinavian peoples who then went on to places like Ogden and Salt Lake City. Immigrants from the British Isles, Germany, and the Russian Empire found the coal mines of the foothills of the Kiamichi Mountains in southeastern Oklahoma compelling because of the relatively high wages they could earn there.

The South failed to attract many immigrants because they believed that they would have to compete with plantation slaves. Moreover, the climate of the Southern states made them less appealing. On the eve of the Civil War only 5 percent of southerners were foreign-born. Immigrants who settled in the South could be found in the port cities of Baltimore, New Orleans, Charlestown, and Savannah. Like areas of the North the newcomers were usually Germans or Irish. After the Civil War southerners held conventions aimed at promoting immigration, but their success was limited. White southerners even enticed Chinese immigrants to work on plantations. The Chinese quickly discovered that plantation work was difficult, and after a few years they left to return to California or opened small shops, largely catering to blacks. Even today a few hundred of their descendants live in the Mississippi delta.

Wherever they went and whoever they were, the immigrants lived and worked under conditions that were far from idyllic. Male workers were always needed in the dangerous construction of the canals and railroads, and strapping Irishmen won a reputation for talent and skill in these construction industries. Irish laborers built the Illinois Central Railroad before the company employed German hands. The Union Pacific used Mexicans, Germans, Chinese, and Irish to get its lines going. In rural areas, prairie fires, blizzards, the pestilence of grasshoppers, and the ravages of storms or long spells of dry weather were not unknown. Food was often scarce. Many Danes in Nebraska wore wooden shoes rather than leather ones; among many of the pioneers, who depended upon the homespun garments that their women made for them, underwear was also considered a luxury that hardier settlers did without. A German in Indiana wrote home in 1842, "We have reduced our requirements for luxuries very sharply: We drink coffee on Sundays only, go barefoot all summer and make our own clothes because we keep sheep and can also make flax."

Life in rural America was exceedingly difficult for women. Farm lands had to be cleared and crops planted and harvested. Women were expected to help with these tasks in addition to rearing children and running the household. Unmarried women carried a major farming burden. Because doctors were rare, women also helped one another in sickness and childbirth. Although immigrants set up ethnic organizations, the church being the most important, to aid in settlement and survival, primitive transportation made communication with friends and family difficult during the harsh winter months. Because of their isolation, rural families were apt to cling to traditional practices and values, in which the women played such a vital role. They spoke in their native language to the children, prepared ethnic foods, and in general conveyed a sense of the Old World culture. It is no doubt true that women in immigrant families were the main keepers of ethnic cultures because of their central role in family life, and in rural America it was possible to resist the process of Americanization more easily than in the cities.

Mass immigration also resulted in new social problems for urban dwellers, especially in congested cities like New York and Chicago. Immigrants who were either unemployed or underemployed, as well as those who were diseased and/or living in poverty, found coping difficult.

For the most part, however, immigrants generally found work wherever they chose to live but often in unskilled jobs where wages were low. In cities like New York, Boston, and Chicago, immigrants composed the bulk of the unskilled laborers, porters, street cleaners, bartenders, waiters, draymen, cabmen, livery workers, and domestics. The Irish could be found as stevedores on docks at every major port of the country. In New England they replaced young American women in the mills and later stepped aside for the French Canadians, who became the mainstay of the region's late nineteenth- and early twentieth-century textile establishments. Germans in New York held menial positions but also qualified as tailors and skilled craftsmen in furniture, cabinet making, and bookbinding firms; in Cincinnati they were dominant in the stove and musical instrument industries. Those Norwegians who did not farm worked in the iron mines and lumber camps in Michigan, in the sawmills and fisheries in the Pacific Northwest, and at other industrial tasks in places as diverse as Tacoma, Cleveland, and Brooklyn.

While many men labored indoors and outside as well, single women often worked as domestics, which they regarded as a vast improvement over similar experiences in Europe. As early as 1860, Irish women constituted two-thirds of the domestics in Boston, but later in the century Scandinavians provided competition. Swedish women, no less than Swedish men, found limited economic opportunities at home, and it became common for late adolescents to seek outside employment. But as with Irish women, employment in the home country offered brutal working conditions with little chance for advancement. They quickly found improved conditions in the United States, generally near other Swedes with whom they could associate during their leisure hours. Letters home indicated that they worked fewer hours, had specified indoor tasks and none outdoors, and that the existence of indoor plumbing provided numerous conveniences. Moreover the young women had opportunities for learning. While they absorbed the New World culture they viewed their new lives as having increased status. Women may still have been subordinate to men but much less so than they had been in the lands these working women had come from. Moreover, they were they treated with affection and respect. One woman wrote home, "I now have a place in a family.... They are concerned for me as if I were their own daughter." A Swedish male also noted differences in treatment in the United States. He wrote to his sister in Europe, "America is the woman's promised land.... A domestic is never asked to clean her employer's shoes, he does that himself."

Most immigrant men expected their wives to stay home, raise the children, and care for the household, for immigrant families often included five or more children. Women also served as midwives to bring their neighbors', friends', and relatives' children into the world. Unmarried women were usually sent to work to contribute to the family income. They found jobs in the nation's growing number of garment shops, in the printing business, as domestics, and as dressmakers. After women married they usually remained at home, but on occasion some still sought outside employment. Others added to their domestic responsibilities, and contributed to the family coffers, by taking in lodgers. One historian described the situation among Irish anthracite miners in Pennsylvania: "in addition to a married couple and their children, households often included other relatives, or a number of boarders, or in some cases a second family. These households were almost ethnically exclusive."

Widows and those whose husbands had deserted them needed to support their children. Socially acceptable work for which they had the necessary skill, such as sewing at home, was not lucrative. Not even the labor of their children, who went to work at an early age, could provide enough income. Thus in much of the United States a strikingly large number of households headed by women lived in a precarious state.

In the West ethnic laborers sometimes worked harmoniously with members of other groups and sometimes less so. Utah's Carbon County housed individuals who, collectively, spoke 36 different languages. From 1860 to 1890, Wilkerson, Washington, workers included emigrants from Croatia, Slovakia, the Western Ukraine, Poland, Italy, and Finland. Despite religious, class, and ethnic differences, they cooperated with one another in political and economic endeavors. Their baseball teams, however, were based strictly on ethnicity.

The Chinese, on the other hand, were shunned in mines, domestic service, and on farms. Forced into narrow economic choices, they opened restaurants and laundries, and also did menial work on farms. Moreover, excluded from the white men's unions, they showed no respect for those who went out on strike. They did not hesitate to work as scabs and strikebreakers. When miners struck in 1875, for example, the Union Pacific Railroad's managers brought 125 Chinese to mine in Rock Springs, Wyoming. Ten years later a similar problem resulted in the further importation of Chinese workers, who refused to join the Knights of Labor. This no doubt precipitated the September 1885 massacre in Rock Springs, where whites killed 28 Chinese laborers, wounded 15 others, and chased several hundred out of town.

The conditions under which Americans and immigrants labored were often appalling. Since American wages were much higher than those in Europe and Asia, emigrants did not realize that there could be economic hardships in the United States, due to a correspondingly high cost of living. In Sweden farmhands earned $33.50 a year, plus room and board. It is no wonder, therefore, that a salary of $40 a month in the Pennsylvania coal mines, $1.25 to $2.00 a day on a railroad construction gang, or $200 a year as an American farmhand would be appealing. Not until they reached the United States and had to cope with the realities of urban squalor or rural depression did the emigrants realize that the American laborer did not lead a princely existence. During the boom times in the Midwest after the Civil War, farm income was relatively high. Wheat sold for $1.50 a bushel, and hard work seemed to ensure prosperity. But in the 1890s wheat prices fell on the world market to 50 cents a bushel. Countless farmers were ruined. There is no doubt that the failure of wheat crops in places like Kansas, Nebraska, Minnesota, and the Dakotas contributed to the decline in migration to those areas in the late 1880s and early 1890s.

Employees in industrial enterprises fared just as badly as those on the farm. In the nineteenth century there was a chronic labor shortage even though at times cities like Boston had more people than jobs. But the pay in most occupations failed to sustain even a modest standard of living. In 1851 the *New York Times* and the New York *Tribune* published estimated budgets for a family of five. The first came to about $600 a year, the second to $539. Yet the wage scales reveal that most employees' yearly incomes fell far short of these figures. A skilled tailor might earn $6 to $9 a week but did not work a 52-week year. Cabinetmakers earned $5 a week, and common laborers took home $20 to $30 a month. A journeyman dressmaker earned $1.25 to $1.50 for a 14- to 16-hour day. In Boston, in 1830, when the annual cost of living was $440, the average working person earned $230; in 1864, when the cost of living rose to $810, the average unskilled laborer made only $465. Real wages increased in the decades after the Civil War, but many immigrant families received only a few hundred dollars a year and had to struggle to maintain a modest standard of living.

Such low wages and yearly incomes make clear why so many immigrants, as well as many native-born Americans, lived in humble and often squalid dwellings. The typical Norwegian in the upper Midwest built a log cabin 12 feet by 12 or 14 feet, with a height of 7 to 14 feet, for himself and his family. The early Dutch pioneers of Michigan lived under bedsheets framed on hemlock branches, with cooking pots outside. When they earned enough to build a more commodious abode, several families shared a one-room log cabin. The German Russians in North Dakota put together homes representative of many others on the Great Plains. Inexpensively built, they had interior walls plastered with a straw- or prairie-grass clay mud and limewashed. Few of the homes had wooden floors since lumber was too expensive and the original occupants did not expect to remain long.

Urban enclaves also left much to be desired. In small cities like Fall River and Holyoke, Massachusetts, French Canadians squeezed into dark, dank, rat-infested tenements that one chronicler pronounced "worse than the old slave quarters." Housing in most of the major urban centers was also appalling. In Boston the Irish resided in "crammed hovels ... without furniture and with patches of dirty straw," in damp cellars that flowed with raw sewage after heavy rains, or in reconverted factory lofts with leaking roofs, broken windows, and no running water. Historian Oscar Handlin, who vividly chronicled their experiences, tells us that in winter the Boston Irish often remained in bed all day to protect themselves from the cold or "huddled together like brutes, without regard to sex, or age, or sense of decency." Similar hovels existed in New York as well. In the middle of the century 18,000 people lived in cellars without light, air, or drainage, and even those residing above them had to use outdoor, and often malfunctioning, privies—winter and summer. Overcrowding was proverbial; half a million people lived in 16,000 dilapidated tenements. The Irish often grouped five or six families in a single flat. Three quarters of the city had no sewers; garbage and horse droppings littered ghetto streets.

The appalling overcrowding of immigrants and lack of proper sanitation led to continual bouts with disease. Slum dwellers suffered from consumption, cancer, pneumonia, diarrhea, and bronchitis. They were also victims of periodic epidemics of typhoid, typhus, and cholera, which spread through the neighborhoods like fires in a parched forest. Cities having large immigrant populations—New York, St. Louis, Cincinnati, and New Orleans—suffered the most from such outbreaks. In 1851 a cholera epidemic hit Chicago, and in one three-block section where 332 Scandinavians (mostly Norwegians) lived, *everyone* died from the disease. Hospitals and lunatic asylums housed disproportionately high numbers of newcomers. In 1850s New York City, 85 percent of the foreign-born admitted to Bellevue Hospital were Irish; so were most of those admitted to Blackwell's Island, the city's asylum.

In rural areas too settlers, poorly versed in the need for proper sanitation, preventative measures, and the benefits of quarantines during bouts with contagious diseases, often fell prey to the ravages of epidemics. In 1898 a wave of diphtheria spread through McIntosh County, North Dakota, yet the German Russians insisted that every member of the family attend all of the funerals of neighbors who perished. As a result all the adults and children in the community either had the disease or had been exposed to it. One cabinetmaker there, who worked day and night building coffins, had to construct three for his own children, ages 12, 10, and 3, who died within a week of one another.

Poverty was another common affliction for the immigrants. Rural folk would sometimes benefit from the generosity of their neighbors, but in the larger cities many of the poor turned to almshouses. Those forced to accept charity also had to tolerate the sanctimonious declaration that they were merely "the indolent, the aged, and infirm who can earn their subsistence nowhere, [but must] become a burden, and often because of their vices, a nuisance to the community." The foreign-born outnumbered the native-born in the poorhouses of the nation in 1850; in some states, like New York, the ratio was greater than 2:1. The problem worsened with the arrival of new immigrants.

Among the most serious difficulties newcomers encountered was American intolerance for ethnic differences. Each immigrant group experienced hostility in countless ways. The best jobs were closed to them, and employers posted signs saying NO IRISH NEED APPLY or some variation on that theme. Institutions dealing with the foreign-born—almshouses, hospital dispensaries, employment bureaus—treated their clients with "a ridiculous, often brutal disdain." Hardly any minority escaped the barbs of the prejudiced. The Germans received abuse from several sides. Temperance advocates did not like their making merry, drinking beer, and ignoring the Puritan Sabbath. Conservatives distrusted radical and reform-minded German exiles from the abortive revolutions of 1848 who supported the abolition of slavery, women's rights, and other liberal causes in America.

Economics, and the alleged lack of morality, in part explain ethnic intolerance. The increase in immigration, especially of many poverty-stricken refugees from Ireland, aroused American fears of having too many poor people. And large numbers of unskilled laborers, it was argued, would depress wages and the American standard of living. Americans also deplored what they considered the immigrants' striking personal deficiencies. A Massachusetts Bureau of Labor Statistics report in the 1880s censured the French Canadians for their lack of "moral character, their lack of respect for American institutions, their failure to become naturalized, and their opposition to education."

Before the Civil War the most important source of conflict between native-born and immigrant was religion. More precisely, the key battles were fought over American objections to Irish Catholics. The underlying issue revolved around the American belief that Roman Catholicism and American institutions, which were based on Protestant concepts, were incompatible. In this view, if Catholics "took over" America, the pope in Rome would rule and religious and political liberty would be destroyed. Samuel F. B. Morse, inventor of the telegraph, believed that there was a Catholic plot to destroy the United States. He held that the Church was sending Jesuit-controlled immigrants to America. Writing in 1835, he asked his countrymen not to be any longer "deceived by the pensioned Jesuits, who have surrounded your press, are now using it all over the country to stifle the cries of danger, and lull your fears by attributing your alarm to a false cause.... To your posts! ... Fly to protect the vulnerable places of your Constitution and Laws. Place your guards; you will need them, and quickly too.—And first, shut your gates."

Morse was not the only impassioned enemy of Catholicism. Militant Protestants wrote sensational exposés of the Church. The most famous of the anti-Catholic diatribes was Maria Monk's *Awful Disclosures of the Ho-*

tel Dieu Nunnery of Montreal, published in 1836. This gothic horror tale was frequently reprinted and sold several hundred thousand copies. According to her inflammatory story, the author was compelled to live in sin with priests in the nunnery and witnessed the execution of nuns for refusing to submit to the men's carnal lusts. She even insisted that babies were strangled and buried in the basement of the Hotel Dieu Nunnery. Such yarns created inevitable controversy. On the one hand, Monk's work was cited by anti-Catholics as proof of their worst fears, and on the other hand, indignant Catholics and skeptical Protestants denounced the book as a fraud. Investigations turned up no evidence to support her charges, and Maria Monk was personally discredited as a prostitute. Nevertheless, many believed her story and the book continued to inflame the passions of the anti-Catholic crusade. Her success encouraged others to publish similar hair-raising studies, and she herself added to the literature by writing *Further Disclosures,* also about the Hotel Dieu. Archbishop John Hughes of New York hardly allayed Protestants' fears in the 1840s and 1850s when he clearly stated, "everyone should know that we [Catholics] have for our mission to convert the world."

Tales of women's experiences in nunneries and the statement from Archbishop Hughes fanned the passions of the day and contributed to anti-Catholic hostility. In August of 1834 an angry mob burned the Ursuline Convent outside of Boston. Nativist violence occurred in other places in antebellum America, including a riot in Philadelphia in the summer of 1844. Most conflicts did not lead to violence but involved controversies over control of church property, religious teaching in the schools, and the general issues of separation of church and state.

Not satisfied with exposés and agitation, the nativists turned to state and national politics for weapons against the detested Catholics. A few nativist political organizations and parties existed prior to 1850, but the major nativist party flourished during the 1850s. Called the Know-Nothings, this large secret organization suffered from a number of sectional disagreements and eventually fell apart as a national movement. At its peak it was held together by a suspicion of the Roman Catholic Church. In 1854 the party scored victories at the polls, won control of several state governments, and sent dozens of congressmen to Washington. The Know-Nothings were strongest in the Northeast and the border states. Once in office the nativists proposed a number of bills to restrict the franchise and to make naturalization a longer process. They also established legislative committees to investigate alleged misconduct in Catholic institutions. Many Know-Nothings who took Maria Monk seriously were convinced that nuns were virtual prisoners in convents, and they petitioned state governments to free these women.

The proposals and investigations produced few results, and did not lead to immigration restriction. The movement failed in part because the party was fragmented, in part because discussions concerning the morality and extension of slavery consumed American political attention in the late 1850s. But most important, despite fears about Catholics and their imagined habits and other alleged evils of immigration, was the fact that Americans welcomed immigrants because they were needed to help the nation expand and develop economically.

Yet even without native hostility, foreigners and their children preferred living in ethnic enclaves and often resisted moving into the mainstream. In some Norwegian communities a "yankee was almost an alien" and a visitor to Scandinavia, Wisconsin, in 1879–80 noted: "On the streets, in stores, one heard only Norwegian. The church was a replica of those at home; the minister wore the vestments of the State Church; the hymnbooks were the same as those used in Norway." A more recent commentator wrote that although his grandparents lived in the United States for more than sixty years, "There's no evidence that they had more than glancing contact with anyone who was not Norwegian."

Several groups, including Irish Catholics, Germans, and Scandinavians, established parochial schools to preserve traditions and thwart assimilation. The French Canadians feared that losing their language would mean losing their faith, which to them meant absolute loss of identity. For the Irish, language presented hardly any problem, but their church claimed their staunchest allegiance. To them nothing seemed as important as keeping the faith. Many sermons and religious tracts of the Irish Catholics, historian Hasia Diner tells us, "linked common schooling with Protestantism, atheism, sexual depravity, and social unrest." In the upper Midwest, among other places, Germans and Scandinavians maintained Lutheran parochial institutions of learning. In 1917 Minnesota alone had over 350 elementary and secondary schools; 270 different German-language texts were in use. On the eve of World War I fewer than one-third of all the parochial schools in the state taught their children in the English language. Most of the rest utilized German, but there were also public schools conducted in Polish, French, Norwegian, Danish, Dutch, and Czech.

Schooling and language were closely tied to religion, and many religious groups split over the appropriate course of behavior and action. Most curricula opted for the maintenance of established values. Among Catholics, liberal cardinals like James Gibbons of Baltimore and John Ireland of St. Paul argued for a gospel of success and accommodation with the members of the dominant society. They favored assimilation, opposed parochial schools, and frowned on Catholic insularity. But the more conservative theologians of the Northeast, like Bishop Bernard McQuaid of Rochester, Archbishop Michael Corrigan of New York City, and William Cardinal O'Connor of Boston, did not agree with their more liberal counterparts. "Clinging to medieval visions of church and society," prize-winning historian Kerby Miller tells us, "the conservatives revered tradition, order, and authority both religious and secular." They feared socialism and progressive change and aligned themselves "with the most reactionary elements of native society. Likewise their refusal to attribute social and spiritual ills to any source other than 'Anglo-Saxonism' (their synonym for Protestantism and materialism) impelled conservatives to segregate their flocks behind rigid ideological and institutional barriers."

Protestants suffered from similar woes. One chronicler of newcomers to South Dakota noted, "The central role of the church as a conservative force that defended cultural continuity with the past cannot be overstated. It was the key to cultural maintenance and local identity in all immigrant communities." Constant admonitions from Scandinavian clergymen that "language saves faith" and knowledge of English promoted loss of heritage permeated the region.

Germans especially clung to their religious traditions and fought bitterly any attempt to interfere with their cultural heritage. In 1889, when Wisconsin and Illinois passed laws requiring some of the education of school-age children to be conducted in English, both Lutheran and Catholic Germans denounced the new measures. Their united opposition led to Republican electoral defeats in both states and the subsequent repeal of the offensive acts. The strong stand Germans took against compulsory education in English reinforced prevailing views about their clannishness. What is more, they did little to alter this impression, making great efforts to maintain the Old World culture. In Nashville, Tennessee, observers noted that the newcomers "used the German language as a weapon to ward off Americanization and assimilation and used every social milieu—the home, the press, and the church—in the fight to preserve the German language and

German customs among their children and grandchildren." Historian Andrew Yox, who wrote about newcomers in the North, reiterated almost the same point.

> The German immigrants who came to America in the mid-nineteenth century established a counterculture they called *Deutschtum*. In medium-sized cities like Buffalo, Cincinnati, and Milwaukee, the German quarter consisted of Gothic steeples, rows of small frame cottages, open-air markets, and the ubiquitous saloon. Unlike the sedate neighborhoods of the Anglo-Americans, the German district rustled with sounds. Beer gardens, brass bands, shops, dance halls, and "slumber-breaking" bells, installed in the steeples to rouse the artisans for work, teamed up to deprive the Yankees of their once-quiet weekends. The German community was younger, more tolerant with regard to beer and dancing, and more populated than the native American sectors. With respect to other immigrant enclaves, the German colony was larger and more developed. In major cities, *Deutschtum* consisted not only of stores and saloons, but banks, hospitals, orchestra halls, and elite social clubs.

Efforts were made to keep everything German; women in particular were admonished "that they must seek to preserve the German spirit in their children." A Texas grandmother, who had come to this country as a 10-year-old girl in 1846, published her memoirs, *Was Grossmutter Erzählt* (1915), in her native tongue and reminded readers that "German family life stands for the preservation of an ideal culture, which can only continue to exert its influence if respected from generation to generation." Most German Americans obviously felt the same way, for at the beginning of the twentieth century it was rare for midwestern Germans to choose mates from other ethnic groups, and on the eve of World War I, 70 percent of the Lutheran churches in St. Louis conducted their services in German. In some German-Russian areas of North Dakota, moreover, church services and Sunday schools in the German language continued into the early 1950s.

Practically every ethnic group that arrived in the nineteenth and twentieth centuries established a variety of organizations, publications, and/ or activities to preserve Old World culture, explain the American scene, and help newcomers adjust to life in the United States. These included, but were not limited to, gymnastic societies, choral and dramatic groups, and newspapers that provided information about the homeland to home-sick emigrants. Germans, being the largest group of immigrants in the nineteenth century, had the most expansive network of organizations and societies. By 1900 over 750 German-language newspapers existed in the United States, 64 of them in North and South Dakota alone. In fact, in 1905 the *Dakota Freie Press* had more subscribers than any English-language newspaper in South Dakota. German daily and weekly papers also dotted the landscape in all of the major American cities.

Germans also enjoyed their ethnic theater, their beer, their convivial picnics, their pleasure-filled Sundays, and their melodious music. While parks all over America had bandstands filled by German oompah bands, their *Liederkranz* (singing societies) and *Sangerbunde* (regional and national associations or song groups) made an even more significant national impact. The *Liederkranz* groups were among the most popular cultural societies in the nation between the end of the Civil War and the advent of World War I. Composed of all-male choruses (some cities had female auxiliaries), they prompted not only choral songs but also classical music, opera, and philharmonic concepts. These singing societies were a major force on the cultural scene in Chicago, Buffalo, Philadelphia, Pittsburgh, Cincinnati, and many other cities. In Louisville, Kentucky, "the Liederkranz was the most prestigious of all the musical organizations," while in Wheeling, West Virginia, there were eleven different German singing societies from 1855 until their demise in 1961 and, we are told, "for many of Wheeling's German citizens the singing societies were a way of life."

The coming of World War I marked the decline of the German American culture. Other Americans demanded 100 percent loyalty and renounced everything and everyone that smacked of "the Hun." Though many resented these pressures, German Americans made a strong effort to conform to the dominant customs and thereby weakened their own heritage.

Scandinavians, who were mostly Lutheran, were more devout and strait-laced than the Germans. No one caricatured them as jolly or frolicsome. Their faith, a stern one that frowned on drinking, dancing, and levity, also provided a complete philosophy of life stressing piety along with the work ethic. This influence was so pervasive and persistent that in 1934 fully two thirds of all the Protestant church members in Minnesota, Wisconsin, and the Dakotas still identified themselves as Lutherans.

The security derived from family, ethnic neighborhood, school, church, society, and newspapers hastened the day when immigrant children or grandchildren could stand securely on their own and move into the main-stream of American life. Having been nurtured in relative security, they had the strength to meet new challenges of becoming Americanized head-on. They knew, however, that the customs that provided a secure ground for their parents or grandparents would not suffice for them in the United States. Girls and women, more sheltered from the outside world than boys and men, took their cues from fathers and husbands, changing their ways to the extent that the head of the household dictated. Yet disclaimers must be made. To be sure, in the German and Scandinavian households tradi-tional values and lifestyles prevailed. In most of these homes women were respected and appreciated for what they were—"good, laborious, submis-sive, and silent housewives." But among some of the German Russians in the Dakotas, women were somehow thought to be of considerably less value to a family unit; one popular saying among them went

When women die, it is not a tragedy
But when horses die, it is a disaster.

Among the Irish, however, women dominated family life. Perhaps be-cause "the tone of male-female relations within Irish families was indeed characterized by intense animosity," as historian Hasia Diner tells us, as well as "a high rate of domestic violence and discord, [and] the frequent desertion of the male breadwinner," wives and mothers emerged as the strong and stable forces in the family. And because so much violence and disorder occurred in Irish families, a larger percentage of Irish females than those of any other immigrant group sought work outside of the home and delayed or refrained from marriage. Political activist Elizabeth Gurley Flynn recalled: "A domestic life and possibly a large family had no attrac-tion for me. My mother's aversion to both had undoubtedly affected me profoundly. She was strong for her girls 'being somebody' and 'having a life of their own.'"

And of those who did marry, Irish women more than any other eth-nic females except blacks appeared in census rolls as heads of family. For example, in 1870 in Philadelphia 16.9 percent of Irish women headed families, compared to only 5.9 percent headed by German females. (Only black families had a higher percentage of female heads in Philadelphia that year.)

The tradition of strong, assertive Irish women provided excellent role models for their daughters, many of whom later became successful as nurses and teachers. Jobs existed for Irish women who wanted to teach, for they spoke English. The public schools did not wish to spend much money educating the growing number of immigrant children pouring into their schools, and Irish women provided them with a supply of low-wage teachers. They soon made up about one fourth of the teachers in many cities. When the parochial school system expanded at the end of the nineteenth century, women constituted the bulk of instructional staff; they even ran some of the schools. Irish women also became nurses and worked in a variety of religious charities. In some of these institutions they held supervisory positions.

Thus, as we summarize the lives, experiences, and adventures of these immigrants, we reiterate that the complexities, the inequities, and the incongruities of so many immigrants' lives combined with the dynamics of American society to foster a new type of individual in the United States. Almost always rooted in and committed to their ethnic heritage, and often desperate to preserve their native cultures intact, these newcomers frequently discovered that the realities of life in both urban and rural America eventually intruded on the values they wished to continue. To a certain extent, of course, modicums of the culture were preserved. But each successive generation viewed itself as more American and less ethnic. And the advent of World War I in 1917 proved a mighty blow to ethnic life in the United States.

3

A New Wave of Immigrants, 1890s–1920s

As the nineteenth century progressed, industrialization spread southward and eastward in Europe. Uprooted peoples left their farms and villages, moved into towns and cities, crossed national boundaries, and traversed the oceans. In this worldwide movement millions of uprooted Europeans dispersed. Warsaw, Berlin, Vienna, Naples, and London were as much inundated by newcomers as were New York, Chicago, and Philadelphia. Germany, France, Brazil, Argentina, and Great Britain received hundreds of thousands of immigrants. However, the United States, with its higher standard of living and reputation for being a land of golden opportunity, attracted the largest number. Between the early 1880s, when southern and eastern Europeans began impacting American immigration statistics, and 1930, when the combination of restrictive legislation and a major depression established barriers, the United States received a total of 27 million immigrants.

After 1890, newcomers from northern and western Europe continued coming to American shores, but they had less impact. Of the 788,992 immigrants of 1882, for example, the nineteenth century's peak year for immigration, 250,630 were from Germany, whereas only 32,159 were from Italy, 27,935 from the Austro-Hungarian Empire, and 16,918 from Russia and the Baltic countries. In 1907, the peak year for early twentieth-century migration, of the 1,285,349 recorded entrants only 37,807 came from Germany, whereas 298,124 came from Italy, 338,452 from the Austro-Hungarian Empire, and 258,943 from Russia and the Baltic States.

Just as the Germans, Irish, and Scandinavians had before them, southern and eastern Europeans were escaping from economic strangulation and despair. Southern Italians, especially, fled horrendous conditions, including unemployment, high birth rates, overpopulation, and cholera and malaria epidemics. Many Italian peasants lived in houses of skew (straw) or even in rock caves and abandoned Greek tombs. Often, one-room shacks housed people and livestock together. An agricultural laborer earned 8 to 32 cents a day in Sicily but rarely worked an entire year. Furthermore, while the population in Italy increased by 25 percent from 1871 to 1905, the economy slackened. Wheat, citrus fruits, and wine, commodities that were the mainsprings of the Italian rural economy, declined drastically in price on the world market. The resulting poverty made some Italian arrivals in the United States declare afterward, "we would have eaten each other had we stayed."

Some northern Italians had left the country earlier in the nineteenth century. After national unification in 1859, though, relaxed emigration restrictions and expanded steamship advertising combined with a depressed economy to induce southern as well as northern Italian men and boys, and a few women, to seek their fortunes in the New World. Many went to Brazil and Argentina, but depressions in those countries in the 1890s encouraged emigrants to opt for the United States even though it too experienced severe economic woes. The comparative prosperity and opportunities here, which were communicated in letters and reported by returning immigrants, finally resulted in a deluge of emigrants, many of whom left Italy through Naples. Between 1876 and 1930 more than 5 million Italians sailed for the United States. Table 3.1 indicates the peak years for Italian arrivals.

Jews ranked second to Italians among the immigrants. In the late nineteenth and early twentieth centuries over 2 million of them left eastern Europe, more than 70 percent coming from Russia. Over 90 percent of the Jews headed for the United States, the remainder going to cities in central and western Europe, Canada, and Latin America. While others were victimized by a changing agricultural economy, the Russian Jews were aliens in the land of their birth. Russian laws, with few exceptions, restricted them to life in enclosed settlements (mostly in eastern Poland and western

TABLE 3.1

Italian Immigration in Peak Years, 1905–1920

YEAR	NUMBER
1905	316,797
1906	358,569
1907	298,124
1909	280,351
1912	267,637
1913	376,776
1920	349,042

Source: Immigration and Naturalization Service, *Annual Reports*

Russia), curtailed their educational and occupational opportunities, and conscripted Jewish youths for years of military service. Things were made still worse by violence. The assassination of Czar Alexander II in 1881 set off a wave of government-condoned pogroms—brutal beatings, killings, and lootings—which lasted for about 30 years. Jews never knew where or when the terror would strike next. A particularly devastating pogrom in the city of Kishinev in 1903 involved 2,750 families; 47 people were killed and 424 were wounded, many Jewish homes were burned, and Jewish shops were pillaged. The massacre received worldwide attention and vastly increased the number of Jews emigrating from Russia. As a consequence of these east European migrations, the Jewish population in the United States soared from about 250,000 (mostly of German descent) in 1877 to more than 4 million in 1927.

The Slavic groups—which included Russians, Ruthenians (Ukrainians), Slovaks, Slovenes, Poles, Croatians, Serbs, and Bulgarians—together accounted for about 4 million of the new arrivals in the United States. Each of these ethnic groups had a distinctive language, set of customs, and historical experience, but most dispersed themselves throughout the country and either set up separate enclaves or blended in with other Slavic groups. Many were mistakenly identified in the census tracts or lumped together as Slavs and otherwise ignored.

The Poles, the largest of the Slavic groups, were counted separately after 1899, and as a result we know that after the Italians and the Jews, they were the third largest element among early twentieth-century immigrants.

Well over a million Poles arrived before World War I; their coming can be attributed to the acute poverty in territory controlled by Russia and the suppression of Polish culture and nationalism in the sections of Poland under Austrian domination. The Poles, like practically all other Europeans, were influenced by letters from compatriots who had already settled in the United States. Many of these were published in newspapers, while others circulated widely in the villages.

Several other groups came to the United States for similar reasons. Among them were about 1 million Magyars from Hungary, perhaps 400,000 Greeks, 233,000 Portuguese, 105,000 Czechs, 70,000 or 80,000 Armenians, and thousands of Syrians escaping from Turkish tyranny; about 90,000 Japanese came from Asia and Hawaii. World War I temporarily interrupted the major flow, but in the 1920s another 800,000 Italians, 160,000 Scots (more than the entire colonial migration from Scotland), almost 500,000 legally accounted-for Mexicans (many more crossed the border illegally), and over 400,000 Germans streamed into this country.

One of the most overlooked groups was the Basques, who settled in the Great Basin (the area roughly between Salt Lake City and the Sierra Nevada Mountains in eastern California, which includes most of Nevada, southeastern Oregon, and southwestern Idaho) at the end of the nineteenth and the beginning of the twentieth centuries. Their homeland, Basque country on the Iberian peninsula in Europe, had been taken over partially by France in 1789 but mainly by Spain in 1839. Since generation after generation of Basques produced larger families than the local economy could absorb, grown children frequently emigrated. There were and are Basques in many Latin American countries, and the Basques also populated California during the Spanish and Mexican periods. Today Boise, Idaho, contains the largest Basque contingent outside the Iberian peninsula. Other Basque colonies are in eastern Oregon, California, Nevada, Wyoming, and Colorado. Since the Basques are Caucasians, they have not been enumerated separately in either immigration figures or census returns. Including members of the second and third generations, there are more than 20,000 Basques in the West today.

In recent decades many Koreans, Asian Indians, and Filipinos have immigrated to the United States in large numbers, but they were not the first of their groups to arrive. Several thousand Koreans went to Hawaii around the turn of the century. They had been recruited to work in the sugar cane fields. Most were males who came to make money and return home, but some came as families; both men and women labored in cane fields. A thousand or so went from Hawaii to the United States, where they usually settled in California. About 80 percent of these Californians were men who became agricultural workers. Asian Indians, numbering 6,500, also came to work in agriculture. Their main location was the Imperial Valley of California. Often called "Hindoos," these overwhelmingly male immigrants from Punjab were Sikhs. In the United States about half married Mexican women. When Congress barred the immigration of Korean and Asian Indian workers, Hawaiian cane growers turned to Filipino men to replace them. Filipinos also came to the West Coast, where they too labored in agriculture, in Alaskan canneries, or as domestic servants. Few brought their families, and like many Chinese, Koreans, and Asian Indians, they lived chiefly in bachelor societies.

Caribbean immigrants, who often went to other places in the Caribbean and Latin America in search of work, also began coming to the United States. Bahamians headed for Florida to pick crops, and after 1900 they tended to settle in Miami where they worked as construction laborers and as service personnel in the expanding tourist industry. A larger group of black immigrants went to New York City. They were mostly English speakers, but some from Haiti and Martinique spoke French, and formed their own communities and published their own newspapers. Cuban immigrants at first arrived as political exiles during the nineteenth century. These were middle-class immigrants, but others came in the late nineteenth and early twentieth centuries to work in the cigar-making industries of Key West and Tampa, Florida.

Arabs also arrived after 1880. These immigrants from Syria or Lebanon, like others, left because of economic reasons. During World War I, living conditions in the Middle East were particularly harsh. But in addition, the people had heard from Protestant missionaries about the wonders of America. The early waves arriving before World War I were mostly Christians. Most settled in New York City; others peddled throughout the United States. As a result, small Arab communities eventually developed in places such as Detroit, Washington, D.C., and Iowa. Other Lebanese immigrants worked in factories in New York City, Maine, and Michigan.

Except for the Irish, the majority of European and Middle Eastern immigrants consisted of young adult males. Among European immigrants, 78 per cent of the Italians, 95 percent of the Greeks, and about half of the Jews were male. From Asia, Japanese immigrants, like the Chinese before them, were overwhelmingly male. Although many men sent for their wives and children, others hoped to make their fame and fortune and return to their native countries. Few made fortunes, but many returned.

Intelligent estimates of how many foreigners returned to their native countries range from a high of nearly 90 percent for the Balkan peoples to a low of 5 percent for the Jews. We do know that in the period between 1908 and 1914, immigration officials recorded 6,703,357 arrivals and 2,063,767 departures. During these years, more than half the Hungarians, Italians, Croatians, and Slovenes returned to Europe. For the most part returnees included a high percentage of single men. A number of Italian men migrated annually to Italy in the fall, returning to the United States the next spring. Availability of jobs determined their movement. During the winter months, many Italians in railroad, construction, and mining work saw no point in remaining unemployed in the United States. From 1908 through 1916, 1,215,998 Italians left. This back-and-forth migration virtually ceased by the mid-1920s after the quota system went into effect.

Eighty percent of the new immigrants settled in the northeastern quadrant of the United States, roughly delineated by Washington in the southeast, St. Louis in the southwest, the Mississippi River, Canada, and the Atlantic Ocean. Two thirds of the immigrants could be found in New York, New England, Pennsylvania, and New Jersey; sizable numbers also gravitated toward states like Illinois and Ohio. Relatively few went to the South.

Major cities, especially New York and Chicago, proved particularly attractive because of the jobs available, their location as major transportation depots, and the presence of compatriots who could help the immigrants adjust to the New World. A majority of the Jews and many Italians remained in New York City. Other groups also found city life desirable. According to the census records of 1910, about three quarters of the population of New York City, Chicago, Detroit, Cleveland, and Boston consisted of immigrants and their children. Foreign enclaves also dominated cities like Philadelphia, St. Louis, Milwaukee, Buffalo, Baltimore, Pittsburgh, and Providence. In 1916, 72 percent of San Francisco's population spoke a foreign language in addition to English.

Although some habitats naturally had more to offer than others, no *area* of the United States escaped the immigrants' attention or proved totally unsuitable to all groups. Thus one could find—then as now—Italians in Louisiana, Michigan, and Colorado; Hungarians and Greeks in Florida; Slavs in Virginia; Mexicans in Illinois; Irish in Montana; Armenians in Massachusetts and

California; Basques in Idaho and Oregon; Serbs and Croatians in Nevada; German Russians in North Dakota; and Jews in Arizona and New Mexico. Foreigners, including the English, Russians, Lithuanians, Poles, Magyars, and Italians, outnumbered the native-born throughout the Oklahoma coal-fields by a margin of 2:1 in 1890. One Oklahoman noted, "You name it and they were all working together here. And they got along just fine too." Certainly these immigrants constituted minorities in the states where they lived, but it is significant that so many places in the United States afforded opportunities to the venturesome.

The immigrants came with high hopes, and although in some places they got on well, in general they were unprepared for the coolness with which so many Americans received them. Like those who had come earlier, the new immigrants were often stereotyped as representatives of some kind of lower species. None of the newer groups escaped contempt. Greeks were physically attacked in Omaha, Nebraska, and forced out of Mountain View, Idaho. A New Englander, observing some Poles weeding rows of onions, commented: "Animals, they work under the sun and in the dirt; with stolid, stupid faces." On the West Coast, San Franciscans created an international incident by segregating the fewer than 100 Japanese students in the city's schools.

Italians, who outnumbered all other twentieth-century European immigrants, were one of the most despised groups. Old-stock Americans called them "wops," "dagos," and "guineas" and referred to them as the "Chinese of Europe" and "just as bad as the Negroes." In the South some Italians were forced to attend all-black schools, and in both the North and the South they were victimized by brutality. In 1875 the *New York Times* thought it "perhaps hopeless to think of civilizing [Italians] or keeping them in order, except by the arm of the law." Other newspapers proclaimed that Italians were criminal by nature, and a supposedly intelligent and sympathetic observer wrote that Italians "are as a race simpleminded and often grossly ignorant." University of Wisconsin sociologist E. A. Ross, one of the Progressive Era's most outspoken bigots, explained that crime in Italy had declined significantly since the migrations began "because all the criminals are here." Americans were fortified in their beliefs about southern Italians because many northern Italians, who had arrived here decades earlier, also regarded their compatriots from the south as "an army of barbarians encamped among us."

Jews experienced similar problems. In colonial America they had not been allowed to vote, and the restriction lasted, in some states, well into the nineteenth century. Not until New Hampshire removed its barriers in 1877 did American Jews have the franchise in every state. Even where there were no Jews, prejudice and misconceptions abounded. On stage Jews almost always appeared as scoundrels. To have portrayed male Jews in a sympathetic or admirable vein, one scholar tells us, "would have been in defiance of the centuries-old tradition that in the drama the Jew must be the villain or the object of derision."

When the east European Jews arrived, they were often scorned, even by German Jews. The Germans, who had arrived in the mid-nineteenth century, did not want Russian, Galician, and Rumanian Jews in their midst. German Jews had achieved considerable success in the United States and had absorbed the nation's values; many had even refurbished their religious practices, bringing them more into line with Protestantism. The stampede of east European Jews, with their long beards, peculiar clothing, and staunch devotion to an orthodox faith that seemed strange to many Americans, threatened members of the established Jewish community. They envisioned, correctly, an increase in anti-Semitic feeling, which would affect their hard-won respectability. Their views were most specifically stated in an 1894 issue of the *Hebrew Standard:* "The thoroughly acclimated American Jew has no religious, social or intellectual sympathies with the east European Jew. He is closer to the Christian sentiment around him than to the Judaism of these miserable darkened Hebrews." But the American Jews could do nothing to stem the east European tide, nor could they stop other Americans from lumping all Jews together. Once they recognized these facts, they reversed their position and did what they could to help the newcomers adjust to life in America.

Although the German Jews eventually reconciled themselves to having their coreligionists from eastern Europe in the United States, other Americans did not. Beginning in the 1870s, latent or often privately uttered anti-Semitism emerged into the open and struck first at those Jews who were the most Americanized. The New York Bar Association blackballed a Jew who applied for membership in 1877; a City College of New York fraternity did the same thing a year later; and a major resort hotel in Saratoga Springs, New York, barred a longtime guest, Joseph Seligman, one of New York City's leading bankers. Thereafter, clubs, resorts, and private schools increasingly turned away Jewish patrons. Hostility toward Jews knew no geographical bounds. In the 1890s, Jewish merchants in the South had their stores wrecked and were harassed by threats to leave town. In a New

Jersey mill town several days of rioting resulted after a local firm hired 14 Jews. By the Progressive Era, open discrimination prevailed in housing and employment. Hotels displayed signs proclaiming NO JEWS ALLOWED, and job advertisements specified CHRISTIANS ONLY.

No amount of prejudice or hostility toward the newcomers, however, prevented employers from putting the greenhorns to work. The industrial sections of the country needed cheap labor and foreigners provided the necessary hands. Older immigrants and native-born workers would not tolerate conditions the immigrants had to accept, and so toward the end of the nineteenth century Slavs and Italians replaced British, Irish, and Germans in Pennsylvania coal mines; Portuguese, Greeks, Syrians, Armenians, and Italians worked alongside French Canadians in the New England textile mills; east European Jews and southern Italians took over the jobs formerly held by the Irish and Germans in New York City's garment factories; and the Japanese on the West Coast did the agricultural and menial tasks that had formerly been the province of the Chinese. The United States was certainly not paradise for the foreigners. However, one immigrant residing in Chicago probably summarized the majority feeling when he wrote to his mother in Europe: "Nowhere there is heaven, everywhere misery, in America no good, but still better than in the [old] country."

Because immigrants felt more comfortable working and living among friends and relatives, ethnic groups concentrated in particular industries and occupations. The Slavic groups located in the mining and industrial regions of western Pennsylvania, Ohio, Illinois, Michigan, and New York. They also provided the bulk of the labor in Chicago's slaughterhouses and Pennsylvania's steel mills, where they were considered desirable because of "their habit of silent submission, their amenability to discipline and their willingness to work long hours and overtime without a murmur"—or, as the Pittsburgh *Leader* bluntly put it, because the east European immigrant made "a better slave than the American." About one third of the Poles also went into farming in the Northeast and the Midwest. They did truck gardening on Long Island, cultivated tobacco, onions, and asparagus in the Connecticut Valley, and planted corn and wheat in the north central Midwest.

Greeks avoided farming but went into industry or operated small businesses of their own. One survey at the beginning of the twentieth century found that about 30,000 to 40,000 of the 150,000 Greeks in the United States were laborers in factories or in railroad construction gangs. But others peddled fruit and vegetables or maintained shoeshine and ice cream parlors, flower shops, restaurants, or confectioneries. The association of Greeks with candy and food was proverbial. Chicago became the center of their sweets trade, and in 1904 a Greek newspaperman observed that "practically every busy corner in Chicago is occupied by a Greek candy store." After World War II Greeks still maintained 350 to 450 confectionery shops and 8 to 10 candy manufacturers in the Windy City. Most Americans still connect the Greeks with restaurants, and for good reason. Almost every major American city boasts fine Greek eating establishments, a tradition that goes back more than half a century. After World War I, for example, estimates were that Greeks owned 564 restaurants in San Francisco alone.

Italians settled everywhere and entered almost every occupation, or so it seems at first glance. They built subways in New York, manufactured cigars in Florida, and made wine in California. In Chicago they manned the stockyards, and in San Francisco they caught fish. They constituted a large segment of New England's textile workers and were second only to the Jews in New York's garment trades. They provided gang labor on railroads and construction projects and worked underground in the bituminous coal fields of Illinois, Kansas, and Oklahoma, the iron mines of Michigan and Minnesota, and the copper and silver mines of Colorado, Arizona, and Montana. In 1894 they constituted all but one of New York City's 474 foreign-born bootblacks; in 1897, 75 percent of the city's construction workers. They moved into public sanitation departments in New York, Chicago, and Philadelphia. In 1911 a federal commission found that they accounted for the largest number of common laborers of any ethnic group in America.

But Italians also yearned for the security of their own businesses, and as soon as they were able, they bought pushcarts or opened small stores. In New York City they dominated the fruit business in all its phases, from produce market to retail outlet. They opened shoe-repair shops, restaurants, groceries, and bakeries. Some made spaghetti, others made candy. Many cut hair, and by 1910 more than half the barbers in New York City were Italian. Italians are also responsible for much of the opera that exists in the United States.

Unlike the Italians, who left Europe for the most part illiterate and unskilled, 67 percent of the Jewish males who arrived in the early part of the twentieth century were classified as skilled workers. This figure compared with an average of 20 percent for all other male immigrants. Most of the Jews utilized their craftsmanship in New York's garment trades, which employed half the city's Jewish workers. On the eve of World War I, in fact, 70 percent of all workers in New York's clothing industry were Jews. Other Jewish workers found jobs in cigar factories and distilleries, as printers and bookbinders, and as skilled carpenters. For the unskilled, a peddler's pushcart often opened the path to settled retail trade throughout the country, while the enormous numbers of Jews, with their special dietary needs, gave rise to the establishment of kosher butchers, grocers, and neighborhood candy stores, which also sold soda water, newspapers, stationery, tobacco, and sundries. Jews also found opportunities in music and the theater, and in the early decades of the twentieth century they made up half the actors, popular songwriters, and song publishers in New York City.

Outside the big cities, in the Rocky Mountain area for example, Basques have been associated with sheep raising in the West's Great Basin. They have been herders, foremen, buyers, transporters, and ranch owners. When they arrived in the 1870s and 1880s, they were valued for their shepherding skills but despised as a minority. Some people referred to them derogatively as "Bascos," likened them to "Chinamen," and described them as filthy, treacherous, and meddlesome. Nevertheless, they maintained their calm and went about their work. Shepherding is a lonely, monotonous task, but the Basques excelled at it. Their culture values people who succeed in physically arduous tasks that also require grit and determination. One analyst opined that the Basque "sees physical labor and adverse working conditions as a personal challenge which affords an opportunity to merit the approbation of his peers." Basques dominated the western sheep industry from the end of the nineteenth century, but they also entered a wide variety of industrial and professional activities.

Many Japanese immigrants on the West Coast became truck farmers. Beginning as farm laborers, they managed to acquire their own places, raising food for local markets. In the Hood River Valley of Oregon they won a reputation for their apple orchards. In cities such as Los Angeles and Seattle they operated small businesses. They ran hotels, fruit and vegetable stands, barber shops, restaurants, and laundries. Whether farms or businesses, these were family enterprises. Japanese men, who began the immigration stream, sent for their wives and children back home. If they were single, they married young Japanese women by proxy. These "picture brides," as they were called, arrived in America without having seen their new husbands. Many were shocked to find men older than they appeared in their pictures. One remarked, "When I first saw my fiancé, I could not believe my eyes. His hair was grey and I could not see any resemblance to the picture I had. He was forty-six years old." But once here, brides worked beside their husbands when the children were in school.

Like most of the immigrant men who preceded them, the latest newcomers expected their wives to stay at home to raise children and run the family. Girls were socialized to become wives and mothers. But immigrant families were so poor that they needed the wages of daughters, who often went to work at an early age. Those few women who came on their own to the New World were expected to live with relatives and contribute to the family coffers until they had families of their own. Work was rigidly segregated by gender, and women usually took low-paying jobs in the garment shops of Chicago and New York or in the mill towns of New England.

Of course, married women could stay at home and earn money just like women of yore. In Johnstown, Pennsylvania, women had few opportunities outside of the home, but with many single men coming to work in the mills, they could take in boarders. The 1900 census found more than half of all east central European households with lodgers. This meant "more overcrowding, less privacy, more drinking and fighting, and an exhausting seventeen hours a day of work for the wife who had to cook, clean, scrub, wash, iron, carry water and do the shopping." Obviously, caring for boarders was undesirable and women tried to avoid it. Thomas Bell's novel of Slovak life, *Out of This Furnace*, noted how when times were good in Pittsburgh's mills, families tried to avoid having lodgers, but all too often, as the statistics make clear, it became an economic necessity.

Women found other ways to earn money while remaining at home. Mothers and daughters did needlework or made artificial flowers to be sold on the streets. One girl told a New York State investigating committee, "When I go home from school, I help my mother to work. I help her earn the money. I do not play at all. I get up at 6 o'clock and I go to bed at 10 o'clock." Reformers at the turn of the century considered home work involving children or in unhealthy occupations such as rolling cigars to be especially harmful to their health, and they gradually convinced legislative bodies to outlaw it. With inspectors in short supply, the laws were not always enforced.

Wherever the newcomers labored, employers sapped them of their energies before replacing them with fresh recruits. Industrial accidents proliferated. The infamous Triangle Shirtwaist Factory fire in New York City in 1911 took 146 lives, mainly young women. One fireman who watched the women leap to their deaths told of the horror. "They hit the pavement just like hail. We could hear the thuds faster than we could see the bodies fall." Construction and railroad workers also frequently met with fatal injuries, as did newcomers in the Pittsburgh steel mills. Even where the workers were fortunate to escape alive, working conditions often ensured irreparable damage to health. In Riverside, California, Armenian cement makers inhaled dust and poisonous gases emitted in the large, overheated grinding rooms. In Chicago, Greek teenagers slaved in shoeshine parlors from 6 A.M. to 8 P.M. Afterward, the boys cleaned the stores before being allowed to return to barrackslike dwellings for a supper of stale bread and watery soup. The yearly earnings of a shoeshine boy were $160 to $180. A Hungarian immigrant complained about his experiences in a Pittsburgh steel mill: "Wherever the heat is most insupportable, the flames most scorching, the smoke and soot most choking, there we are certain to find compatriots bent and wasted with toil." In New York home sweatshops, whole families bent over coats and suits with their sewing needles.

In labor camps, where many immigrant men worked, conditions were as bad as in the cities, if not worse. Armed guards patrolled isolated labor camps in Georgia and West Virginia, and beatings with iron bars and gun butts kept the men at their jobs. When a Hungarian immigrant tried to escape from a Georgia lumber camp, his bosses went after him with trained dogs. When they caught him, he was horsewhipped and then tied to the buggy for the return trip. Peonage, though illegal, was widely practiced. Eventually, charges were brought against this particular lumber camp and the owners had to stand trial. As the Hungarian peon recalled, a peculiar kind of justice was enacted. "Of all things that mixed my thinking in America," he later wrote, "nothing was so strange as to find that the bosses who were indicted for holding us in peonage could go out free on bail, while we, the laborers, who had been flogged and beaten and robbed, should be kept in jail because we had neither money nor friends." In a West Virginia labor camp Italian workers slept in wooden boxcars where "the dirt of two years covered the mattresses. Roaches and bedbugs livened the walls and held undisputed sway of the beds and their immediate surroundings.... All doors were closed at night. No windows, no air. Nothing seemed to have been left undone to reduce human beings to animals." The workday for these men lasted from 5 A.M. to 4 P.M. with an hour off for lunch. They were never given morning breaks because the *padrone* who controlled them resisted: "The beasts must not be given a rest. Otherwise they will step over me."

Greek and Italian *padrones,* or labor agents, exercised great control over the immigrants. The *padrones,* who had come to the United States earlier, spoke English and arranged jobs and found living accommodations for their later-arriving compatriots. Men and boys were sent to railroad and construction gangs, lumber camps, and factories. A *padrone* collected the salaries of every one under him, or else a prior fee for placement, and kept a portion for himself as his commission. They also performed sundry tasks like writing letters and sending money back home for those unable to do so themselves. Often, and accurately, accused of taking advantage of those who placed their trust in him—the record of abuses committed by the *padrones* is replete with reports of decrepit rooming houses and vanishing payrolls—the *padrone* nonetheless performed the valuable services of easing the adjustment to the New World and of obtaining a man's initial position for him. In 1897 two thirds of the Italian workers in New York were controlled by *padrones,* but as the immigrant numbers increased and the states began to regulate labor agents, the need for these intermediaries lessened. By the beginning of the twentieth century in Chicago and on the eve of World War I in New York, the number of *padrones* had declined considerably.

Although new immigrants had little trouble finding jobs—either with or without the assistance of the *padrones*—the wages paid rarely provided for a family's subsistence. One scholar discovered that in a Pittsburgh steel district where a family needed $15 a week to survive, two thirds of the recent immigrants earned $12.50 a week, while the other third took home less than $10. Tales abound of garment workers earning 8 cents an hour; others made $1.25 for a full week's work. Prior to World War I, residents of New York City required a yearly wage of $876 to maintain a minimum standard of living, yet most families earned less. Among all immigrants, Armenians, Jews, and Greeks generally fared better than Poles, Slovaks, southern Italians, and Serbs.

Wages were especially low for immigrant women who found jobs in the garment industries, in laundries, or as domestics. Yet these jobs were more desirable than others. Less fortunate women who arrived alone and without money ended up as prostitutes in the nation's red-light districts. Indignant and moralistic reformers sometimes exaggerated the extent of the "white slave" traffic, but prostitution certainly existed. One muckraking journalist described the plight of some of these women in New York City.

Just north of Houston Street are the long streets of signs where the Polish and Slovak servant-girls sit in stiff rows in the dingy employment agencies, waiting to be picked up as domestic servants. The odds against these unfortunate, bland-faced farm girls are greater than those against the Galician Jews. They arrive here more like tagged baggage than human beings, are crowded in barracks of boarding-houses, eight and ten in a room at night, and in the morning the runner for the employment agency takes them with all their belongings in a cheap valise, to sit and wait again for mistresses.... Just below this section of Poles and Slavs lies the great body of the Jews.... These girls are easily secured.... In many cases the men who obtain control of them do not even speak their language.

With working-class life so desolate, union organization made firm headway. Garment workers in New York and Chicago went out on strike in 1910 and after long struggles finally won the right to collective bargaining. In an industry run by tyrannical foremen and profit-hungry owners, unions like the Amalgamated Clothing Workers and the International Ladies' Garment Workers' Union (ILGWU) pioneered efforts to establish safety and sanitary codes and to obtain shorter hours and higher wages. The people in the garment trades—owners, workers, and union organizers—were predominantly Jewish (and secondarily Italian), and this was the case well into the twentieth century. In 1924 Jews constituted 64 percent of the ILGWU members, and as late as the 1940s they made up 75 percent of the members of Dressmakers Local 22 in New York City. As the decades passed, however, Jews concentrated in the upper echelons of management in both factories and unions and were replaced in the rank and file by blacks, Latin Americans, and Asians.

Although trade union leaders were usually men, there were exceptions. One of the most notable examples of women leading strikes occurred in the "Great Uprising" of 1909 in the shirtwaist factories of New York City and Philadelphia when 20,000 workers walked out and began the process of organizing the industry. Jewish women and girls became leaders in these activities and in organizing unions. In Philadelphia the organizer was only 17 years old, and four of the other prominent strikers ranged in age from 12 to 14 years. They were not "helpless girls" but "committed activists" as their protagonists observed. A Philadelphia newspaper referred to the local group as the "girl strikers." Despite their youth and gender, however, these activists won recognition for their union, management reduced working hours from 56 per week to 52½ per week, and all the workers received a small wage increase.

Some historians have suggested that it was not the poor working conditions of the shops alone that triggered female activism, but also the radical culture of their European background. Others think that Jewish families gave their young women more freedom than did Italian families, and this may account for the greater Jewish participation. Whatever the exact cause, young Jewish women took the lead, answered the call, and played a major role in organizing garment workers. Many of these women, such as Rose Schneiderman and Clara Lemlich, remained active in union and radical politics for years.

Garment workers who struck in 1909 had the support of middle-class reformers, and two years later their cause was greatly strengthened by the Triangle Fire. While the strikes of New York's women garment workers became famous, historians have noted that Polish women struck Detroit's cigar makers in 1916 and Italian, Polish, Lithuanian, Greek, Syrian, Armenian, and Portuguese daughters and wives participated in the Lawrence, Massachusetts, textile strike of 1912.

While members of trade unions and skilled workers fared better than unskilled immigrants, many newcomers nonetheless managed to improve their lot. The number of hours devoted to the job declined, which gave them a few more hours each week for leisure. A drop from 62 hours to only 55 might seem small by contemporary standards, but it was a huge decline for laborers. By the 1920s skilled workers were on the job only 48 hours each week. With increased free time, some men spent more time in the saloons after their hours of labor. But for many immigrants with more time for leisure there was the attraction of dance halls, picnics, and holidays. The silent motion pictures also had great appeal. These early movies, called nickelodeons, were short and most important were silent. Immigrants with limited English could enjoy them. The early movies were at times bawdy and with low-life scenes, which had a great attraction for immigrants seeking laughs. Vaudeville too appealed to immigrants with its humor and music.

Declining food prices in the late nineteenth century also enabled families to have funds for needs other than housing and food. Because of the inflation after 1900, real wages rose only at a modest amount. With the coming of World War I, employment was plentiful but prices also rose.

During the war government officials encouraged immigrants to buy Liberty Bonds to help finance the war and to exhibit their patriotism with slogans such as "Are You 100 Percent American? Prove it! Buy U.S. Government Bonds." During the fourth Liberty Bond drive in 1918 nearly half of those purchasing Liberty Bonds were immigrants or the children of immigrants. Immigrants also used their savings to purchase homes. A government commission reported in 1911 that one fifth of immigrants owned their own homes, a figure similar to that of native-born Americans. Certainly a major goal was to have one's own place. In Thomas Bell's novel *Out of This Furnace*, about immigrants working in the mills of Pittsburgh, a housewife remarked that she and her husband "wanted to live well, to live in a nice house away from the mill."

Such gains hardly resembled the spectacular rise of Andrew Carnegie, an immigrant from Scotland, but these improvements were important achievements for immigrant families. In addition to owning homes and participating in the growing consumer culture, immigrants were also able to send money to the Old World to support their loved ones or to provide the all-important passage money to America.

The beginnings of union organization and the continuous replenishment of workers at the lowest job levels by newer immigrants provided minorities with opportunities to upgrade their positions and move away from the slums. It is remarkable, in retrospect, how people survived and continued to work and hope for better lives when they were mired in such depressed conditions. Whole neighborhoods were filthy, foul smelling, and overcrowded. In cities like Boston, New York, and Chicago houses adjoined stables, and offal, debris, and horse manure littered the streets. Piles of garbage in front of buildings or in narrow passageways between houses gave rise to stomach-turning odors and a large rat population. Population density was astronomical, some sections of Chicago, for example, having three times as many inhabitants as the most crowded portions of Tokyo and Calcutta. In 1901 a Polish neighborhood in the Windy City averaged 340 people per acre, and a three-block area housed 7,306 children. In the late nineteenth and early twentieth centuries Italian sections of New York, Philadelphia, and Chicago seemed little better. One survey taker found that 1,231 Italians were living in 120 rooms in New York; another reporter could not find a single bathtub in a three-block area of tenements. In Chicago a two- or three-room apartment might house an Italian family of parents, grandparents, several children, boarders, and cousins. A 1910 survey revealed that many of Philadelphia's Italian families had to cook, eat, and sleep in the same room, while most shared outhouses and a water hydrant—the only plumbing facility available—with four or five other families. In addition, many Italians kept chickens in their bedrooms and goats in their cellars. In 1901 New York passed a tenement-house law requiring that all new buildings have windows 12 feet away from the opposite building, toilets and running water in each apartment, and solid staircases within each structure. But it was many years before a majority of the newcomers occupied such houses.

Although members of various groups shared similar working and housing conditions, it would be a mistake to suggest that they also had common aspirations. All, of course, desired decent homes, well-paying jobs, and the opportunity to maintain their own lifestyles free of strife. But ethnic groups differed in cultural ethos and the ways in which they chose to attain their goals. Their attitudes toward family, education, religion, success, philanthropy, and community affairs differed considerably. Moreover, values of the various groups frequently collided with the dominant strain in this country, a factor that sometimes created new problems.

The non-British minority groups spoke a foreign language when they arrived in America, and this placed an immediate stigma upon them. For their own emotional security they chose to live in neighborhoods inhabited by people like themselves; as a result they had even less reason to learn English quickly. Immigrant women felt particularly isolated because they rarely left the insulated community. Many of the men were also cut off from interaction with other groups, especially when they worked with their compatriots in similar occupations, a situation that further retarded the assimilation process. As one Italian put it, "When I arrived in New York I went to live with my *paesani* [countrymen]. I did not see any reason for learning English. I did not need it for everywhere I lived, or worked or fooled around, there were only Italians." Habits of dress, food preparation, and religious practices were also retained by the immigrants. But children, educated in the United States, could not accept or feel completely at home with all of their parents' ways. Although they did not sever cultural ties, immigrant children tried to harmonize as much of their parents' values as they could with the demands of American society. Inevitably, such efforts created intergenerational strains. Good manners, hard work, frugality, and religious devotion dominated the values of East European Slavs. Slovenes (a plurality of whom settled in Cleveland, Ohio), Slovaks, and Poles, all devoted to their Catholic faith, also wanted their own ethnic parishes. These groups, as well as the Italians, saw little value in education for their children above the elementary grades. Teen-aged children were expected to work, give their wages to their parents, and act in ways beneficial to their families, not just themselves.

Italians, for example, placed little importance on *individual* success or accomplishment. A person was supposed to enhance the family's fortune or honor, not his or her own. Only members of the family and their close blood relations were considered important and trustworthy. All outsiders were strangers to whom one had no responsibilities. Family honor had to be defended to the death, if necessary, but society's laws were of little moment. "Individual initiative was virtually unknown," one scholar tells us, and "all actions had to receive the sanctions of tradition and custom." Most of the Italian immigrants seemed to follow the advice contained in a southern Italian proverb: "Do not make your child better than you are."

The Italian *contadini* (peasants), who had a history of oppression, linked education with class, status, and nobility. It was regarded as something that peasants—and women—could not aspire to. Education might be financed with surplus wealth, but most immigrant families could barely sustain themselves on what they earned. The *contadini* also had other reasons for being wary of the schoolhouse. In Italy, historian Rudolph Vecoli tells us, "educated persons were regarded with mistrust; in the old country, the priest and professor had been among the exploiters. Immigrant parents prized education solely for its utilitarian value; reading in itself was thought to be an idle, and perhaps injurious, pastime." Southern Italian immigrants therefore did not encourage their children to excel in reading. As soon as the law allowed, they pulled their offspring out of school and sent them to work. Material advancement was what counted.

Some Italians, of course, did not subscribe to these views. The first American of Italian descent to become a governor and a U.S. senator, Rhode Island's John O. Pastore, had a mother who was impassioned with achieving American middle-class respectability. She made her sons wear fresh shirts every day and admonished them, "Make yourself liked; make people respect you." New York City's first Italian American school principal recalled his father's urging, "Go to school. Even if it kills you." But these were the exceptions. Before World War II, few immigrant Italians graduated from high school or attended college. One survey of Italian children in St. Louis found that a majority went beyond the sixth grade for the first time in the 1930s. In 1940 only 1 percent of residents on the "Hill"—the

Italian area in St. Louis—had graduated from high school, and only 13 percent had done so in 1970.

Southern Italian attitudes toward religion and the Church also differed considerably from those of most Americans and other immigrants. Nominally Roman Catholic, Italians as a whole did not share the Irish dedication to the faith. Unlike American Protestants, who are not always dutiful in their attendance at church services but who tend to maintain a respect for the institution and its members, most Italians regarded the church as "a cold and almost puritanical organization." Moreover, they looked upon the priests as they had in Italy, "as lazy, ignorant hangers-on who merely earned their living off the community." It was not that Italians lacked religious beliefs, but rather that their customs differed from those of the dominant Irish Catholics. They were flexible about doctrine, ignorant of many traditional aspects of Roman Catholicism, and devoted to their festivals and *festas*. The southern Italian immigrant feared "the evil eye" and its effects, and, as one historian tells us, "through the use of rituals, symbols, and charms, they sought to ward off evil spirits and to gain the favor of powerful deities."

Irish domination of the American Catholic Church caused further problems. The Irish hierarchy looked down upon the Italians. One said, "When they are told that they are about the worst Catholics that ever came to this country, they don't resist, or deny. If they were a little more sensitive to such remarks they would improve faster. The Italians are callous as regards religion." An 1884 census of 50,000 Italians in New York City showed that 48,000 of them "neglected church services." Italian men left it to the women to attend mass and to keep the faith. One scholar remarked of his father, "Typical of males of contadino origins, my father had been an infrequent churchgoer, attending Mass only on major holidays like Christmas and on those traditional occasions when family loyalty made presence compulsory—weddings and funerals."

Eventually the Church appointed Italian-speaking priests to serve in predominately Italian parishes. Father Antonio Demo, who headed a parish from 1898 to the Great Depression, helped his New York flock find jobs and deal with authorities; he even worked with Protestant groups on mutual concerns. Italian women were also recruited by Church officials to train as nurses and teachers. As successive generations of Italians Americanized, they adhered more closely to the standards of the Roman Catholic Church in the United States.

Immigrant Italians rarely united for community programs. Southern Italians were devoted to their families and had some loyalty to members of their villages or communities in Italy, but they lacked an overall ethnic commitment. Italian mutual-benefit societies existed in the United States, but for the most part they helped comparatively small numbers. Regional dialects and lack of widespread written communication, as well as a diversity of thought, actions, and lifestyles, divided Italians of different provinces and regions and made any kind of group organization almost impossible in the United States. Not until 1967, in fact, did the Italian-American Civil Rights League band together to protect and defend those of Italian descent from abusive treatment by other Americans.

On the other hand, Jewish success in this area won the admiration of numerous groups. In 1908, when the New York City police commissioner asserted that many criminals were Jewish, Jews protested vigorously. A New York Italian newspaper remarked approvingly: "The Jews are all connected to each other, and, when they believe a patent offense has occurred to their colony, they act as one man."

Pogroms in Russia from 1903 to 1906 provided a focus for organized Jewish efforts to help their brethren in distress, and led to the formation of the American Jewish Committee, an organization composed of and representing the Americanized German Jewish community. The Committee pledged itself to protect the civil rights of all Jews throughout the world. In 1913 midwestern Jews organized another defense organization, B'nai B'rith's Anti-Defamation League (ADL), four weeks after an Atlanta jury convicted a Jew, Leo Frank, of murder primarily, as B'nai B'rith and other Jews saw it, because he was a Jew. The ADL, dedicated to combating prejudice in the United States wherever it existed, was the first such general defense organization founded in this country, and over the years has been quite successful in curbing the effects of prejudicial behavior.

Jews differed from Italians in a number of other ways. The east Europeans were more religiously observant, and, unlike the Italians, becoming more American for Jews meant a weakening of religious ties. Moreover, the Jewish faith embodies ethical prescriptions that make charity a social obligation, and most Jews still accept that view. For those who seek honor and prestige within the Jewish community, philanthropy is a necessity. Respect and appreciation go to those involved in humanitarian endeavors.

This sense of *noblesse oblige,* combined with fears that east European Jews would exacerbate anti-Semitism among non-Jews, motivated German and Americanized Jews to help the newcomers adjust to life in America. To acculturate their European cousins, German Jewish individuals and agencies supported educational institutions that trained foreigners to speak English, started a Yiddish-language newspaper for Lower East Side ghetto dwellers, and funded the Jewish Theological Seminary to train Americanized Conservative, rather than Orthodox, rabbis. No efforts were spared to bring Jews into the mainstream of American life. And to prevent them from becoming a burden on society, wealthier and more established Jews in the United States financed homes for orphans, delinquents, and unwed mothers as well as new Jewish hospitals.

East European Jews accepted whatever assistance they got; they also endeavored to provide their own facilities. They too established charitable organizations to help the needy, and devoted themselves to the quest for culture. Between 1885 and 1915 they started over 150 Yiddish-language newspapers, journals, and yearbooks. The best known of those was Abraham Cahan's *Forward*. At its height before World War I, it was the ghetto's leading daily and over the years the most widely read Yiddish newspaper in this country. In addition, Jews established successful theater groups, and participants like Paul Muni, Jacob Adler, and Molly Picon went on to Broadway and Hollywood. East European Jews attended concerts and lectures and afterward moved on to the most popular cultural institution on the Lower East Side, the cafe or coffeehouse, where they would debate endlessly about plays, poets, pianists, politics, and the direction society was taking.

More than anything else, however, the Jews sought knowledge. Jewish parents believed that education was one of the greatest gifts they could give to their children. Many Jews believed that "there's no use living if you haven't got an education." To emphasize this point one Jewish girl wrote, "If you have learning you'll never lose your way." New York City's Educational Alliance had a regular daily attendance of 500 and a waiting list of 1,000 for English classes, which were given at all hours of the day and 6 evenings a week. The poorest Jewish families saw to it that their children attended public school, and teachers generally praised the youngsters for their industry and deportment. By 1915 Jews made up 85 percent of the student body at New York's free but renowned City College, one fifth of those attending New York University, and one sixth of the students at Columbia. Like all other immigrant groups, Jews were more enthusiastic about educating boys than about teaching girls. But Jewish women had a tradition of literacy in the Old World. Whereas Italian and other immigrant families took their girls out of school as soon as possible, Jewish parents were much more supportive of female education. It no doubt helped that Jews were better off than many other immigrants and did not always have to send young women to work. There were also practical reasons for educating girls: well-trained women could help their husbands and fathers in the many small family businesses. And as the white-collar economy began to expand after 1910 it offered a wider variety of opportunities. Teaching was another profession open to women. During the Great Depression of the 1930s, over half the women college students in New York City were Jewish. They later provided the greatest number of new public school teachers.

Jews who lived outside New York City did not have a million-plus coreligionists to support a full and rounded community life. Accordingly, most relinquished Old World customs at a faster pace. It is for this reason, in fact, that first- and second-generation New York City Jews remained where they landed. Rural areas, small towns, and even some of the bigger cities simply could not provide the cultural and educational opportunities as well as the Jewish sense of community so essential to these east European newcomers.

Other immigrants also sought to maintain their own cultures in the United States. For the Magyars in America, both social and religious life revolved around the Church. The Poles were also devoted to the Roman Catholic Church and supported the institution generously. On the other hand, they thought less highly of education or advancing their children's positions in society. For most of the east central European Catholic peasants, home ownership was clearly the primary goal. Children may have been expected to learn to read and write, tutored in the group's rich history and traditions, and inculcated in the precepts of their faith, but as one Polish-American second-generation male complained, "Immigrant parents often thoughtlessly sacrificed their children's future to the exigencies of their own survival, sending them off to jobs when they should still have been in school or college."

Some parents, however, made decisions about education deliberately and without qualms, and in this regard their views were reinforced by the local priest, who "urged 'hard-working creatures of God' to exercise humility and patience suitable for their condition planned by 'Almighty Providence.'" Many ethnics agreed with such pronouncements. Too much education, they believed, was inappropriate for their youth.

Two scholars, Ewa Morawska and Helene Lopata, have written exten-
sively on this phenomenon. Morawska explains that among east central
European Slavs:

> Popular consensus in the village still considered education acquired by
> formal schooling to be a pursuit for the nobility, a fancy of the higher or-
> ders; "It is all right for the rich man, but not for a poor, stupid peasant."
> In the virtually unanimous testimony of eyewitnesses—peasant-born
> memoirists, writers, publicists, and politicians—prolonged schooling
> and too-visible concern with formal education alienated those peasants
> who possessed it from the rest of the village. For most, the only accepted
> and comprehensible purpose of schooling for a peasant son at the turn of
> the century was still the priesthood.

Helene Lopata, writing about the Poles, describes the almost identical
thought patterns:

> The traditional peasant attitudes toward formal education were very neg-
> ative, intellectual matters being defined as the province of the nobility
> and the intelligentsia; schooling was seen as an economic waste and a
> source of intergenerational problems.... The only school system the im-
> migrants trusted to rear their children was the parochial school, which
> was expected to teach them Polish Catholicism and moral values.

Among most of the Slavs and southern Italians, education past the age
of 14 was deemed wasteful due to the family's loss of their children's
income. Morawska found in her research, in fact, that many priests in
Johnstown, Pennsylvania, as a matter of course signed papers indicat-
ing that underage children were in fact a year or two older so they could
obtain work legally. Other religious Catholics, like Mexicans and French
Canadians, shared these beliefs. One scholar has written, in fact, that
among French Canadians "formal schooling was devalued. Education
beyond a basic level—reading, writing, and simple arithmetic—was required only for children who would join a religious order." It would take
several generations before these views began to change; not until after
World War II, and especially since the 1960s, do we find significant re-
evaluations of such thoughts among the descendants of the Slavs, Italians, and French Canadians.

On the other hand, in those groups that recognized the importance of education as a tool for socioeconomic advancement, children and grandchildren of immigrants moved into the middle and upper classes much more quickly than did individuals whose parents frowned on too much learning. Among those who prized education were the Czechs, Japanese, Armenians, and Greeks. Japanese immigrants, who by law could never become citizens, often made incredible sacrifices so that their children might go to high school and college. Armenians surpassed all other incoming groups between 1899 and 1910 with a literacy rate of 76 percent. Once in this country they, along with the Japanese and Greeks, "devoured" education. A common admonition of the Armenian parent to his child went, "My son, don't be ignorant like me—get an education and be a man." "The Czechs," on the other hand, "came from a country where universal compulsory education was strictly enforced. A sense of literacy was thus ingrained in the Czech immigrant, and it was not unusual for parents to aspire toward a college education for their children in the United States." Greek children, no matter how poor their parents or how lowly their status, were "socialized to postpone immediate gratifications for a future goal. For a majority of Greek parents, that goal was to see their children ... move up the social scale through the avenue of education, business, and commerce outside the Greek ethnic community."

The Greeks also tried to instill in their children the language and heritage of the old country while making sure they became accomplished in the United States. They encouraged their offspring to prepare for the professions, especially law and medicine, because in Greece these were considered the most prestigious fields. One scholar tells us that among Greek Americans "education of the young became a byword in community after community," while a Chicago schoolteacher claimed, "I think I have found the Greeks the brightest and quickest to learn." Greek American children performed their required chores, but when someone asked one man why his 14-year-old son was not out working, the father responded, "My boy will stay in school. He must study at home after school. He must be a good student; he must become a good man."

In the Greek American community the *kinotitos*, or community councils, was the governing body of the people. It provided for the establishment of churches and schools, hired and fired priests and teachers, and exerted a continuing influence on Greek affairs. The feelings of the group were almost always reflected in the actions and statements of the *kinotitos*.

For recreation, the Greeks flocked to their *kuffenein,* or coffeehouses. These served as community social centers where men smoked, drank, conversed, and played games in what became literally places of refuge after a hard day of work or escapes from dank and dreary living quarters. No Greek American community was without its *kuffenein,* and one chronicler reported that in Chicago before World War I "every other door on Bolivar Street was a Greek coffee house."

Many of the ethnic groups that came to the United States felt an attachment or loyalty to their native countries, but none surpassed the Greeks in their devotion to, or involvement with, the homeland. In the United States, Greek Americans divided into factions and argued vigorously the ramifications of politics in Greece. Many Greeks were fervently attached to their mother country and hoped to return. Although large numbers remained in the United States, they were slow to take out American citizenship, which to many meant a renunciation of their heritage.

Like the Greeks, the east central European Slavs remained attached to their compatriots and were reluctant to become American citizens. The ocean crossing did not lead to changed values or outlooks, and unlike the fiercely independent Greeks, the Slavs in general did not perceive the United States to be a place where additional effort would increase their opportunities to move up the socioeconomic ladder. Nor did they seem to consider social mobility a realistic possibility for their children. They accepted the so-called natural superiority of the upper classes as part of God's order on earth and these views, which were sanctioned by both religion and custom, were deeply ingrained in them. They resisted pressures to Americanize and lived the life encapsulated by an old Galician village proverb: "There is not equality among angels in heaven; there will never be any on earth. A peasant is always a peasant, a gentleman a gentleman: Amen."

The numerous fraternal and social organizations immigrants established further attested not only to their reluctance to relinquish their heritage and beliefs but also to their desire to enrich their lives in America among compatriots who shared their values. Among the groups actively promoting the maintenance of traditional cultures were the South Slav Socialistic Federation, which played a key role in aiding Yugoslav workers in the United States; the Ukrainian Women's Alliance (which became the Ukrainian Woman's League of America in 1925), which taught illiterates how to read while promoting" the goal of a national Ukrainian state in Europe; and the Croatian Catholic Society, formed in Gary, Indiana, in 1922. The Greeks had two major ethnic associations: GAPA (Greek American Progressive Association) and AHEPA (American Hellenic Educational Progressive Association), organized in Atlanta in 1922. The former strove to perpetuate the Greek culture; the latter wanted to help smooth the path to acculturation. The variety of ethnic associations across the country also included the Garibaldina Society—Italian, formed in Los Angeles in 1885; the Young Men's Serbian Society of Tonopah, Nevada; and the Hungarian Verhovay.

Along with the ethnic societies were numerous newspapers that recorded the groups' events. In the larger cities, like Chicago and New York, the different immigrants often had a choice of several daily and weekly newspapers in their own languages. In some of the smaller communities, however, choices of foreign-language newspapers were understandably smaller or nonexistent. Among some of the numerous periodicals that recounted events in the old country and offered suggestions for coping with life in America were the *Ukrainian Chronicle,* the *Slovenian Proletarac,* and the *Bolletino del Nevada.* In the 1920s, among the foreign-language press in Utah, an observer listed *Beobachter* (German), *Bikaben* (Danish), *Utah Nippo* (Japanese), and *To Fos* (Greek).

In another area of the West, the Basques also took pride in and strove to maintain their culture. Their language is Europe's oldest, although the Spanish takeover of Basque lands in 1839 caused it to become diluted with Spanish words; it is so complex that in this country most of the children have not learned it and speak only English. Although the Basques married one another during the first generation, the passage of time and their involvement with other people made this difficult to continue. Nonetheless, the Basques do gather periodically. Since 1928 they have held an annual Sheepherder Ball in Boise, and there is also a midsummer St. Ignatius Day picnic to honor their patron saint. Many western universities have made an effort to preserve Basque culture. The University of Oregon has a collection of Basque songs and stories; the University of Nevada offers a course in the Basque language; and the University of Idaho collects Basque historical items.

Ethnic organizations were often segregated by gender. Just as men ran political groups and worked outside the home, they dominated the formal ethnic groups. Yet women had their own organizations in churches and participated in social and union activities. Women of German ancestry dominated the elite clubs of St. Cloud, Minnesota, Jewish women attended the educational programs offered to their communities, and Italian women

participated in the street religious *festas*. In the informal world of immigrant life, men and women frequently went separate ways. The saloon or
bar culture was basically for men. Describing Polish workers, one historian
noted, "Men had their own world—the corner saloon, where immigrant
males could meet their friends and drink away the tiredness of the day."
Sporting clubs were also for men. Italian men, for example, went to neighborhood saloons to play cards or to the local parks to play bocce. Urban immigrant boys played stickball in the streets, or if they were lucky, attended
the numerous clubs to play basketball.

Women's economic role in the home was also a social role, for the home
was "woman's place." They spent their free time meeting with friends and
relatives or participating in church activities. They often frowned on the
male saloon culture. Stories abound in immigrant communities of men
drinking up their earnings or deserting their wives. Immigrant organizations aided those in distress, but not always successfully; and as noted, the
plight of women heading households with many small children was precarious at best. For young single women the world of "cheap amusements"
proved attractive. They went to amusement parks, attended dances, and
patronized nickelodeons, so common in immigrant neighborhoods. These
women were being introduced to the emerging world of consumerism,
which in the long run would take them away from their ethnic communities. During the twentieth century, movie houses, department stores, mass
advertising, radio, and the other forms of an emerging mass culture would
have a profound influence on the lives of immigrants and their children.

Growing consumerism and greater distance from Old World culture was
part of the ongoing process of Americanization. Once begun, assimilation
could not be stopped. For most groups each succeeding generation had
fewer ties to the old country and was more directly involved with American
society. Children and grandchildren forgot the language of previous generations, joined trade unions that cut across ethnic lines, and moved away
from urban ghettos. In this fashion they gained a strong foothold in the
mainstream of American life.

Europeans and Asians were not the only migrants to America in this
era. Also important were Mexicans. However, it is difficult to think of the
Mexicans as newcomers, especially those in New Mexico and southern
Colorado who can trace their ancestry back many centuries. Santa Fe, New
Mexico, was founded in 1609, twenty years before the Puritans set foot in
New England. After the United States annexed the Southwest, Mexican

immigrants crossed the border in search of work. Ever since, the history of the Mexicans in the United States has been tied to the history of the Southwest. The modern migration began with the completion of the south-western railroads, the expansion of cotton planting in Texas, Arizona, and California, and the agricultural revolution in the Imperial and San Joaquin valleys in California. These industries needed cheap labor, and the Mexican workers provided it. Mexicans made up more than 60 percent of the common laborers on the railroad track gangs, in the mines of Arizona and New Mexico, in agricultural fields in Texas and California, and in the numerous packing plants on the West Coast. They also dominated the labor supply in the sugar beet states as far north as Montana and as far east as Ohio.

The coming of Mexican laborers coincided not only with the rapid growth and development of the Southwest but also with the curbing of immigration from China and Japan and later from Europe, and with the revolutionary upheavals in Mexico beginning in 1910. Mexican workers, cowboys, shepherds, and ranch hands had crossed the Mexico-U.S. border frequently and easily between 1850 and 1910, just as others had moved north and south or east and west within the United States. There was no border patrol before 1924, and American immigration officials were more concerned with keeping out Asians than with tracking down Mexicans. But as southwestern agriculture developed it demanded hundreds of thousands of cheap, mobile laborers who could pick the crops quickly, then move on to other areas and harvest whatever else was ripe. In Texas the migratory farm workers usually started in the southern part of the state in June, then moved eastward and eventually westward for the later harvest in the central part of the state. In California, on the other hand, more than 200 crops are cultivated and the growing season ranges from 240 to 365 days, keeping workers busy all year.

Before 1910 most of the Mexican migrants were temporary laborers, but after the upheaval caused by the Mexican Revolution many permanent settlers arrived. Although the overwhelming majority were lower-class agrarian workers, the migration also included artisans, professionals, and businessmen whose property had been destroyed by the violence accompanying the revolutionary chaos.

The Mexican Revolution spurred movement, but so too did a number of other factors. From 1877 to 1910 Mexico's population increased from 9.4 million to 15 million without a commensurate increase in the means of subsistence. A small percentage of *haciendados* (feudal barons) controlled most of the country's land, which was tilled by the agricultural proletariat. There existed between hacienda owners and their laborers a patron-peon relationship, and each role was well defined. As the economy boomed, though, prices rose while daily wages remained constant or even declined to an amount well below that needed to care for a family. At the beginning of the twentieth century the construction of the Mexican Central and Mexican National railroads, as well as the opening of mines in northern Mexico, encouraged movement.

Once the exodus from central and eastern Mexico began, many workers saw no need to stop at the border. Wages in the United States were at least five times higher than in Mexico and American businessmen avidly sought foreign peons. As two scholars who have studied Mexican migration pointed out, their inability "to speak English, their ignorance of personal rights under American law, and their recent experience as virtual serfs under the exploitative dictatorship of Porfirio Díaz made them ideal workers from the growers' viewpoint." The northward migration brought about 10 percent of Mexico's population to the southwestern borderlands.

The first Mexican migrants in the twentieth century were overwhelmingly males, mostly transient, who found work on the railroad track gangs. They lived in boxcars and moved from place to place with the Southern Pacific or the Santa Fe or the Chicago, Rock Island, and Pacific. By 1910 they could be found from Chicago to California and as far north as Wyoming. They were cheap laborers who worked for $1 to $1.25 a day, less than their predecessors—the Greeks, the Italians, and the Japanese. Employers found Mexicans desirable because of their tractability and their willingness to work at more arduous jobs for longer hours, at lower wages, and in worse living conditions than the Europeans or Asians. Many of today's Mexican American *colonias* (settlements) originated as railroad labor camps. Women accompanied some of the men heading north and they too found employment in the low-wage sectors of the economy. In El Paso and other Texas cities with Mexican populations, women worked largely as domestics in the homes of European Americans or as service workers in the growing tourist industries. Some women also joined their husbands in the fields during harvest time. As the canneries of California expanded, they began to employ women. One historian noted, "the canning labor force included young daughters, newly married women, middle-aged wives and widows. Occasionally three generations worked at a particular cannery—daughter, mother, and grandmother."

With the influx of Mexicans, El Paso, Texas, became a major placement center and assembly point for workers in an arc of 22 states reaching from Louisiana to the state of Washington. Three major railroads passed through this border city, where railroad, mine, and seasonal agricultural employers recruited. Representatives from labor-contracting companies also took thousands of immigrants to distributing centers in Kansas City, Missouri; Los Angeles; and San Antonio.

After 1910 more Mexican newcomers found work in agriculture rather than on the railroads. Nonetheless, the major southwestern railroad employed more than 50,000 Mexicans. During World War I, European immigration fell drastically, American residents went off to war, and the expanding southwestern agricultural acres needed hands. As a result the laws governing contract labor were temporarily suspended in 1917, and those Mexicans who were otherwise ineligible for immigration visas were brought in to cultivate the crops and work the harvest. The depression of 1921–22 left many of them unemployed, but then the return of prosperity and the immigration restriction acts of 1921 and 1924 curbed European immigration, thereby stimulating a further demand for Mexican labor. Large southwestern agricultural growers put great pressure on Congress to exempt Mexicans from the quota for their area, and their intensive efforts succeeded. To be legally admitted to the United States, Mexicans still had to pay fees for visas and medical examinations, show that they were literate and not likely to become public charges, and prove that they had not violated the contract labor laws. These restrictions, plus an inadequately patrolled border (not until 1924, in fact, was money appropriated for a border patrol), made it easier for Mexican agricultural workers to enter illegally than to go through the rigmarole of formal application. Scholars estimate that in the 1920s there were at least 450,000 documented immigrants, and about the same number without appropriate immigrant papers. The 1920s immigrants worked primarily in the agricultural areas of five southwestern states—California, Texas, Arizona, New Mexico, and Colorado—as well as in the Michigan sugar beet fields and in the industrial areas in and around Chicago, Detroit, Milwaukee, and western Pennsylvania. Chicago's Mexican population, in fact, shot up from 3,854 in 1920 to 19,362 ten years later, and the city claimed the largest Mexican population east of Denver.

As for schools, one scholar remarked of the El Paso schools, "From their inception El Paso public schools segregated most Mexican children in practice if not legally." But prejudice was by no means limited to education. For those immigrants who sought to mix more with other Americans, societal prejudices until about the 1980s formed an almost insuperable barrier. Although discrimination existed throughout the American Southwest, it was not entirely uniform. For example, Mexicans were expected to live in their own *barrios,* and if they did find housing elsewhere it was usually in deteriorating neighborhoods. They were often blocked from using many public recreational facilities, could obtain mostly menial and relatively unskilled jobs, and in general were expected to accept a subordinate role in society. In New Mexico, however, there was a tradition of Hispanic participation in government, and upper-class Americans of Mexican background moved easily throughout society. In New Mexico also, those of Mexican descent, regardless of class, have been active in local politics, and their numbers (until recently almost half the population) have determined where and when they could hold office. In Colorado, Mexican *colonias* date back to the 1850s, and there too prejudice existed but was not intense. Nor was Arizona, despite its segregated schools and movie theaters, a particularly harsh place for Mexicans.

But in California and especially in Texas, bigotry toward Mexicans was extreme. In the Lone Star State, with its strong southern heritage, Mexicans encountered more overt discrimination than anywhere else in the country. Restaurants and merchants routinely refused to serve them; kindergarten teachers called their children "greasers"; churches held separate services "For Colored and Mexicans." One Texas farmer told an interviewer "You can't mix with a Mexican and hold his respect, it's like the nigger; as long as you keep him in his place he is all right." And during World War II, when the Mexican government, incensed at the treatment those of Mexican ancestry received in Texas, refused to allow braceros to work in the state, one Mexican American weekly noted: "The Nazis of Texas are not political partners of the Führer of Germany but indeed they are slaves to the same prejudices and superstitions."

Like other groups, Mexicans created organizations to improve their low position in American society. The most important group was the League of United Latin American Citizens (LULAC), which as the title indicates was open to Mexicans born in the United States or those who had naturalized. LULAC, founded in Texas in the 1920s, was not a large organization. Its aim was to end discrimination against Mexican-American citizens. One of its main victories was to have the U.S. government and the state of Texas to declare that Mexicans were white and should not be subjected to the legalized Jim Crow laws that sanctioned segregation and denied southern black Americans the right to vote. However, as the above discussion indicates, Mexicanos were treated as second-class citizens and segregated by custom even though they were considered white. Nor could LULAC prevent the mass deportations of Mexican immigrants that occurred during the Great Depression.

4

Ethnic Conflict and Immigration Restriction

Although immigrants contributed to the accelerated pace of American growth and development, native-born Americans rarely considered their presence an unalloyed blessing. Periodically, different groups of Americans wanted to curtail the immigrant traffic, but the overriding national need for more people and the commitment to the idea of America as a haven for the distressed prevented serious legislative curbs. During the colonial period, the Scots-Irish and the Germans were subject to hostile barbs from earlier arrivals and selective taxation by colonial governments. While John Adams was president, in 1798, the period required for foreigners to be in the United States before applying for citizenship was temporarily increased from 5 to 14 years. In the middle of the nineteenth century the Know-Nothing Party again raised the issue of too many foreigners, but it evaporated before it could mount a lengthy campaign.

Between 1875 and 1924, however, pressure groups succeeded in getting Congress to reduce the number of immigrants allowed to enter the United States. Congress enacted its first restrictive law in 1875 when it banned prostitutes and alien convicts from American shores. Seven years later a more comprehensive law excluded lunatics, idiots, and people likely to become public charges. In 1884 further legislation eliminated contract laborers. These measures reflected a growing fear of certain types of people, but kept out relatively few of those who sought entry into the United States.

More important, the Chinese Exclusion Act of 1882 was the first proscription of an ethnic group. The enactment of this law was the culmination of a vigorous West Coast campaign against the Chinese, and it reversed the welcome they had received after the gold rush in the early 1850s. In 1852, for example, the governor of California, seeking new sources of labor for the state, characterized the Chinese as among "the most worthy of our newly adopted citizens."

The negative picture of the Chinese originated before they came to America, with American missionaries, merchants, and diplomats who had sent back derogatory pictures of China and the Chinese. At first, these images were not widely known. Nevertheless, they did prepare public opinion for the growing hostility toward Asians, especially as immigrants from Asia increased from approximately 40,000 in 1860 to over 100,000 in 1880. Although a few opponents of the Asians insisted that Chinese laborers were virtual slaves in this country, most West Coast workers, whether native or foreign-born, claimed that these people depressed wages and consequently were unfair competition. In the 1860s, when the race to complete the transcontinental railroad was in full swing and jobs were abundant, this charge mattered little. When the railroad was finished, and especially during the depression of the 1870s, anti-Chinese feelings became virulent in California. One legislative committee in the state, appointed in 1876 to investigate the Chinese in their midst, concluded that "the Chinese are inferior to any race God ever made.... [They] have no souls to save, and if they have, they are not worth saving."

Behind much of the anti-Chinese sentiment was racism, the belief that there were vast cultural and racial differences between whites and Asians. The Chinese were accused of having low morals, specifically of practicing prostitution and smoking opium; of low health standards; and of corrupt influences and practices. One advocate of restriction told a congressional committee in 1877:

> The burden of our accusation against them is that they come in conflict with our labor interests; they can never assimilate with us; that they are a perpetual, unchanging, and unchangeable alien element that can never become homogeneous; that their civilization is demoralizing and degrading to our people; that they degrade and dishonor labor; that they can never become citizens.

The movement to ban the Chinese from America centered in California. Mobs assaulted them, legislatures burdened them with special head taxes, and city ordinances harassed their hotels and laundries. The most vigorous opposition came from Dennis Kearney and the Workingmen's Party in the 1870s. One manifesto of this group declared, "The Chinaman must leave our shores. We declare that white men and women, and boys, and girls, cannot live as the people of the great republic should and compete with the single Chinese coolie in the labor market.... To an American, death is preferable to life on a par with the Chinaman."

The 1875 law banning prostitutes was in part aimed at Chinese women, and the Chinese Exclusion Act of 1882 was a response to intense pressure from throughout the nation. Loopholes in the law allowed for some immigration, however, and this sparked further agitation and violence in the West. In 1885 a Tacoma, Washington, mob drove out Chinese residents and burned their homes, and incidents of violence occurred elsewhere. More Chinese were harassed in Arizona in 1886 than in any other year. While awaiting further congressional action California passed its most far-reaching anti-Chinese law. This measure barred most Chinese from entering the state and required those already there to register with state officials. In 1892 additional congressional legislation virtually ended Chinese immigration and restricted the civil rights of those still in this country.

Following these restrictions, overt violence against the Chinese ceased, and agitation for tighter laws and controls gradually subsided. Yet the prejudice against the Chinese remained. Discrimination in jobs and housing was common after 1890, and derogatory images of Chinese Americans appeared in the media. Newspapers played up stories of prostitution, gambling, and opium dens in Chinatowns. "Chinks" and "John Chinaman" were sobriquets frequently used to describe Chinese Americans. The prejudices and discrimination lasted well into the twentieth century. State laws against interracial marriages, for example, were part of the legacy of racial prejudice, and Chinese aliens were not eligible for citizenship until after 1943, when Congress repealed the exclusion laws.

In part, Americans transferred their prejudice after the Japanese began arriving in California and Hawaii in the 1890s. Again the focus of hostility and agitation was California, where most of the Japanese lived. Arguments similar to those used against the Chinese were employed to assail Japanese immigrants. "The Japs must go," shouted one demagogue; and the United States Industrial Commission reported in 1901 that the Japanese were "far less desirable" than the Chinese. "They have most of the vices of the Chinese, with none of the virtues. They underbid the Chinese in everything, and are as a class tricky, unreliable and dishonest."

And yet the racism directed against the Japanese was not the same as the anti-Chinese feeling. Whereas the Chinese were considered coolies who depressed American wages, at times the Japanese were considered too successful, especially in California agriculture, where they became efficient workers and growers. Unlike China, Japan was becoming a world power at the beginning of the twentieth century. Instead of showing contempt for Japan, many racists became alarmed by her growing power. The fear was expressed in the "yellow peril" scare just after 1900, an imagined invasion of the United States by hordes of Asians. Congressman Richmond Pearson Hobson of Alabama insisted that the "yellow peril" was already here, and he further warned: "the Japanese are the most secretive people in the world," and were "rushing forward with feverish haste stupendous preparations for war.... The war is to be with America." The Hearst press in California insisted that "every one of these immigrants ... is a Japanese spy."

Growing fear of and antagonism toward Japanese immigrants reached a crisis after the turn of the century. Led by labor groups, delegates gathered in San Francisco in 1905 to organize the Asiatic Exclusion League. A year later, the San Francisco Board of Education ordered the segregation of all Asian pupils. Of the city's 25,000 schoolchildren only 93 were Japanese, but the public was outraged at reports that older Japanese boys were sitting next to little white girls in classes. The Japanese government protested the order, and Theodore Roosevelt's administration found itself faced with a full-fledged diplomatic crisis. Federal pressure on the San Francisco school board led to the rescinding of the new policy. In return the Japanese, in the Gentlemen's Agreement of 1907, promised to restrict exit visas for laborers who wanted to go to the United States. The agreement short-circuited a confrontation but did not prevent those Japanese already here from pursuing the American dream. Reputedly hard workers and shrewd businessmen, they amassed a great deal of property before the California legislature, in 1913, prohibited aliens ineligible for citizenship from acquiring land. The act, based on a provision of the naturalization laws limiting citizenship to incoming whites and descendants of Africans, failed because the Japanese continued acquiring property in the names of their American-born children or under legal corporate guises.

Californians may have been especially concerned with Asian minorities, but the most widespread American hostility was directed at Roman Catholics. The growing Catholic immigrant population after 1880 once more stirred up Protestant bigotry. Even more than before the Civil War, the Roman Catholic Church appeared aggressive and powerful as Irish Catholics succeeded in politics and Catholic leaders spoke without restraint in public.

School issues in particular kindled ethnic tensions. Catholics found the Protestant orientation of American public schools offensive and developed their own parochial schools. Although the Church encouraged all parishioners to send their children to these schools, only a minority—mostly of Irish background—chose, or could afford, to do so. This led in turn to Catholic demands for state aid for parochial schools, a proposal that further enraged Protestants. Local elections often centered on the school issue, as did the 1880 election in New York City, for example. The Democrats had nominated William R. Grace, a Roman Catholic, for mayor, and this incensed a number of the city's Protestants. The *New York Times* stated the prevalent anxieties clearly:

> If the Irish Catholics should happen, for instance, to control the Mayoralty, the Controllership, and the Board of Aldermen, they would very soon be able to reconstitute the Board of Education, to place Catholic Trustees over certain schools, to put in Catholic teachers, to introduce Catholic textbooks, to convey public funds to Church schools under some guise which would elude the law, and, in fact, to Romanize our whole system of public education.

In the end Grace won the election, and the fears expressed by the *New York Times* proved groundless. But the anxieties remained.

Boston, with its large Irish population, was also a hotbed of dispute. In 1889 a teacher in a public high school defined indulgences in a manner that was considered offensive by a Catholic pupil. The Church protested and the Boston School Committee reprimanded the teacher, transferred him from history to English (a "safer" subject), and dropped a disputed text. Aroused Protestants organized and in the next election won control of the school committee.

At the national level the issue of religion and the schools intruded and divided political parties. In 1875 James G. Blaine, the House Republican leader, proposed a constitutional amendment to ban governmental property and financial aid for the use of any school or other institution under the control of any religious sect. Although the amendment never passed, the issue prompted considerable debate.

At bottom much of the conflict centered on the belief held by many Protestants that Catholicism was a menace to American values and institutions. This view was not as strong as it had been before the Civil War. Nevertheless, many Protestants believed that a large proportion of American Catholics were under the thumb of Rome and were unwilling to accept American values. Some militant Protestants insisted that Catholics had divided loyalties and should be denied the ballot until they took an oath of allegiance renouncing the supremacy of the pope. A prominent Protestant clergyman, Josiah Strong, expressed much of this anxiety in his popular *Our Country: Its Possible Future and Its Present Crisis* (1885), in which he argued that Catholics gave their foremost allegiance to the Church, not to the United States of America. Protestants like Strong were also agitated because of the Roman Catholic Church's opposition or indifference to the temperance crusade.

The largest anti-Catholic organization to appear in the late nineteenth century was the American Protective Association (APA). Founded in 1887 in Clinton, Iowa, by Henry Bowers, the APA had a large following until the mid-1890s; at its peak it claimed 2.5 million members. Appealing mainly to working-class Protestants in the Rocky Mountain states and the far West, the APA pledged its members' support of public schools, immigration restriction, and tougher naturalization laws. To fight the so-called Roman menace, APA members organized boycotts of Catholic merchants, refused to go on strike with Catholic trade unionists, and vowed never to vote for a Roman Catholic for public office. The growing political power of Catholics was especially alarming to the organization, which claimed that "although only one-eighth of the population of the United States was Catholic ... one-half of all the public officeholders were Catholics ... Catholics were favored in the Civil Service examinations, and ... all civil servants were forced to contribute to Catholic charities."

Hysteria peaked in 1893 when many believed a rumor that the pope had written a letter ordering Catholics to exterminate all heretics in the United States. Some Protestants armed themselves, and the mayor of Toledo called out the National Guard to halt the coming slaughter. The rumor soon proved groundless and fraudulent, of course, but members of the APA quickly found other aspects of Catholicism to fight.

The association never formed a political party, but it did enter politics. It supported candidates, usually Republicans, who were against the Catholic Church and lobbied for particular pieces of legislation. The association backed state compulsory school-attendance laws and, at the national level, became embroiled in a dispute over Indian schools. Under federal policy established during the Grant administration, contracts were granted to church groups to operate Indian schools. Thus federal funds were going to parochial schools, which horrified the APA. The association threw its support behind efforts to eliminate the contract system and substitute public schools for the church-supported ones.

In spite of the widespread hostility to Catholicism among non-Catholics, the appeal of the association was limited. The movement crested in the 1890s and then fell apart. Other issues were more important to American voters in the 1890s, and the APA found itself plagued by internal disputes. Republicans used the APA, but they discovered that it was not important politically. Anti-Catholicism took other forms after 1895.

In addition to the religious prejudice directed at Catholics, hostility toward Jews grew in the late nineteenth century. Anti-Semitism was aggravated by the economic depressions that plagued Americans, on and off, from 1873 through 1896. The German Jews, who arrived in the United States in the middle of the nineteenth century, prospered despite the existing prejudices because there were few, if any, economic barriers to those who were enterprising. Their prosperity in the face of widespread unemployment and despair reinforced the old Shylock image of a cunning and avaricious Jew demanding his pound of flesh. One southern patrician noted, for example, "it is quite the fashion to caricature the Jew as exacting his interest down to the last drachma." He then pointed out, perhaps half in envy and half in respect, that in the hardest of times the Jew "has money to lend if not to burn and before he is ready to execute his will he owns the grocery store, the meat-market, the grog-shop, the planing-mill, the newspaper, the hotel and the bank." The extremist fringe in the free-silver movement saw the Jew as the archenemy foisting an international gold standard on beleaguered American farmers who were fighting for silver, "the people's money."

The presence of east European Jews, who started coming to the United States in the 1870s, aggravated existing anti-Semitic feelings; and as already noted, all Jews faced growing social and economic discrimination. As Jewish immigration from eastern Europe increased, anti-Semitism helped to kindle the movement for immigration restriction. In 1906 a member of President Theodore Roosevelt's immigration commission told an investigator that the "movement toward restriction in all of its phases is directed against Jewish immigration."

Alongside religious antagonisms, immigrants also confronted economic conflicts. Many workers opposed immigrants on the grounds that they depressed wages and were potential strikebreakers. The Knights of Labor called for a ban on contract labor, as did a number of labor leaders. Organized labor, with a high proportion of foreign-born workers, was reluctant to support general immigration restriction, but labor leaders were becoming more critical of immigration in the 1880s and in the economically depressed 1890s. In 1897 the American Federation of Labor (AFL), America's largest labor union, finally supported a literacy test as a means of limiting immigration.

Although employers needed workers for the nation's growing industries, at times they were uneasy about immigration. Labor disturbances, fairly common in the late nineteenth century, were frequently blamed on foreign agitators. In 1886 policemen broke up a peaceful protest meeting in Chicago. Before the crowd could be dispersed, however, a bomb exploded, killing seven policemen. Although no one knew who threw the explosive, the press blamed foreigners. One newspaper declared, "The enemy forces are not American [but] rag-tag and bob-tail cutthroats of Beelzebub from the Rhine, the Danube, the Vistula, and the Elbe." Another said the German anarchists accused of the crime were "long-haired, wild-eyed, bad-smelling, atheistic, reckless foreign wretches, who never did an honest hour's work in their lives."

Especially important in the growth of nativism was Americans' awareness of the increased immigration from southern and eastern Europe. These new immigrants were considered undesirable, unassimilable, and hostile or indifferent to American values. Stereotyped images of Slavs, Italians, and Jews predominated. A retired superintendent who had worked in the Pennsylvania steel mills from the 1880s through the 1930s recalled, "Racism was very distinct then.... We all called them Huns, Dagos and Polacks." To the nativist, Italians suggested an image of crime and violence. As a Baltimore newspaper put it, "The disposition to assassinate in revenge for a fancied wrong is a marked trait in the character of this impulsive and inexorable race." Such hostile sentiments led to the lynching of eleven Italians in New Orleans in 1891. After the murder of a police superintendent, suspicion focused on the local Sicilian community and several Italians were indicted. City officials called for stern action but the jury refused to convict. An angry mob then took matters into its own hands and lynched the accused men.

Late nineteenth-century Americans were increasingly receptive to pseudo-racial thinking that classified European nationalities or ethnic groups, such as Slavs, Jews, and Italians, as races. Such thinking emphasized differences and deemed one "race" to be superior to another. This point of view found increasing support in the early twentieth century. Not surprisingly, racists regarded earlier immigrant groups as more desirable. One alarmed nativist said, "it is only in recent years that new, more ignorant and therefore more dangerous elements have entered into the problem of immigration.... The Irish and German tides were ebbing, while those of Southern and Eastern Europe were both increasing and threatening. None but an optimist ... can view it without concern."

Just as religious prejudice, economic rivalry, and intellectual racism generated opposition to immigration, so did politics. Urban reformers noted with apprehension the rise of the Irish in urban politics. Reformers, usually old-stock Americans, believed that political machines built on immigrant votes were corrupt and inefficient, the protectors of prostitution, graft, and saloons. Prostitution was considered a virtual immigrant monopoly. A reform group in the 1890s declared, "Unless we make energetic and successful war upon the red light districts ... we shall have Oriental brothel slavery thrust upon us.... Jew traders, too, will people our 'levees' with Polish Jewesses and any others who will make money for them. Shall we defend our American civilization, or lower our flag to the most despicable foreigners—French, Irish, Italians, Jews, and Mongolians?" When the power of the immigrant-supported machine was broken, they argued, American cities would be reformed.

Many reformers, however, attributed political corruption to business influence. They noted that immigrants supported machines because the machines helped them. Clean up the immigrants' environment, and the machine would lose its following. Yet graft and the social ills of American cities, combined with the concentration of immigrants in the urban ghettos, too often led native-born Americans to blame political chicanery on immigrants.

Conflicts also arose among the immigrants themselves. Many of the newcomers distrusted and disliked one another. Irishman Dennis Kearney, leader of the California Workingmen's Party, led the assault on the Chinese, and English-born Samuel Gompers of the AFL favored immigration restriction. Within the ranks of labor some foreign-born unionists did not want members of ethnic groups other than their own in their unions. Foreign-born Protestants within the APA did not trust Catholics. Within the Catholic Church, Germans, French Canadians, Italians, and Poles resented Irish domination. As one Polish journal remarked in 1900, "is it that the Irish want to dominate the Catholic world? Can't Polish Catholics have as much freedom as the other nationalities? Isn't the United States a land of Freedom? It is, but that is no reason that the Irish should have more preference than any other nationality."

Europeans arrived in America with fears and prejudices that did not disappear. When German votes killed a proposal to teach Bohemian in a Chicago school, Bohemians retorted, "Finally, since impudence, selfishness, obstinacy and insolence is excessively rooted in the minds of all Germans, almost without exception, how then could we expect, even in this land of freedom to receive any support from them?" An American writer of Norwegian ancestry recalls his grandmother admonishing members of the family never to trust a Swede. "The essence of her counsel," the grandson wrote, "was that Swedes were a strange, cold, selfish, sneaky lot and that any contact with them could only have unhappy consequences."

The intense xenophobia in the United States, among both older Americans and more recent arrivals, pointed inevitably in one direction: immigration restriction. Although the Chinese were banned in 1882 and the first restrictive federal immigration law excluded certain classes of immigrants, the legislation did not greatly affect the flow of newcomers. Bigots called for drastic limitations. The time had come, they insisted, to decide whether the nation was "to be peopled by British, German and Scandinavian stock, historically free, energetic, progressive, or by Slav, Latin and Asiatic races, historically downtrodden, atavistic, and stagnant." The most popular scheme for stemming the tide was the literacy test. Led by the Immigration Restriction League, founded in Boston in 1894 by Boston blue bloods, agitation for federal action grew. The literacy test, which required immigrants over 16 to be literate in some language, made no distinctions among nationalities or races, but the intent of the proposal was clear. Since proportionately more northern and western Europeans than southern and eastern Europeans were literate, the requirement would have barred many of the latter groups of immigrants from the United States.

The literacy test, supported by the Republican Party, finally passed in 1896, only to be vetoed by President Grover Cleveland, who insisted that America should remain an asylum for the oppressed of Europe. The president also rejected the inference that the new immigrants were less desirable than the old: "It is said," he declared, "that the quality of recent immigration is undesirable. The time is quite within recent memory when the same thing was said of immigrants who, with their descendants, are now numbered among our best citizens." The literacy test's proponents attempted to muster votes to override the veto, but they failed. And then, after 1896, prosperity returned and the tide of nativism ebbed.

But it resurged quickly. By 1901 President Theodore Roosevelt spoke in a different vein than Cleveland had a few years earlier. Stirred by the recent assassination of President William McKinley by an anarchist, Roosevelt called for a comprehensive immigration act to keep out "not only all persons who are known to be believers in anarchistic principles or members of anarchistic societies, but also all persons who are of a low moral tendency or of unsavory reputation ... who are below a certain standard of economic fitness to enter our industrial field as competitors with American labor." He also called for an educational test to ascertain the capacity of immigrants to "appreciate American institutions and act sanely as American citizens." Roosevelt insisted that his proposals would decrease the "sum of ignorance" in America and "stop the influx of cheap labor, and the resulting competition which gives rise to so much of the bitterness in American industrial life, and it would dry up the springs of the pestilential social conditions in our great cities, where anarchist organizations have their greatest possibility of growth." Congress responded in part to the president's request by excluding anarchists in 1903 and, four years later, "imbeciles, feeble-minded [persons] and persons with physical or mental defects which might affect their ability to earn a living."

In 1907 Congress also appointed a joint Senate-House commission to investigate the "immigration problem." The new commission, known by the name of its chairman, Senator William Paul Dillingham of Vermont, issued a 42-volume report in 1911. Its main assumption was that the newer immigrants from southern and eastern Europe were more ignorant, more unskilled, more prone to crime, and more willing to accept a lower standard of living than previous immigrants from northern and western Europe. Although the Dillingham Commission preferred a literacy test rather than a ban, it also suggested that restrictive legislation could be based on a percentage of each nationality group already in the United States. This alternative was ignored at the time but would be revived in the 1920s.

Congress responded to the Dillingham report with passage of another literacy bill in 1913, but once again a president would not sanction it. William Howard Taft, heeding protests from friends favoring liberal immigration policies, acknowledged an "abiding faith" in American institutions to exert a positive influence upon newcomers "no matter how lacking in education they may be.... The second generation of a sturdy but uneducated peasantry," he continued, "brought to this country and raised in an atmosphere of thrift and hard work, and forced by their parents into school and to obtain an instrument for self-elevation, has always contributed to the strength of our people, and will continue to do so."

The outbreak of World War I and American entry into the war in 1917 broke the dam holding back the tide of nativism. On the eve of America's declaration of war Congress again passed a literacy bill, and when President Woodrow Wilson for a second time refused to approve it, Congress overrode his veto. The act also created an Asian "barred zone," which excluded most Asians and added to the list of banned immigrants.

In the heated atmosphere of wartime, patriots insisted upon 100 percent Americanism. Radical opponents of the war and German Americans who were suspected of having pro-German sentiments or of being secret agents of the Kaiser became targets of unrestrained hysteria. Theodore Roosevelt led the attack and insisted that "the men of German blood who have tried to be both German and American are not Americans at all, but traitors to America and tools and servants of Germany against America." Superpatriots attacked German Americans, their organizations, and their press. Libraries removed German books from their shelves, and several states, among them Delaware, Iowa, and Montana, prohibited public schools from teaching German. Sauerkraut was renamed "liberty cabbage," orchestras refused to perform German music, and towns, business firms, and people hastily anglicized their German-sounding names. The governor of Iowa issued a proclamation urging citizens not to use foreign languages in public, and the governing body of Nye County, Nevada, passed a resolution to the effect that use of another language in a publicly designated area would be deemed evidence of disloyalty. Angry mobs sometimes smashed German stores or burned German books. That most German Americans were loyal to the nation and supported the war effort did not seem to matter.

Although they were not as suspect as German Americans, some Irish Americans also came under attack. Many people of Irish ancestry were un-enthusiastic about fighting a war in alliance with Great Britain, regarded as the enemy and oppressor of Ireland. A few who were critical of the Wilson administration found themselves in difficulty with the law.

The xenophobia unleashed by the war reached new heights in the 1920s. Although German and Irish Americans now found more acceptance, im-migrants and their children were generally suspect. The nation assumed an isolationist mood; old-stock Americans rejected Europe and her peoples and insisted on conformity and loyalty to the United States. Terms like "wop" appeared regularly in newspapers like the *Pocatello* (Idaho) *Tribune*, and about the only time minorities found stories about themselves in the daily newspapers was when they were involved in crimes, industrial ac-cidents, or sports events. Ewa Morawska observes, "The same young men from Slavic and Magyar homes who, as American soldiers fighting in Eu-rope during World War I, had been praised by the *Johnstown* [Pennsylvania] *Tribune* as 'our Johnstown boys' and lauded for heroism in the struggle 'in defense of their country' (the United States) were again labeled 'foreigners' after they returned to the city" at the end of the war. The Russian Revolu-tion, a by-product of the war, added to the fears of things foreign. Ameri-cans believed that radical ideology, which was considered a foreign import, had to be stamped out or suppressed. Radical groups were hounded and members physically assaulted, and Attorney General A. Mitchell Palmer's Justice Department rounded up aliens in spectacular raids and deported them during the Red Scare of 1919. Patriotic groups bombarded Congress with petitions proclaiming that the time had arrived "when Americans should assert themselves and drive from these shores all disloyal aliens."

While conservative and patriotic groups feared radical agitators flooding America with their Bolshevik ideas, union leaders feared cheap labor. The 1920s were lean years for organized labor, as the unions lost more than a million members. In 1918 the AFL, anxious about the problems of indus-trial reconversion after the war, called for a two-year halt in immigration. Some labor union leaders not only used the old cheap-foreign-labor argu-ment but also warned about the social dangers of immigration. The Eng-lish-born Gompers, president of the AFL, defended restriction: "America has not yet become a nation." He noted that it was "honeycombed with 'foreign groups' living a foreign life," and this would continue if the na-tion's door remained open to all comers.

The 1920s have been described as a tribal era during which ethnocentrism and xenophobia ran wild. No development better illustrates this situation than the activities of the Ku Klux Klan, the largest nativist organization of the 1920s, which claimed over 4 million members at its height. Founded in Georgia in 1915, the Klan had a spectacular growth rate in the early 1920s and for a brief period exerted considerable political clout in several states, including Indiana, Alabama, Texas, and Florida. Klansmen thundered at liberal Protestantism and modern ideas and demanded Prohibition enforcement and compulsory Bible reading in the public schools. But the focus of their credo was anti-Catholic and anti-immigrant, and they wanted to keep African Americans "in their place." Hiram W. Evans, the Klan's imperial wizard, believed that the "old-stock Americans," the "Nordic race," had "given the world almost the whole of modern civilization." And he insisted that aliens from eastern and southern Europe should be kept out of the United States.

The Klan's response to immigration and minorities was merely an extreme version of what many old-stock white Protestants believed. Prohibitionists, for example, insisted there was a sinister connection between liquor, cities, and immigrants. One liberal clergyman proclaimed, *"national Prohibition is* the highest mark of distinctively American morality and citizenship" and warned, "there is already too much congestion of immigrants in the great cities.... If we are to have an American civilization we must assimilate the stream of newcomers. If we do not assimilate them they will adulterate us with an admixture of old-world morals. A straw in the wind is afforded by the recent referendum in Massachusetts on the liquor issue. The entire state went overwhelmingly dry except the large immigrant filled cities, and they went so overwhelmingly wet as to give the state as a whole a wet majority."

In Michigan, Henry Ford's *Dearborn Independent* published anti-Semitic diatribes. Many of its vitriolic writings seem to have come directly from passages in the *Protocols of the Elders of Zion.* This fake "document," concocted by the Russian secret police at the turn of the century, charged there was a Jewish plot to establish a world dictatorship. During the decade, anti-Semitism even reached the hallowed gates of Harvard University when the institution's administration established a Jewish quota, thereby prompting one Jew to dub the school an "intellectual Ku Klux Klan."

Discriminatory practices and thoughtlessness characterized Americans throughout the country in the 1920s and 1930s, and people of a variety of foreign ancestries suffered through many humiliating experiences. A number of individuals changed their foreign-sounding names to anglicized versions, either for better economic opportunities or merely to avoid unnecessary comments from others. Sam Divanovich of Tonopah, Nevada, for example, became Sam Devine because he thought it would "sound better and not cause as much comment." In Morrelville, Pennsylvania, in the 1930s, teachers often incorrectly characterized students of east central European descent as "Slavish." "At school I went as Thomas," one man later recalled, "because my teacher would not pronounce or spell my own [name]." His wife had a similar experience. Her surname was "Tomasovich, but the teacher spelled it Tumoski; she did not bother to get it right." A child of Polish American parents remembered that she never raised her hand in elementary school to speak. "I was afraid I'd make a mistake.... American children called us 'Hunky.'... We felt inferior." One man voluntarily misidentified himself and explained why: "I usually say I'm Russian. If you say you're Ukrainian, the guy tells you, 'Jesus Christ, what's that?' and you have to go into the whole history of Ukraine and explain to the guy what you mean. It is easier to just say that you are Russian."

Ideological racism, another facet of American nativism, peaked in the early 1920s. The eugenics movement in America after 1900 had warned of the dangerous effects of bad heredity. Eugenicists argued that poor hereditary, rather than environmental, factors produced unalterable human inequalities. Many Americans supported racist thinking. Popular writers such as Madison Grant and Lothrop Stoddard enjoyed a vogue in the 1920s. Grant's *The Passing of the Great Race* and Stoddard's *The Rising Tide of Color* preached a racism that could easily be applied to immigration restriction. Grant declared

these new immigrants were no longer exclusively members of the Nordic race as were the earlier ones who came of their own impulse to improve their social conditions. The transportation lines advertised America as a land flowing with milk and honey, and the European governments took the opportunity to unload upon careless, wealthy, and hospitable America the sweepings of their jails and asylums. The result was that the new immigration ... contained a large and increasing number of the weak, the broken, and the mentally crippled of all races drawn from the lowest stratum of the Mediterranean basin and the Balkans, together with hordes of the wretched, submerged populations of the Polish Ghettos.

A follower of Grant argued that continued immigration would inevitably produce "a hybrid race of people as worthless and futile as the good-for-nothing mongrels of Central America and Southeastern Europe," while a psychologist, flushed with uncritical use of intelligence test results, proclaimed that the "intellectual superiority of our Nordic group over the Alpine, Mediterranean and Negro groups has been demonstrated."

What these racists were saying was that the peoples of southern and eastern Europe were not "white." To be sure, Italians, Greeks, and others were legally white, and immigration authorities and census takers marked them down as white. For naturalization and immigration purposes even Syrians and Armenians were white. The courts ruled that only Asians were not white and could be excluded as persons ineligible for naturalization. "As free white persons" southern and eastern Europeans could become citizens and they did drink out of the white water fountains in the South. Nor were they required to use the "colored" waiting rooms in train stations or sit in the back of streetcars and buses. Calling them not quite white was simply saying that Italians, Jews, Greeks, and others were distinct and inferior peoples.

Given the intense nativism of the 1920s, the issue was not *whether* there would be immigration restriction but *what form* it would take. Aside from the recent immigrants, few Americans, regardless of background, resisted restriction. Congressmen representing urban areas with heavy concentrations of the foreign-born attacked the proposed laws and their racist assumptions, but they lacked the votes to sustain their views. Over 800,000 newcomers arrived in 1921, and foes of immigration had visions of another immigrant invasion after the wartime lull. Stories circulated of between 5 and 20 million Europeans ready to descend upon the United States.

In 1921 Congress established the principle of restriction based on nationality and placed a ceiling on immigration from Europe. The 1921 law limited, for a one-year period, the number of entrants of each nationality to 3 percent of the foreign-born of that group in America based on the 1910 census. Under this stopgap measure approximately 358,000 were eligible to come from Europe. Congress extended the law twice before passing the Johnson-Reed Immigration Act of 1924.

The Johnson-Reed law continued the qualifications enacted in the past, such as the exclusion of anarchists, prostitutes, illiterates, and those likely to become public charges, and tightened the quotas established three years earlier. It cut the number of immigrants to 2 percent of the foreign-born of

each group based on the 1890 census, further discriminating against southern and eastern nations, which was exactly what Congress wanted to do.

The case of the Greeks shows how moving the base year back from
1910 to 1890 and lowering the percentage helped Congress accomplish its
purpose. In 1910 there were 101,282 Greeks in the United States. Under the
1921 act, they were therefore entitled to a yearly quota of 3,038 people (3
percent of 101,282). But the 1924 act, by lowering the percentage and setting
the base year back to 1890, when census takers counted only 1,887 Greeks
in this country, cut the quota to 38 (2 percent of 1,887), or about 1 percent of
what the 1921 law had allowed. Similar cuts affected Italians, east European
Jews, and Slavs. Thus an ostensibly objective change of base years and a
one-point decrease in the percentage drastically curtailed immigration opportunities for those that Congress desired to exclude. The quota based on
the 1890 census was meant to be temporary. The Johnson-Reed Act established National Origins Quotas, based on the white population according
to the 1920 census and that went into effect in 1929. While basing quotas
on the entire white population and not simply the foreign-born increased
the numbers from southern and eastern Europe, it still drastically reduced
their totals from the annual figures before World War I. The new system
provided for 153,714 immigrants from Europe (Asians were already barred
in 1924, Western Hemisphere natives were not restricted, and African and
other colonies came under the quotas for the European nations that controlled them). Each European nation received a number based on its share
of the American white population in 1920. English, Germans, and Irish
received the bulk of the allotments.

Passage of the Johnson-Reed Act marked the end of an era in American
history. Asians had already been excluded, for the most part, but for Europeans the nation had had an open door. The act ended this virtually free
immigration policy. Although the United States modified its restrictions
after World War II, it never again opened its gates to unlimited numbers.

Immigration restrictions of the 1920s, combined with the severe depression of the 1930s, achieved the effect that restrictionists desired. But the
laws did not curtail ethnic conflicts, and the nation continued to experience
tensions over immigration and intergroup relations throughout the twentieth century and into the twenty-first century.

Shortly after the final quota system went into effect in 1929, President
Herbert Hoover requested that the State Department use its administra-
tive powers for a tight enforcement of the laws. In particular, the "likely to

become a public charge" provision of the immigration codes was invoked, for America experienced a deep economic depression during the 1930s and did not want foreign laborers to compete with the growing numbers of unemployed native-born workers seeking jobs. Actually, few from any land tried to immigrate to America during the early years of the Great Depression. Only 23,068 came in 1933; 28,470 in 1934; and 34,956 in 1935. In several years more people left than arrived; there were simply not enough jobs to go around, and relief benefits were few and inadequate.

Before the immigration acts and the Depression combined to curb the numbers of newcomers, Filipinos moved into Hawaii and California to fill the labor gap created by the restriction on other Asians. Because the Philippines was then a commonwealth of the United States, there were no legal barriers to population movement; the enormous needs of the sugar planters in Hawaii and the farmers in California provided the spur.

Filipinos had been immigrating to Hawaii to work for the sugar and pineapple planters since the Gentlemen's Agreement of 1907 with Japan had reduced Japanese emigration. During the next quarter century the Hawaiian Islands welcomed 125,000 Filipinos. In the 1920s, however, when California growers feared that Congress might impose quotas on Mexicans, they turned to the Filipinos for labor. Filipinos came to the mainland from Hawaii and directly from the Philippine Islands. According to 1920 census figures, there were only 5,603 Filipinos on the mainland, but 10 years later they numbered 45,208. Other sources estimate that there may have been more than twice that number. Some 90 percent of the Filipinos were single, male, and under 30 years of age. They worked in northern and central California farms and vineyards. Stockton, California, with a concentration of perhaps 4,000 to 8,000 Filipinos, became known at the end of the 1920s as the Manila of California. Other sizable settlements formed in San Francisco, Seattle, and Portland.

The commonwealth status of the Philippines also permitted substantial numbers of Filipinos to be recruited for the U.S. armed forces, especially the navy. This accounted for the presence of Filipino communities in the San Diego and Los Angeles areas. A majority of these recruits made the military their career and left the service only upon retirement. The armed forces provided them with security and, more important, with the chance to bring their families to the United States. In the navy the Filipinos were usually assigned to mess halls and as personal attendants to high-ranking personnel.

The Depression and American prejudices caused many Filipinos to lose their jobs during the 1930s. A congressional act of 1934, which promised the Philippine Islands their independence in 1946, also established an annual Filipino quota of 50 immigrants. The quota, plus the fact that many Filipinos returned home, cut their numbers in West Coast agriculture; by 1940, 90 percent of those who remained in California were working in such personal domestic service jobs as bellboys, houseboys, cooks, kitchen helpers, and waiters.

The depression of the 1930s curtailed immigration; and many Mexicans and their American-born children were encouraged—even forced—by local government officials to return to Mexico. More than one third of the Mexican American population was removed between 1929 and 1940. About half the Mexicans who remained in the United States experienced severe deprivations. In Gary, Indiana, social workers found them living without furniture and with only boxes for tables and the floor for beds. Moreover, they fell victim to tuberculosis and rickets, and malnutrition was common among their children. One report, noting the poor housing, the large numbers of unemployed, and the deteriorating health, observed, "The agony and suffering that all of these people endure is beyond comprehension of any who have not experienced it." Southwestern agricultural wages fell from 35 cents to 15 cents an hour. In Texas, Mexican cotton pickers, working from sunrise to sunset, were lucky to earn 80 cents a day; other Mexican farm workers had to be content with 60 cents a day. In California by the late 1930s migratory Mexican families averaged $254 a year, and even there American whites were given preferential treatment. By 1939, in fact, more than 90 percent of the Golden State's field workers were dust-bowl refugees who had replaced the minority group members. In 1940 one investigator found that most of the Mexican agricultural workers in Hidalgo County, Texas, earned less than $400 a year. That same year a quarter of the Mexican children between 6 and 9 years of age worked in the fields with their parents; 80 percent of those in the 10- to 14-year age group did so as well.

As economic conditions improved in the late 1930s, the numbers of European immigrants rose again. More important motivating factors than economics, however, were the triumph of fascism in Germany in 1933 and the coming of war in Europe six years later. As the Germans annexed Austria (1938) and Czechoslovakia (1939) and then crushed Poland (1939) and conquered Norway, Denmark, the Netherlands, Belgium, and France in the spring of 1940, hundreds of thousands fled in terror, and more would have left had they been able to do so.

Though millions of political and religious dissenters were persecuted by Hitler's regime, Jews stood out as the major victims. Plagued by legal and other harassments, they sought asylum in other countries. After accepting as many as they thought they could absorb, the nations of the world refused further modification in their immigration policies. Until October 1941, Hitler permitted almost all Jews to leave the country if they chose to do so; unfortunately, most could not find any nation to accept them. During World War II the horrors perpetrated by the Nazis were legion, but before the mass exterminations in the concentration camps, perhaps the worst single episode occurred on the night of November 9–10, 1938 (now known as *Kristallnacht*). The government sanctioned a savage assault on German Jews, and throughout the night people were beaten, stores were looted, and homes, hospitals, and old-age institutions were burned; at least 20,000 people were rounded up for deportation to concentration camps. The barbarity of these actions evoked worldwide denunciation. President Franklin D. Roosevelt declared, "I myself could scarcely believe that such things could occur in a twentieth-century civilization."

Nevertheless, U.S. immigration laws remained intact, and the American government made few allowances for the victims of Hitler's terroristic policies. Americans feared economic competition from immigrant workers, for with almost 10 million unemployed in the United States, job prospects for newcomers were dim. The likelihood that additional new people in the country would become public charges and swell overburdened relief rolls was not discounted either. A few Americans also believed that spies and fifth-column agents would enter as refugees if quotas were increased. Especially important in the decision was the intense nature of anti-Semitism in the United States at the time. Both Protestant and secular newspapers wrote about it, but the Catholic Church, and Catholics in general, found Jewish support for the Republican cause in late 1930s Spain galling. Moreover, for many Americans of all stripes the word "Jew" was often used synonymously with the word "communist," and most Americans did not want any more of them in this country.

President Roosevelt was aware of American hostility toward Jews yet he also sympathized with the refugees' plight, as did a number of other Americans who urged the government to assist them. Roosevelt instructed members of the consular service to grant refugees 'the most humane and favorable treatment under the law," which enabled some applicants the opportunity of coming to America. Generally, however, the President allowed the State Department to handle the refugee problem. Unfortunately, anti-Semitism existed in the State Department too, and its influence resulted in a rigid application of the visa policy against Jewish applicants. Typical of this attitude was that of the Assistant Secretary of State, Breckenridge Long, who had charge of refugee affairs after 1939. In a 1941 diary entry he indicated approval of another man's opposition to further immigration. "He said," Long wrote, that "the general type of intending immigrant was just the same as the criminal Jews who crowd our police court dockets in New York.... I think he is right."

The State Department position probably reflected the majority viewpoint in the United States. When, in 1939, Senator Robert F. Wagner of New York and Congresswoman Edith Rogers of Massachusetts proposed a measure to allow 20,000 German refugee children between the ages of 6 and 14 years into the United States above the quota limit, patriotic societies like the American Legion and the Daughters of the American Revolution denounced it. In speaking against the legislation a spokeswoman for the Ladies of the Grand Army of the Republic warned that Congress might "decide to admit 20,000 German-Jewish children!" A year later, however, when mercy ships started bringing children from Great Britain to the United States, patriotic organizations voiced no opposition, and congressional mail ran heavily in approval. Over 15,000 American families volunteered to take one of the British children, with "a blond English girl, 6 years old" the most popular choice.

Anti-Semitism reached new heights in the United States in the late 1930s. Groups like the Silver Shirts and the German-American Bund thundered against the Jews. Bigots saw the "hidden hand of international Jewry" around every corner, and patriots organized "Buy Christian" campaigns. The most influential and well-known anti-Semite was the radio priest Father Charles E. Coughlin. Originally a supporter of the New Deal, Coughlin turned against Roosevelt and increasingly used anti-Jewish and anticommunist arguments in his broadcasts and journal, *Social Justice*. This journal reprinted excerpts from the discredited *Protocols of the Elders of Zion* and carried a speech by the German Propaganda Minister Joseph Goebbels. *Social Justice* had an estimated circulation of over 300,000, and millions heard Coughlin's radio voice. In 1940 and 1941 public opinion polls revealed that 17 to 20 percent of the nation considered Jews "a menace to America." Another 12 to 15 percent admitted that they would support an anti-Semitic campaign, and still others indicated that they would be sympathetic to such a campaign.

Despite the bigotry, though, Jews as well as others who came to America under the quota system received hospitable treatment. A host of organizations like the National Refugee Service, the Hebrew Immigrant Aid Society, and various ad hoc groups stood ready to assist the newcomers in finding jobs, housing, and friends.

European arrivals in the 1930s included a number of eminent intellectuals and scientists. Albert Einstein was perhaps the best known of the illustrious immigrants, as they have been called, but other Nobel Prize winners also came during the decade. Among the most noted were Thomas Mann, the writer; Bruno Walter and Arturo Toscanini, the conductors; Paul Tillich, the theologian; Béla Bartók, the composer; and Enrico Fermi, the physicist. Several of the scientists who came played key roles in the development of the atomic bomb.

Those who arrived in the 1930s usually adjusted to America more readily than most of the millions who had come before them. For the most part the professionals and refugees were well educated, knew some English, and had contacts and skills that they could utilize in the United States. Fleeing in terror from Europe, they were eager to become American citizens and to participate in American society. One such refugee was Henry Kissinger, who would later serve as President Richard Nixon's chief foreign policy adviser and in 1973 would become America's first foreign-born secretary of state.

Not all could adapt as well. Béla Bartók, the composer, never felt at home in America and died in relative obscurity and poverty in New York City in 1945. Some, like Thomas Mann, returned to Europe after the war. Others who lacked the contacts of an Einstein or a Toscanini had to take jobs where they could find them, often beneath their educational levels and skills. The fact that some of them left families and friends behind to an unknown fate added to their anxieties.

Concern that fifth-column agents would enter America if quotas were relaxed may have been one factor blocking a change in immigration laws, but fear of sabotage by enemy aliens already here was even greater during World War II. Consequently, the federal government interned over 25,000 Germans, German Americans, and Germans living in Latin America but transferred by their governments to the United States during the war.

Since we were also at war with Italy, Italians living in this country were at first considered "enemy aliens" and forced to register with the federal government. Fifty thousand Italians and Italian Americans lived on the West Coast. Those whose dwellings were near the ocean were relocated and all were forced to abide by a nighttime curfew.

Japanese people born abroad (Issei) and Japanese Americans (Nisei) fared much worse than either the Germans or the Italians. Those living in the far western states were incarcerated in relocation centers that some critics likened to concentration camps.

Certainly the fear of espionage, heightened by the surprise attack on Pearl Harbor and rumors of attacks to come on the mainland, was a real factor in prompting the federal government to intern Japanese Americans. In spite of the fact that no acts of espionage or sabotage by Japanese Americans were uncovered in either Hawaii or California, the boards of supervisors of eleven California counties solemnly declared that "during the attack on Pearl Harbor ... the Japanese were aided and abetted by fifth columnists of the Japanese." One U.S. senator insisted

A Jap born on our soil is a subject of Japan under Japanese law; therefore he owes allegiance to Japan.... The Japanese are among our worst enemies. They are cowardly and immoral. They are different from Americans in every conceivable way, and no Japanese ... should have a right to claim American citizenship. A Jap is a Jap anywhere you find him, and his taking the oath of allegiance to this country would not help, even if he should be permitted to do so. They do not believe in God and have no respect for an oath. They have been plotting for years against the Americans and their democracies.

Even when others pointed out that no espionage had been reported, proponents of internment argued that that merely proved the danger was greater, for the Japanese were tricky, sneaky, and underhanded, plotting for the right moment to subvert America. Ironically, the absence of overt sabotage was held against them. It was, said General John DeWitt, "a disturbing and confirming indication that such action would be taken!"

In Hawaii, where martial law had been established, armed guards watched over several thousand second-generation Japanese Americans as they worked at building bridges, roads, and airfields. The camps established in the United States by President Franklin D. Roosevelt's executive order 9066 led to the interment of 110,000 persons, most of whom were native-born U.S. citizens. Hasty removal meant hardship and suffering. Given only five days' notice, those interned could take only what they could carry; the government sequestered all other belongings. Not only were the financial losses great, but conditions in the relocation centers were miserable. At first the Japanese were placed in temporary quarters, including a hastily converted racetrack that lacked basic amenities. Eventually the government built ten camps, most of them in barren desert country, hot in the summer and cold in the winter. The surroundings were drab and unattractive, complete with barbed wire, military police, and, in some instances, machine guns. One Japanese American woman wrote of her experience at Camp Minidoka, north of Twin Falls, Idaho.

> When we first arrived here we almost cried and thought that this was a land that God had forgotten. The vast expanse of sagebrush and dust, a landscape so alien to our eyes, and a desolate, woe-begone feeling of being so far removed from home and fireside bogged us down mentally, as well as physically.

Gradually conditions improved, except for internees at the Tule Lake, California, camp, who were considered especially disloyal.

One of the sorriest episodes of the Japanese American internment was the reaction of the U.S. Supreme Court. Several Japanese Americans challenged the government's policy and took their cases all the way to the highest court. In 1943 in *Hirabayashi v. U.S.*, and in 1944 in *Korematsu v. U.S.*, the justices upheld military curfews as well as the evacuation. Three dissenting justices—Owen Roberts, Frank Murphy, and Robert Jackson—scorned the government's policy and attacked the racial prejudice that supported it. But the majority accepted the argument that internment of these immigrants and their American-born children served the national interest in wartime.

Most Japanese Americans were permitted to leave the internment camps by July 1943, but both the Issei and Nisei feared the nature of their reception in other parts of the country. Some of the most bitter renounced their American citizenship and returned to Japan. The vast majority, though, elected to return to California despite federal efforts to relocate them elsewhere. Anti-Japanese groups opposed their return. Bumper stickers appeared declaring NO JAPS WANTED IN CALIFORNIA, and a few incidents occurred, especially in the Central Valley of the Golden State. Veterans' groups urged boycotts of reopened businesses, and a few rocks were thrown and shots fired into homes. In Oregon an American Legion post removed the names of local Japanese American servicemen from the public honor roll, and other American Legion posts on the West Coast banned Japanese American servicemen from membership.

Yet the opposition gradually subsided, and, aided by church and liberal civic groups, Japanese Americans were able to find homes, jobs, and increasing acceptance. However, they reclaimed only about a tenth of their $400 million in forfeited holdings. In 1948 an anti-Japanese proposition on the California ballot to make the alien laws harsher was defeated by 59 percent of the voters. Although over 40 percent still favored restrictions against the Japanese, this was the first time in California history that an anti-Japanese referendum had been defeated. In 1952 the California Supreme Court declared the 1913 Alien Land Act unconstitutional. Also in 1952, in the McCarran-Walter Immigration Act, Congress lifted the ban on Asian immigration and the exclusion of Asians from citizenship. Japanese Americans still faced discrimination in the 1950s and 1960s, especially in housing and jobs, but the situation had changed drastically from pre–World War II attitudes and practices. By the 1960s public opinion polls revealed that most Americans considered Japanese Americans desirable citizens, trustworthy people, and loyal to the United States. Nevertheless, the trauma for those interned has not been completely overcome. A generation after the camps closed, one Japanese American admitted, "My father still trembles when he talks about this experience." On Memorial Day 1974, some Japanese Americans whose children had difficulty believing the stories of their parents' hardships made a pilgrimage to the Tule Lake camp. In Klamath Falls, Oregon, where a few had stopped to pay respects to those who died at Tule Lake, a woman passing by rolled down her car window and shouted, "You're on the wrong side of the ocean."

It was also during World War II that two particularly heinous events involving Mexican Americans took place in Los Angeles. One, in 1942, involved the arrest and conviction of a gang of teenage boys for murder although the prosecution presented no evidence at the trial to justify their conviction. Existing community prejudices, combined with the unkempt and disheveled appearance of the youths (the prosecuting attorney instructed the sheriff to prevent them from bathing or changing their clothes during the first week of the trial) sufficed to bring forth a guilty verdict. Similar miscarriages of justice reflecting community prejudices have been rendered in other sections of the country toward other minority group members at different times, but few have been marked by such gross disregard of evidence. Unable to raise bail, the defendants were forced to spend two years in San Quentin prison before a California appeals court unanimously reversed the lower court's decision "for lack of evidence" and reprimanded the trial judge for his behavior during the proceedings.

The other event that won national attention and pitted Mexican Americans against Anglos took place in June 1943. The Zoot Suit Riots involved Mexican American youth sporting the then faddish zoot suits: baggy trousers with high waists and tight cuffs, long coats with wide shoulders and loose backs, and broad-brimmed flat hats. On the evening of June 3, 1943, a group of sailors was assaulted while walking in the Mexican *barrio*. The sailors claimed that their assailants were Mexicans. They reported the incident to the police, who returned to the area but could find no one to arrest. The following night 200 sailors took the law into their own hands, went into the Mexican district of Los Angeles, and beat up every zoot suiter they could find. One naval officer explained their mission: "We're out to do what the police have failed to do, we're going to clean up this situation." Not surprisingly, the Los Angeles police did nothing at the time to deter the servicemen from their course. For the next few nights sailors, soldiers, and marines paraded through the streets of Los Angeles indiscriminately attacking Mexicans in what *Time* magazine called "the ugliest brand of mob action since the coolie race riots of the 1870s." It took the intervention of the Mexican government with the U.S. Department of State to curb military leaves in the Los Angeles area, which put an end to this mob action. The Zoot Suit Riots led to the formation of the Los Angeles Commission on Human Rights in 1944, but the new organization did little to alter established prejudices.

[5]

The Door Opens Again

Immigration from the Eastern Hemisphere, World War II to 2008

When World War II ended in 1945, the Daughters of the American Revolution, the American Legion, the Veterans of Foreign Wars, and several other patriotic groups called for a ban on immigration for five to ten years. However, Congress passed legislation to bring 205,000 displaced Europeans to our shores within three years; added to that figure in 1950; and continued to increase the numbers of immigration permits, rather than restrict them, during the next decades. Despite the narrow McCarran-Walter Immigration Act, which essentially reiterated American beliefs in the 1924 policies established by the Johnson-Reed Act, special legislation to aid individual groups in dire circumstances characterizes the Congresses of the past five decades. The new policies reflected a more liberal and generous spirit in American society, but they also represented a response to communist expansion and the sense of Christian obligation that many Americans felt required us to provide a refuge for those escaping from tyranny. Not to be overlooked as an element in this change is the strength of ethnic lobbying organizations. Before World War II these groups shied away from opposing the views of patriotic organizations, but in 1946 they recognized that favorable legislation would come about only through petitioning and influencing Congress. Then special-interest legislation, and a completely revised immigration bill in 1965, worked their way into the statute books.

But before legislation could be passed the temper of the country had to change. Anti-Semitism peaked in 1945–46, then began to subside. The changed perception of minorities was aided by a popular Hollywood film, *The House I Live In,* in which Frank Sinatra made a plea for tolerance in 1945; the publication of books like Laura Z. Hobson's *Gentleman's Agreement,* and Carey McWilliams's *A Mask for Privilege,* which exposed the depth of anti-Semitic feelings in this country; the Supreme Court's decision to outlaw restrictive covenants in housing; President Harry S. Truman's 1948 proposal for a civil rights program; and increased American prosperity.

Postwar public opinion polls, for example, indicated that fewer Christians believed Jews to be greedy, dishonest, or unscrupulous; and overt anti-Semitism, so common in the 1930s, became less frequent and less respectable. Accompanying the drop in prejudicial attitudes toward Jews was the decline of social and economic discrimination. Universities and professional schools eliminated Jewish quotas, and business firms that had been averse to hiring Jews modified their policies. Changes in major corporations and law firms came slowly. A symbolic landmark was established in December 1973, when E. I. du Pont, the world's largest chemical company, chose Irving S. Shapiro, the son of east European Jewish immigrants, as its president and chief executive officer.

Another persistent theme in American history, anti-Catholicism, also subsided after World War II. Conflict between Protestants and Catholics continued over aid to parochial schools, a proposed American ambassador to the Vatican, the relations of church and state, publicly sponsored birth control clinics, and abortion. But the deep emotional strife of the past eased greatly. The ecumenical movement of postwar society brought Protestants, Catholics, and Jews together in new areas of cooperation. In this same spirit Pope Paul VI visited the United States in 1965, conducted a prayer service before 70,000 people in New York's Yankee Stadium, and received a warm welcome. In 1979 and 1987 the charismatic Pope John Paul II made similar tours and met with even more enthusiastic receptions.

While decreasing anti-Semitism and anti-Catholicism were essential for the enactment of new immigration legislation, the laws, which made possible the admission of many Asians and blacks from the Caribbean and Africa, would not have been possible without a decline in racial prejudice. While Chinese and Japanese immigrants had been scorned and were the first ethnic groups to be banned, they found growing acceptance in post–World War II America. Educational and employment opportunities began to open up for their children, and by the middle of the 1960s many state legislatures had outlawed racial discrimination. The most far-reaching of these measures came at the height of the civil rights movement. In 1964 Congress banned discrimination in public accommodations, education, and employment; it then passed the Voting Rights Act of 1965, permitting practically all adult Americans to register to vote.

The decline of prejudice can be explained by several factors. The fear of divided loyalties that was so potent in World War I and, to a lesser extent, in World War II did not materialize during the Cold War. Prejudice is also strongly correlated with levels of income, religious intensity, and education. As incomes and education increased and as religion became less of a commitment and more of a social identification, tolerance grew. Education did not guarantee the end of prejudice, but there is no doubt that rising levels served to dampen the fires of bigotry. A highly educated public seemed more willing to accept ethnic differences. At the same time, minority members of European and Asian groups absorbed the dominant values of society as they went though the public schools, state colleges, and universities. Finally, as a result of the immigration laws of the 1920s, the nation had achieved a general balance of ethnic groups. The fears of old-stock Americans that hordes of aliens might undermine American traditions and destroy existing institutions declined. The foreign-born percentage of the population steadily decreased from about one seventh in the 1920s to less than one twentieth by the 1970s. America was becoming a more homogenized nation as the grandchildren of Asian and European immigrants came to be indistinguishable from one another or, indeed, from those whose ancestors came here before the American Revolution.

The abatement of ethnic conflict and the general prosperity begun during the war created a climate suitable for the modification of the severe immigration acts. The revision of immigration policy actually began during World War II when Congress, largely because of foreign policy considerations, repealed the Chinese Exclusion acts in 1943. Two years later Congress passed the War Brides Act, which enabled 120,000 wives, husbands, and children of the armed forces to immigrate to the United States. The newcomers were mostly German and English, but Congress amended the act to include Asian women, and as a result nearly 10,000 Chinese women came to America. Also during the war Filipinos who served either in the navy or army were permitted to become U.S. citizens. In 1946 the legislators passed new laws that gave India and the Philippines small quotas of

100. Filipinos who had been naturalized could then bring their spouses to the United States.

Then Congress turned its attention to refugees. World War II caused enormous damage to homes and factories in cities and towns throughout Europe, and reshuffling of national boundaries left many people unable or unwilling to return to their native lands. Some had collaborated with the Nazis during World War II and feared retribution; others scorned the communists; still others could not endure going back and rebuilding their lives amid the ruins. As a first step in alleviating the problem President Truman issued a directive on December 22, 1945, requiring that, within existing laws, American consulates give preference to displaced persons in Europe. About 40,000 people benefited from this order before Congress abrogated it with the passage of the Displaced Persons (DP) Act of 1948. The legislation resulted from intensive lobbying on the part of a newly formed Citizens Committee on Displaced Persons, which emphasized that 80 percent of the displaced persons were Christian. The DP Act won approval only after it had been mutilated by opponents of a liberal immigration policy. It was worded to favor agriculturists, exiles from the Baltic states, and those of Germanic origin. President Truman signed the bill reluctantly, denouncing the provisions that, as he put it, discriminated "in callous fashion against displaced persons of the Jewish faith." In 1950, after most of the Jewish refugees had gone to Israel, Congress amended the 1948 act and eliminated the offensive stipulations. Ultimately about 400,000 people arrived in the United States as a result of the two DP laws.

These acts only scratched the surface of the immigration problem. Postwar dislocations and the onset of the Cold War exacerbated the difficulties of readjustment, and millions more still sought entry into the United States. To cope with the needs of these people, as well as to contain the voices of their friends and relatives in the United States who wanted immigration policies liberalized, in 1947 both houses of Congress established a committee to look into the question. Subcommittees carefully studied the old laws and the mass of rules, regulations, and proclamations governing immigration. Senators and representatives gathered data, heard testimony from 400 people and organizations, and then recommended that the basic national origins system remain intact. While rejecting theories of Nordic supremacy, the committee held, nonetheless, "that the peoples who made the greatest contribution to the development of this country were fully justified in determining that the country was no longer a field for further colonization and, henceforth, further immigration would not only be restricted but directed to admit immigrants considered to be more readily assimilable because of the similarity of their background to those of the principal components of our population." McCarran warned, "We have in the United States today hard-cored, indigestible blocs which have not become integrated into the American way of life but which, on the contrary, are our deadly enemies." The proposed legislation became the McCarran-Walter Immigration Act of 1952. It maintained the national origins system and strengthened security procedures.

The McCarran-Walter Act liberalized immigration in two areas: it repealed the ban on Asian citizenship and granted nations in the Far East minimum annual quotas of 100 each. This was not a controversial change in 1952. The removal of some restrictions against Asians did not mean the end of racism in immigration policy, for the 1952 act contained other discriminatory provisions. Those of European background born in the Western Hemisphere were eligible to come from their nations of birth, but Asians in similar circumstances were not. People with one Asian parent were charged to that parent's home country. Thus a person of Italian and English descent who was born in Mexico, which was a nonquota nation, could enter the United States easily, whereas a person of French and Japanese descent who was born in Mexico would be charged to the Japanese quota. The intent of Congress was clear: to admit few people of Asian heritage. The McCarran-Walter Act also set a quota of 100 for several of the West Indian nations. President Truman, who favored broadening immigration laws and eliminating these provisions and the offensive National Origins Quotas, vetoed the bill but Congress overrode his veto.

Within a year after the McCarran-Walter Act had become law, efforts were made to modify it. President Eisenhower wanted to admit more refugees, and in 1953 when the Displaced Persons Act expired Congress enacted the Refugee Relief Act, which admitted another 200,000 Europeans and a few hundred Asians. Passed at the height of the Cold War, the measure was meant to aid refugees as well as escapees from communist-dominated areas.

Liberals who wanted broad alterations in the law were disappointed, but Congress made a number of other changes during the 1950s and early 1960s along the lines of the Refugee Relief Act. After the abortive Hungarian Revolution of 1956, Congress passed a law that admitted another 29,000 refugees, chiefly Hungarians, but including Yugoslavians and Chinese. Some

31,000 Dutch Indonesians, another uprooted group, came in under a law passed the next year. The United Nations declared 1960 World Refugee Year and Congress responded with the Fair Share Law, which opened the doors of this country for more immigrants.

In addition to congressional actions, Presidents Dwight D. Eisenhower, John F. Kennedy, and Lyndon B. Johnson used the executive powers they possessed under the existing immigration laws to relax restrictions. Thus 30,000 refugees entered after the 1956 Hungarian Revolution as parolees without visas, ineligible for permanent alien registration until Congress made them eligible. President Kennedy ordered the admission of thousands more, especially the Hong Kong Chinese and Cubans who sought refuge after Fidel Castro's seizure of power in 1959.

Additions to the basic immigration law made it possible for many to come who did not qualify under the quota system. In the early 1960s most immigrants were of this sort. By then the political climate was more conducive to immigration reform and not piecemeal action. In 1963 President Kennedy urged Congress to eliminate ethnic discrimination and the national origins system, which he insisted lacked "basis in either logic or reason. It neither satisfies a national need nor accomplishes an international purpose. In an age of interdependence among nations, such a system discriminates among applicants for admission into the United States on the basis of the accident of birth." After President Kennedy's death, President Johnson called on Congress to enact the Kennedy proposal. Following extensive hearings, a new immigration bill passed overwhelmingly in 1965. Designed to be fully effective in 1968, the act abolished the National Origins Quotas system and made other modifications in immigration policy.

Although the national origins proviso disappeared, an overall limitation remained. Only 170,000 people, excluding parents, spouses, and minor children of American citizens, were allowed to enter the United States from outside the Western Hemisphere. No nation in the Eastern Hemisphere was permitted to have more than 20,000 of this total, although immediate relatives were not counted. The United States still had a selective policy for immigrants, but now Congress put in place a preference system that favored family unification, occupational skills, and refugee status. Seventy-four percent of the slots were reserved for family members. Occupational visas accounted for 20 percent of the 1965 law's categories, and refugees received the smallest allotment.

Liberalization of the law for Asians and Europeans accompanied a shift in policy toward Canadians and Latin Americans. In the 1965 law Congress placed a limit—120,000—on immigration from the Western Hemisphere (immediate family members of U.S. citizens were exempt from the limit). The Johnson administration had not pressed for this restriction, but a majority in Congress feared the possibility of a massive increase in Latinos, especially Mexicans. The limitations were modified to admit Cuban refugees. Western Hemispheric immigration increased after 1965 and the Latino presence in the United States became more pronounced.

In the 1970s Congress added to the reforms begun in 1965 and shaped a worldwide uniform immigration policy. In 1976 Congress created a preference system for the Western Hemisphere and placed a 20,000 limit on all its nations, excluding immediate relatives of American citizens. This provision affected Mexico, which sent several times that number to the American Southwest annually in the early 1970s. Friends of Mexico said that the United States had a special relationship with its neighbor to the south and should make allowances, but Congress thought otherwise. The limit on Mexico helped other Latin American nations, however. Whereas Mexico had previously taken up about a third of the Western Hemisphere's overall quota, now other nations could increase their share. In 1978 Congress completed the reforms begun in 1965 when it created a worldwide ceiling of 290,000 quota places annually (not counting immediate family members of U.S. citizens) by combining the Western and Eastern Hemisphere totals; it also established a uniform preference system for all nations. This system reiterated clauses from the 1965 act that emphasized family unification, occupation, and refugees.

Congress also passed several other immigration acts after 1978, nearly all of which led to further increases in immigration. The legislators tried to regularize refugee flows by passing the Refugee Act of 1980. It set the "normal flow" of refugees at 50,000 and established procedures and programs to handle refugees. Five thousand slots were set aside for persons seeking asylum. Refugees were persons screened abroad while those seeking asylum were already in the United States. The figure of 50,000 was almost always exceeded by presidents who wanted to admit more refugees. Refugees were defined as persons with a "well-founded fear" of persecution on the grounds of race, national origin, religion, political belief, or membership in a particular group. Most refugees before 1980 were persons fleeing communism, and anti-communists continued to be the main refugees for another decade.

In 1986 Congress passed the Immigration Reform and Control (Simpson-Rodino) Act. It gave an amnesty to nearly 3 million undocumented aliens in the United States. In the future, employment of undocumented aliens would be illegal, but this provision was poorly enforced.

Another far-reaching bill was the Immigration Act of 1990 that increased immigration 35 percent by giving more visas for those with skills in demand in the United States. During the 1990s Congress did limit benefits to immigrants, but the measure did not reduce immigration.

The immigrant issue emerged again after the bombing of the World Trade Center in New York City on September 11, 2001 ("9/11"). Tighter security measures were put into place, especially for persons entering from the Middle East or Muslim nations, but no cuts in the basic framework of the law were made. In 2006 and 2007 both the Senate and the House turned once again to the immigration situation when it was estimated that there had been another huge increase in undocumented immigrants crossing the Mexican border. With President George Bush supporting a bipartisan approach to immigration, the senators debated a temporary workers program, an amnesty for many of those illegally in the United States, additional fences along the border, and shifting the focus of regular immigration to increase persons needed for their skills. These proposals were killed in the Senate. Thus the 1990 immigration law, along with more security and a larger border patrol, remained the framework of the nation's immigration policy.

After World War II, Europeans at first dominated immigration flows. Many had experienced the horror of war, and they faced language barriers, shortages of funds and skills, and the culture shock of a new environment. Often they were discouraged about the chances of finding good jobs. "I knew I would have to start at the bottom of the employment ladder, but I had no idea that the bottom rung was so far underground," lamented one newcomer. Moreover, many DPs had been through the hardships of concentration-camp life, including malnutrition and physical torture, which made adjustment still more difficult. Those fleeing communism often escaped with only the clothes on their backs.

Yet these people had some advantages. Whether they were fleeing from communism or released from DP camps, the general climate was probably more friendly to immigrants than it had been at any other time in modern American history. A host of private organizations and governmental agencies stood ready to assist them. Jewish groups that had actively assisted refugees in the 1930s continued their efforts. The United Service for New Americans, formed in 1946, was especially helpful to Jewish DPs. Various other European ethnic and religious groups, as well as federal, state, and local governments, assisted still more. In 1957, Hungarians fleeing after the Russian army had crushed the Hungarian Revolution were flown in and quartered temporarily at Camp Kilmer in New Jersey. A federal program begun in 1960 and implemented by the Department of Health, Education, and Welfare aided Cuban refugees; by 1980 over $1 billion had been spent on them. Later the Department helped the Chinese and the Vietnamese, among others. Often public and private agencies worked closely together to ease immigrant adjustment. Moreover, many refugees from communism found Americans sympathetic to their anticommunist views. By comparison, then, most newcomers probably experienced fewer problems than had nineteenth- and early twentieth-century immigrants. Prior to the 1970s they were fortunate too in coming during a period of relative prosperity after World War II, when jobs were available.

Although the enactment of special legislation enabled many southern and eastern Europeans to emigrate as refugees, expellees, or displaced persons, many came under the regular immigration laws, especially the 1965 act. American communities of Italians, Portuguese, and Greeks, among others, used the law to bring in their relatives.

Between 1960 and 1975 over 20,000 Italians arrived annually and settled in places where other Italians had gone, such as New York and New Jersey. They found not only friends and relatives who helped them secure jobs and housing but also churches, stores, and community organizations with familiar names. On the streets they heard their native tongue. After economic conditions improved in Italy in the 1970s fewer sought work in northern Europe or the United States. As a result, immigration from Italy fell off drastically after 1975; only 1,284 Italians arrived in 1995.

Portuguese too were aided by passage of the 1965 immigration act, though they were not as numerous as Italians. The act made their migration possible, and a military coup in 1974 provided a motive for many urban professionals, tradesmen, and entrepreneurs to leave, though a majority were not of the elite. Most emigrés left from Portugal, but a few came from the former Portuguese colonies of Angola and Mozambique in Africa. A few others were from the Cape Verde Islands, but Cape Verdians received their own quota upon the Islands' independence in the 1970s;

about 1,000 of these Portuguese speakers settled in the United States in 1995. Portuguese immigration averaged about 10,000 annually in the 1970s, but was only 2,611 in 1995. Newark, New Jersey, was the largest center of new Portuguese immigrants. The "Ironbound" district, as it was called, consisted of rundown shops and factories when the Portuguese began to arrive in the 1960s. Because of its size, many documented and undocumented Portuguese settled there. As one alien put it, "We are totally invisible. No one knows about us. Being illegal is just a label that doesn't mean anything." The Ironbound's thriving community consisted of restaurants, shops, and homes for newcomers. "I thought I was still in Portugal," remarked one. Brazilians, who spoke Portuguese, began to settle there in the 1990s.

Greeks were a third European group to benefit from the 1965 law. Between 1960 and 1980, 170,000 Greek immigrants arrived, generally settling among compatriots in Chicago and New York City. In New York they headed for the Astoria section of the borough of Queens, and another 20,000 or so located in Chicago. A Hellenic American Neighborhood Action Committee began in New York in 1972 to help immigrants adjust in their new circumstances. Despite a good education many Greeks accepted menial jobs in restaurants, coffee shops, construction, and factories. But enterprising families refused to stay at the bottom and soon purchased businesses of their own. In 1980 *Newsweek* asserted that the Greeks had all but "taken over [New York City] coffee shops."

The changing policies of postwar America also led to an increase in immigration compared to the lean years of the Great Depression. Whereas only 528,000 people arrived in the 1930s and 120,000 during World War II, the numbers grew substantially after 1945. In 1978 they passed 600,000; they were averaging 600,000 annually in the 1980s. During the 1990s immigration reached an all-time high of nearly 10 million arriving from foreign lands. From 2000 to 2007 immigration averaged roughly one million annually. These figures do not include undocumented aliens. The Simpson-Rodino Act of 1986 gave an amnesty to nearly 3 million persons. Unauthorized immigration declined for a few years after 1986, but in the mid-1990s it began to rise again. Experts estimated that 11 million undocumented immigrants lived in the United States in 2008. The large increases in immigration meant that the proportion of the American population that was foreign-born also increased. Only 4.8 percent of Americans were foreign-born in 1970, but the figure reached approximately 12.5 percent in 2008.

[TABLE 5.1]

Legal Permanent Resident Flow by Region and Country of Birth: Fiscal Years 2004 to 2006

(Countries ranked by 2006 LPR flow)

REGION/COUNTRY OF BIRTH	2006 NUMBER	2006 PERCENT	2005 NUMBER	2005 PERCENT	2004 NUMBER	2004 PERCENT
Total	1,266,264	100.0	1,122,373	100.0	957,883	100.0
REGION						
Africa	117,430	9.3	85,102	7.6	66,422	6.9
Asia	422,333	33.4	400,135	35.7	334,540	34.9
Europe	164,285	13.0	176,569	15.7	133,181	13.9
North America	414,096	32.7	345,575	30.8	342,468	35.8
Carribbean	146,771	11.6	108,598	9.7	89,144	9.3
Central America	75,030	5.9	53,470	4.8	62,287	6.5
Other North America	192,295	15.2	183,507	16.4	191,037	19.9
Oceania	7,385	0.6	6,546	0.6	5,985	0.6
South America	138,001	10.9	103,143	9.2	72,060	7.5
Unknown	2,734	0.2	5,303	0.5	3,227	0.3
COUNTRY						
Mexico	173,753	13.7	161,445	14.4	175,411	18.3
China, People's Republic	87,345	6.9	69,967	6.2	55,494	5.8
Philippines	74,607	5.9	60,748	5.4	57,846	6.0
India	61,369	4.8	84,681	7.5	70,151	7.3

[TABLE 5.1] (continued)

Legal Permanent Resident Flow by Region and Country of Birth: Fiscal Years 2004 to 2006

Cuba	45,614	3.6	36,261	3.2	20,488	2.1
Colombia	43,151	3.4	25,571	2.3	18,846	2.0
Dominican Republic	38,069	3.0	27,504	2.5	30,506	3.2
El Salvador	31,783	2.5	21,359	1.9	29,807	3.1
Vietnam	30,695	2.4	32,784	2.9	31,524	3.3
Jamaica	24,976	2.0	18,346	1.6	14,430	1.5
Korea	24,386	1.9	26,562	2.4	19,766	2.1
Guatemala	24,146	1.9	16,825	1.5	18,920	2.0
Haiti	22,228	1.8	14,529	1.3	14,191	1.5
Peru	21,718	1.7	15,676	1.4	11,794	1.2
Canada	18,207	1.4	21,878	2.0	15,569	1.6
Brazil	17,910	1.4	16,664	1.5	10,556	1.1
Ecuador	17,490	1.4	11,608	1.0	8,626	0.9
Pakistan	17,418	1.4	14,926	1.3	12,086	1.3
United Kingdom	17,207	1.4	19,800	1.8	14,915	1.6
Ukraine	17,142	1.4	22,761	2.0	14,156	1.5
All other countries	457,050	36.1	402,478	35.9	312,801	32.7

Source: U.S. Department of Homeland Security, Computer Linked Application Information Management System (CLAIMS), Legal Immigrant Data, Fiscal Years 2004 to 2006.

The millions of immigrants arriving after 1945 settled in all parts of the United States, but 75 percent of them found homes in six states: California, New York, Texas, Florida, New Jersey, and Illinois. Ellis Island is now a popular tourist attraction; today most new arrivals come through airports. Los Angles is the leading center for immigration with New York City as second. Mexicans and Central Americans would simply come across the southwestern border. New York attracts many immigrants from the Caribbean, Europe, and Asia, while Los Angeles and California receive Latinos and Asians. Los Angeles was 72 percent Anglo in 1960 but by 1980 people of European ancestry comprised only 40 percent of the city's population. Texas, too, has seen a large increase of Latinos.

However, in the last two decades the dispersal of immigrants has been striking. The six states that attracted three quarters of newcomers still remained the home for many, but the figure dropped to only 62 percent. Few Asians had gone to the South before 1945, but in the last 20 years 20 percent of all Asians went there in search of new opportunities. The *Atlanta Journal-Constitution* told of Koreans in the Atlanta area in 1999, "Drop a load of dirty clothes at practically any dry cleaners and the business owner is likely to be Asian—Korean actually." In the same year, 80 Korean Christian churches flourished in the Fort Worth, Texas, area. Koreans were not unique in their wide dispersal. Hmong refugees from the Vietnam War were found in Wisconsin and Minneapolis, while Chinese could be found in nearly all parts of the United States. Asian Indians operated motels not only in California and Vermont but in all states stretching from California to the Carolinas.

Many of the newcomers, especially the more prosperous ones, avoided the large cities in finding a place for their new lives. In 1986 the Census Bureau reported that half of the millions arriving between 1975 and 1985 had settled in suburban areas rather than central cities, and the trend continued after that date. And the newcomers often lived among other Americans, not in ghettoes of their own ethnic groups. While the Asian population of New York City doubled in the 1970s, it tripled in the city's suburbs. In nearby Bergen County, New Jersey, an official suggested that the Asian population was growing even faster after 1980. A Japanese journalist who lived in prosperous Scarsdale, New York, remarked that the late-night commuter train from New York City was dubbed "the Orient Express," because so many Asian fathers were on it. Outside Los Angeles, Monterey Park became the nation's first Asian-American city or suburb. Sometimes called "Mandarin Park" by those who disliked the changing demography, it was over half Asian (mostly Chinese) in 1994 but had been 85 percent white in 1960.

Immigration will continue to be dominated by developing nations, at least in the near future. Knowledge about the United States is plentiful around the globe and so is the desire to emigrate. Commenting on the situation in Israel, one scholar noted, "Communications are dominated by the 'big eye' of television where the American influence is large, indeed almost inescapable." He noted that in nations throughout the world, "Millions share sleepless nights pondering the machinations and incredible complexities of the Ewings of 'Dallas'—in about as many tongues and accents as one could care to conjure. Blue jeans are the great leveler of the twentieth century, popular as much in Leningrad as in Louisville. Every man's dreams and expectations tend somehow to be spun out in Hollywood and on Madison Avenue rather than in centers closer to home." American movies were no less popular than TV, and in the 1990s French officials, among others, complained about what they believed to be the negative influence of Hollywood productions. Travelers from the United States were almost sure to find McDonald's fast-food restaurants in the major cities of the world. In 1997 the State Department announced that the backlog of people awaiting immigrant visas to the United States was nearly 4 million, with countries such as India, the Philippines, and Mexico topping the list.

Newcomers from Asia were radically changing the nation's Asian communities and having an impact on American demography. Except for the Japanese, immigrants accounted for the majority of the population of Asian-American communities in the United States. Whereas from 1951 to 1960 only 25,201 people entered the United States from mainland China, Taiwan, and Hong Kong, during the next 35 years over a million arrived. The impact of such immigration was potentially staggering when one realizes that fewer than 250,000 people of Chinese ancestry lived in the United States in 1960. Smuggling rings that appeared in the 1980s brought in illegal workers from China for a hefty price. Once here they found themselves virtual indentured servants, forced to work 60 or more hours a week at low wages to pay off those who had smuggled them in. Moreover, the newcomers settled in a few American cities, such as San Francisco, New York, and Honolulu, substantially swelling the numbers already there. San Francisco's Chinatown more than doubled its population from 1952 to 1972, and New York City's Chinese population grew from 33,000 in 1960 to over 300,000 in 2008. By 1980 New York's Chinese

[TABLE 5.2]

States Ranked by Percent Change in the Foreign-Born Population: 1990, 2000, and 2005

(Table sorted by 2006 figures)

STATE	1990 ESTIMATE	2000 ESTIMATE	2005 ESTIMATE	CHANGE 1990 TO 2000 PERCENT CHANGE	CHANGE 1990 TO 2000 RANK	CHANGE 2000 TO 2006 PERCENT CHANGE	CHANGE 2000 TO 2006 RANK
Delaware	22,275	44,898	68,722	101.6%	18	53.1%	1
South Carolina	49,964	115,978	176,018	132.1%	11	51.8%	2
Nevada	104,828	316,593	475,914	202.0%	3	50.3%	3
Georgia	173,126	577,273	859,590	233.4%	2	48.9%	4
Tennessee	59,114	159,004	236,516	169.0%	6	48.7%	5
Alabama	43,533	87,772	130,049	101.6%	17	48.2%	6
Arkansas	24,867	73,690	107,346	196.3%	4	45.7%	7
North Carolina	115,077	430,000	614,198	273.7%	1	42.8%	8
Arizona	278,205	656,183	929,083	135.9%	9	41.6%	9
Indiana	94,263	186,534	263,607	97.9%	20	41.3%	10
Kentucky	34,119	80,271	111,724	135.3%	10	39.2%	11
Virginia	311,809	570,279	773,785	82.9%	25	35.7%	12
Oklahoma	65,489	131,747	175,987	101.2%	19	33.6%	13
Nebraska	28,198	74,638	99,500	164.7%	7	33.3%	14
Utah	58,600	158,664	210,500	170.8%	5	32.7%	15
Colorado	142,434	369,903	489,496	159.7%	8	32.3%	16
New Mexico	80,514	149,606	197,251	85.8%	24	31.8%	17
Maryland	313,494	518,315	683,157	65.3%	28	31.8%	18
New Hampshire	41,193	54,154	71,200	31.5%	43	31.5%	19

[TABLE 5.2] (continued)

States Ranked by Percent Change in the Foreign-Born Population: 1990, 2000, and 2005

STATE	1990 ESTIMATE	2000 ESTIMATE	2005 ESTIMATE	CHANGE 1990 TO 2000 PERCENT CHANGE	CHANGE 1990 TO 2000 RANK	CHANGE 2000 TO 2006 PERCENT CHANGE	CHANGE 2000 TO 2006 RANK
Minnesota	113,039	260,463	339,236	130.4%	12	30.2%	20
Washington	322,144	614,457	793,789	90.7%	22	29.2%	21
Texas	1,524,436	2,899,642	3,740,667	90.2%	23	29.0%	22
Kansas	62,840	134,735	173,394	114.4%	14	28.7%	23
Florida	1,662,601	2,670,828	3,425,634	60.6%	29	28.3%	24
Missouri	83,633	151,196	193,690	80.8%	26	28.1%	25
Idaho	28,905	64,080	82,040	121.7%	13	28.0%	26
Mississippi	20,383	39,908	51,044	95.8%	21	27.9%	27
Alaska	24,814	37,170	47,066	49.8%	33	26.6%	28
Wisconsin	121,547	193,751	245,006	59.4%	31	26.5%	21
Pennsylvania	369,316	508,291	636,567	37.6%	36	25.2%	30
South Dakota	7,731	13,495	16,852	74.6%	27	24.9%	31
Wyoming	7,647	11,205	13,929	46.5%	35	24.3%	32
Oregon	139,307	289,702	359,867	108.0%	16	24.2%	33
Iowa	43,316	91,085	112,299	110.3%	15	23.3%	34
Connecticut	279,383	369,967	452,358	32.4%	42	22.3%	35
Ohio	259,673	339,279	412,352	30.7%	44	21.5%	36
United States	**19,767,316**	**31,107,889**	**37,547,789**	**57.4%**	—	**26.7%**	—
New Jersey	966,610	1,476,327	1,754,253	52.7%	32	18.8%	37
Massachusetts	573,733	772,983	908,271	34.7%	39	17.5%	38

[TABLE 5.2] (continued)

States Ranked by Percent Change in the Foreign-Born Population: 1990, 2000, and 2005

STATE	1990 ESTIMATE	2000 ESTIMATE	2005 ESTIMATE	CHANGE 1990 TO 2000 PERCENT CHANGE	RANK	CHANGE 2000 TO 2006 PERCENT CHANGE	RANK
Illinois	952,272	1,529,058	1,773,600	60.6%	30	16.0%	39
Maine	36,296	36,691	41,956	1.1%	51	14.3%	40
Michigan	355,393	523,589	598,651	47.3%	34	14.3%	41
West Virginia	15,712	19,390	21,948	23.4%	49	13.2%	42
Rhode Island	95,088	119,277	134,390	25.4%	47	12.7%	43
California	6,458,825	8,864,255	9,902,067	37.2%	37	11.7%	44
North Dakota	9,388	12,114	13,378	29.0%	46	10.4%	45
Louisiana	87,407	115,885	125,204	32.6%	40	8.0%	46
New York	2,851,861	3,868,133	4,178,962	35.6%	38	8.0%	47
Montana	13,779	16,396	17,512	19.0%	50	6.8%	48
Vermont	17,544	23,245	24,182	32.5%	41	4.0%	49
District of Columbia	58,887	73,561	73,820	24.9%	48	0.4%	50
Hawaii	162,704	212,229	210,162	30.4%	45	-1.0%	51

Note: The term foreign-born refers to people residing in the United States who were not United States citizens at birth. The foreign-born population includes lawful permanent residents (LPRs), legal nonimmigrants (e.g., persons on student or work visas), those admitted under refugee or asylee status, and persons illegally residing in the United States. For information on sampling and nonsampling error, contact the U.S. Census Bureau.

Source: Table generated by Jeanne Batalova of the MPI Data Hub (Migration Policy Institute). Estimates for 1990 and 2000 are from the U.S. Census Bureau, 2006 American Community Survey.

population was the nation's largest, living in the old Manhattan Chinatown and new settlements in the boroughs of Queens and Brooklyn. From 1990 to 1994 another 60,000 Chinese could be found in the city. The rapid influx strained housing. In the mid-1980s some experts estimated that nearly 2,000 new immigrants were searching monthly for apartments in New York City's Chinatown. In addition, restaurants and garment shops also sought Chinatown locations. The old Chinatown spread north into Little Italy and east into the famed Lower East Side, the home of tens of thousands of Europeans decades before. Capital to purchase housing for people and businesses came from Hong Kong, where uneasy investors feared the transfer of that colony's control from Great Britain to China, which took place in 1997. As a result, commercial rents were higher in Chinatown than in most areas of the city.

Taiwan and Hong Kong were the main sources for Chinese immigrants from the 1960s to the 1970s, but then the United States recognized the People's Republic of China (PCR) and after 1981 included it in the national immigration system. As a result, immigration from the PRC grew rapidly after 1981. In the 1980s, 170,807 arrived and that figure doubled during the next decade. Another 480,000 entered from 2000 to 2005. After 1990 the PRC figures were triple the combined total of Taiwan and Hong Kong. Many had been students, and by 2005 the 63,211 Chinese students accounted for roughly 10 percent of the total enrolled in 2001–2002. While most returned to China, several thousand each year became legal permanent residents (LPRs) each year. Of China's 69,967 LPRs in 2005, over 20,000 were admitted under the occupational categories. When the Chinese government brutally crushed the Tiananmen Square democratic revolt in 1989, there were 48,212 Chinese students in the United States. Many became vocal about the communist government's action. They spoke to the media and signed petitions of protest. Suddenly their status was threatened, for they feared if they returned to China they would come into immediate conflict with the Chinese government. As a result of this threat the administration and Congress passed special legislation to permit them to stay in the United States and eventually become official immigrants.

The scientific community of America was disproportionately foreign-born. From the end of World War II until the 1960s, scientists and engineers came to the United States, from Great Britain and Canada especially, and Germany was not far behind. Most of these immigrants found jobs in private industry, but a considerable number taught and did research in

American universities. Many had originally come with a temporary visa or as students but elected to remain in this country.

In 1961 the foreign-born made up about 5 percent of the American population but 24 percent of the members of the National Academy of Sciences. The national Register of Scientific and Technical Personnel estimated in 1970 that 8 percent of the nation's professional scientists were born and had received their secondary education abroad. Of the 43 American holders of Nobel Prizes in physics and chemistry up to 1964, 16 were of foreign origin. Of the 28 Americans receiving Nobel Prizes in medicine and physiology, 8 were foreign-born.

The situation in medicine was similar as American hospitals increasingly became dependent upon immigrant physicians for their staffs. In 1950 only 5 percent of new medical licenses were granted to foreign graduates, but by 2008 this figure reached 20 percent. In 1970, more immigrant doctors came to America than were graduated that year by half of the nation's 120 medical schools. In New York City, where nearly 30 percent of foreign-born doctors settled, 70 to 80 percent of the residents and interns of some hospitals were immigrants. After changes in the law in 1976 the proportions began to decline. Even so, by 2008 there were 35,000 Indian physicians practicing in the United States, and they comprised 10 percent of the nation's anesthesiologists.

While immigration laws and procedures favored the admission of scientists, engineers, and doctors from abroad, attractive conditions in America were also essential to lure them. A study done by the National Science Foundation in mid-1970 revealed several reasons for immigration. Many, such as the Cubans, disliked their political situations at home, and others were curious about life in America. Insufficient opportunities for research also drove some out. But above all, existing opportunities made the United States seem like the land of golden opportunity. Most of the newcomers cited a higher standard of living, lower taxes, and higher salaries as major factors inducing emigration. About half said that their salaries in America were at least twice what they would have been in their homeland.

Regardless of the educational and income levels of the new Chinese immigrants, there was one major difference between them and the Chinese who came before World War II: they lived in family-based societies rather than the old bachelor ones. The new Chinese immigrants arrived as families, and their new communities were family-oriented. Women raised the children and labored outside of the home as well. Some were professionals while others worked alongside their husbands in the many restaurants and small shops. Thus Chinese immigration and settlement patterns began to resemble those of so many European immigrants.

The bulk of Chinese immigrants were employed in the service sector, usually at low-paying jobs. Many were desperate to escape from China where they believed that their future at home was bleak, yet immigrant visas were hard to come by. As a result, many from Fujian province in southern coastal China were willing to pay thousands of dollars to get to America. While smugglers along the border with Mexico were tabbed "coyotes," the Chinese smugglers were called "snakeheads." In their trek to America many endured miserable conditions only to find that the available jobs in America paid scarcely enough to live on, let alone make regular payments to the snakeheads. Their plight was brought to light when the ship, *The Golden Venture*, ran aground off the coast of Long Island in 1993. The undocumented immigrants, who had promised to pay $30,000 for the trip and who had been living in a smelly hole for four months, jumped from the ship, but some drowned. The remaining 286 would-be immigrants were taken into custody. Some later obtained asylum but others were eventually returned to China.

The kinds of jobs the Fujianese found were mostly menial. A dispute between a Vietnamese restaurant and its Fujianese workers in upper Manhattan in 2007 highlighted the experience of many Asians. The Saigon Grill was actually owned by Simon Nget, a Cambodian, who had spent two years in a refugee camp before coming to America. He had a takeout and delivery business. His Fujianese employees, who knew little English, delivered up to 40 orders per night on bicycles, at times in dangerous neighborhoods. Such employment was about the only jobs they could find. One Chinese immigrant from Seattle who made four trips before finally making it to America and finding decent employment said, "If I go back to China, and I tell them 'In the United States it's tough, you have to work hard,' they don't believe it. We should ... [let] them know that not everywhere in America is Mountain of Gold."

Next to Mexico and China, the Philippines sent more people to America than any other country. In 2005, 1,593,421 foreign-born Filipinos lived in the United States, and they amounted to 4.5 percent of the immigrant population. Many were married to American soldiers and sailors. When the American bases in the Philippines closed in 1993, the number married to U.S. citizens dropped radically. However, Filipina women sought still another way to migrate to the United States: as mail-order brides. Thousands of ads were placed in newspapers circulating in the United States. Congress passed a marriage fraud act to halt this practice, and the Immigration and Naturalization Service (INS) scrutinized the women when they applied as prospective brides to be married to Americans. These laws did not take into consideration another problem. Some women who entered such arrangements found themselves caught in marriages marked by violence, but they were afraid to leave the marriage because they would lose their green cards. The number of fraudulent marriages is not known, but the number was not large, though Filipinos were estimated to constitute about one half of the mail-order brides in the United States.

The vast majority of Filipino men and women entered under the occupational and family unification provisions of the 1965 immigration act. They had ample reason to do so. In the years of the Ferdinand Marcos dictatorship, begun in 1972 and supported by the United States, there was little dissent. But even when democracy returned, a bleak economy did not improve. Many Filipinos lived in poverty and others barely managed to surpass that threshold. Because they had awareness of American culture, they looked to the United States. Like those who came before World War II, many immigrants took laboring jobs. However, some fared better because of their knowledge of English and worked in the service sectors of the American economy.

The occupational preferences for professionals in 1965 gave them the opportunity to migrate. In the first five years of the new law, over 17,000 Filipino professionals immigrated to the United States, and in the first 20 years of the new law, 25,000 entered. No group stands out more in this migration than nurses. Most entered under the regular preferences but the Congress also passed legislation that permitted temporary workers to enter as nurses. Later, in 1989, legislators permitted the nurses to adjust their status and become immigrants.

The admission of nurses proved to be controversial. Various studies indicated that there was no nursing shortage and that Americans (mostly women) would remain as nurses if their wages were improved. Wages did improve in American hospitals, but large urban hospitals insisted that they could find enough nurses. In the mid-2000s the recruitment policies of such hospitals continued, and administrators warned that there was a potential for more than 100,000 vacancies in the future, and they had to find nurses from abroad. Filipino nurses were willing to fill the gap. In 2006 a skilled nurse in the United States made an average of $50,000 a year.

Filipino physicians also benefited from the changing immigration law, and thousands headed toward the United States. Like the nurses, many found employment in large urban hospitals. By the late 1970s, when Congress enacted new restrictions on foreign-born physicians, there were reportedly 9,000 Filipino doctors in the United States. They continued to arrive after 1980, but not in such large numbers. By 2007, of all practicing foreign physicians in the United States, India furnished the largest number. The Philippines ranked second. Because nurses had an easier time getting into the United States, it was reported in 2004 that physicians were being retrained to labor as nurses in the United States. One doctor said, "Before, I did not want to go abroad, because I thought people who left were failures here. But I know I could get $40 an hour as a nurse abroad. There's no place for Filipino doctors, but nurses—yes."

A majority of Filipinos were women. The reason for this is that many Filipino professionals were women or the spouses of servicemen, a situation quite unlike the pre-1945 migrants. Yet in one respect the latest immigrants resembled the old pattern: their choice of states of preferred settlement. The states with the largest number of Filipinos were California and Hawaii. In Hawaii they constituted almost half of the foreign-born population. In California the largest urban concentrations were Los Angeles and San Francisco. The 2000 census indicated that nearly one half lived in California alone. There were also large numbers in New York and New Jersey. Like so many of the other immigrants after 1990, the largest percentage increases were in areas where few had gone before.

A high proportion of the women went to work for pay, and as a result Filipino-American family incomes were higher than the American average. Like so many other immigrants, they read ethnic newspapers catering to them and worried about the struggle for democracy and economic development in their homeland. They also joined ethnic organizations; but Filipinos, because of their fluent English and high levels of education, did not form ethnic ghettoes. Unlike most other Asian groups, they were apt to intermarry during their first decades in the United States.

More noticeable than Filipinos but fewer in numbers were Koreans. They received attention because of conflicts with African Americans and because they were at the center of the Los Angeles riots of 1992, which destroyed many of their businesses. Few Koreans lived in the United States before 1950. Then came a few students, a few businessmen, and—after the

Korean War ended in 1953—wives of American servicemen. The Korean War had an impact on Korean society, for the penetration of American culture triggered immigration. Koreans learned of our country from the wives of American servicemen and from students, many of whom remained in America after completing their educations. Korean newspapers also told of life here; in 1976 one series of articles was published as a book, *Day and Night of Komericans,* which became a bestseller. However, knowledge was one thing, the law was another; not until the 1965 immigration reform act was it possible for many Koreans to emigrate. First came doctors and nurses, and once they were settled they sent for their relatives.

The 1990 census counted just under 800,000 Koreans, most of whom had arrived since 1960. The largest community was in Los Angeles, but there were also important Korean populations in New York City and Chicago. Many economically successful Koreans, such as medical professionals, lived in the suburbs. Koreans in Los Angeles mixed with other groups, including Mexicans, Samoans, and Chinese, but the city had a Koreatown and the Koreans themselves had a rich community life. For Koreans an important institution was the church. Because so many were Protestants, they affiliated with Presbyterian and Methodist congregations, but they also began to hold separate services. In 1985, the First United Methodist Church of Flushing, in Queens, New York City, had only 30 members in its English-speaking congregation but 450 in its Korean congregation. In many suburbs, where the more prosperous Koreans lived, Koreans held services in their language, even though many of them spoke English well.

Koreans also formed business associations to assist their many economic enterprises. No other immigrant group so easily found a niche in small business. In the 1970s they were successful in running small grocery and vegetable stores in predominately black neighborhoods, replacing Jewish and Italian merchants. In the 1980s and 1990s they branched out and opened nail salons, dry cleaners, and liquor stores. The immigrants running these shops were often college-educated men and women who worked long hours while keeping their stores open late at night. Korean businesses were especially noticeable in New York City and Los Angeles, but they also moved into declining neighborhoods in cities like Newark, New Jersey. El Paso, Texas, had only one Korean store in 1982; three years later 30 more were reported. In that Texas city, as elsewhere, Koreans quickly earned a reputation for successful merchandising. As one El Paso merchant put it,

"They're moving in like crazy—it seems every space that's available, they take it. They're very hard-working and industrious."

Urban Korean merchants in predominately African American areas found themselves in the midst of growing conflicts. Some black residents claimed that the Koreans insulted them, would not hire them, and did little to help the local community. Black groups organized boycotts of Korean stores, forcing several to close and leading to violence in a few cases. But no one could have predicted the upheaval that occurred in Los Angeles in 1992. When a white jury refused to convict white police officers of beating a black man—an event broadcast on television—blacks and Latinos in the city erupted. Korean stores in the ghettoes were attacked and more than 2,300 were destroyed, resulting in $350 million worth of damage. Although community leaders tried to patch up the differences and bring groups together, many Korean merchants refused to reopen their stores; they blamed the police for inadequate protection.

Unlike Koreans, India received a quota of 100 three years after the repeal of the Chinese exclusion acts gave China a quota of 105. However, Indians did not have war brides or refugees arriving before the repeal of the National Origins Quotas in 1965. Thus only a few Indian immigrants came between 1946 and 1965. Then a major movement of people from India to the United States began, and in 2005 over 84,000 Indian immigrants were recorded, second only to Mexico. By 2005 the census bureau reported that there were 1.4 million foreign-born Indians in the United States, behind persons of Chinese ethnicity and Filipinos, and of course Mexico, which accounted for nearly a third of the foreign-born population in that year.

It is uncertain how many Indians came to America, because many came from nations that had substantial Indian populations. When Uganda's Idi Amin expelled Indians in the 1970s, most went to the United Kingdom or to Canada, but some settled in the United States. It was not unusual for families to settle in several places before coming to the United States. Ravina Advani, for example, went to Hong Kong from India and then to Sierra Leone in Africa. From there he finally came to America. A few other Indians came from African nations such as Kenya, while an even larger flow entered from the West Indies and South America. Indians had settled in Guyana and Trinidad (often as indentured workers) in the nineteenth century, and maintained their own communities; in post-1945 some chose to migrate to the United States.

The immigration of Indians to America differed from the small movement of the early twentieth century. Then, few women came, and most of the men were Sikhs, who worked in American agriculture, with the largest number in the Imperial Valley of California. For the most part, these were uneducated workers. Modern Indian immigration was of families. Moreover, Indians had the highest level of education of any post-1945 immigrants. Some estimates suggested that 80 percent of Indians were college graduates, with roughly one half holding degrees beyond the bachelor level. Among these newcomers were many doctors; Indian immigrant physicians were the largest group of the foreign-born doctors, with an estimated 42,000 practicing medicine in the United State. Indeed, Indians accounted for 5 percent of all American doctors. In 1981 they organized the American Association of Physicians of Indian Origin to deal with their concerns about discrimination. The organization also took up issues relating to persons of Indian origin who were studying in American medical schools; by the early 2000s the students numbered 10,000.

The lure of medical practice was not limited to physicians. By 2000, Indian nurses had heard the call of a potential nursing shortage in the United States. Like so many Filipina nurses, they spoke English. As the U.S. government made certification easier in 2002, Indians answered the call; as one official put it, "It is boom time for nurses in India." Hospitals and organizations dealing with the shortage of nurses in American hospitals began to look to India as well as the Philippines and Canada for recruits. In 2003 the Commission on Graduates of Foreign Nursing Schools announced the opening of an office in Bangalore, its first in India in 30 years.

Other lucrative fields for highly educated Indians were in computers, sciences, and economics. In 1990 when Congress established a new guest worker program for temporary high-tech experts, Indians furnished one half of the workers in the first years of the program. Thousands of students first came to American schools, then became immigrants. Some worked for American corporations, utilizing their skills in the research departments, but by 2000 a number of Indians were returning to organize their own firms at home, where labor was cheaper. With development of the Internet a number of American corporations began to outsource jobs that required only lower-level tasks, but also a knowledge of English. Corporations also found that they could easily work with newly organized Indian businesses. By 2003, Texas Instruments employed 1,000 persons in India, and Indians provided 30 percent of Motorola's software personnel. Others founded their own firms in the United States, and still others taught in colleges and universities in the United States. The 2000 census recorded more than 5,000 Indians teaching in American universities. In some fields, such as economics, they were numerous enough to establish their own associations.

Indians in engineering sometimes found that field the way to the top. A remarkable success story was that of Mysore L. Nasgaria. The youngest of 11 children, he came on a scholarship to study engineering at Brigham Young University in Utah. After graduating he landed a position in engineering in New York City. In the mid-1980s he began to work for New York City's Metropolitan Transit Authority, and by 2003 he became head of capital construction for the authority.

Indians have also purchased service stations, but the most notable businesses were motels, many run by persons with the surname Patel. By 1985 an estimated 80 percent of California's independent motels were operated by Indians. They then branched out and won the concessions for over a quarter of the Days Inn chain motels. One wag labeled these "Potels."

Indians spoke English and were generally not ghettoized. They often lived near their places of work: universities, hospitals, and corporations. Because they were so highly educated and taught in colleges and universities, there were often a few Indian families in places such as Middlebury and Burlington, Vermont, where IBM located a major establishment. Another IBM facility, in Boulder, Colorado, employed Indians, as did high-tech industries on the West Coast. Indians formed their own organizations, bound together as Sikhs or Hindus. Among some groups, ethnic identity was maintained within the larger Indian community. Bengalis began to hold their own cultural events and publish a magazine. One leader remarked of the annual conference, "The struggle now is to make sure that this second generation, which was raised in America and sees itself as very American, rightly so, does not lose touch with its language and its music."

The entrance of South East Asian refugees had little to do with the Hart-Celler Immigration Act of 1965. Rather they came to America without regard for the preference system and instead entered after the fall of Vietnam to the communists in 1975. Presidents and then Congress admitted them outside the refugee quota of only 10,200 annually. President Lyndon Johnson had escalated the war in Vietnam in 1965, with little thought that U.S. policy would fail in Vietnam and that America would admit over one million refugees as a result. These people did not necessarily represent highly skilled immigrants such as the Indians or many Koreans and Filipinos.

Many, after enduring horrendous hardships, arrived in the United States with few skills, no English, and little knowledge of American culture. They came in several waves, the first being those who were airlifted from Saigon after it fell to the communists in the spring of 1975. Others crossed into Thailand or fled by ship; they were known as "boat people." About 170,000 eventually ended up in the United States. In 1978 a new crisis developed as communists tightened their control over members of the business class, many of whom were ethnic Chinese. As the crisis spread to Laos and Cambodia, endangered Hmong hill tribesmen who had fought against the communists with the backing of the CIA sought refuge in Thai camps. The bloodbath of Pol Pot's Cambodian Khmer Rouge government sent shock waves through the world. Over a million were killed, and thousands of Cambodians fled across the border to Thailand. In the 1980s the United States and Vietnam agreed upon an "Orderly Departure Program" to process directly relatives of those who had already settled in the United States. A law passed by Congress created a program for the children fathered by American servicemen and Vietnamese mothers to come to the United States. Many had no knowledge of their fathers and some were abandoned by their mothers. The refugee flow began to slow in the mid-1990s after the United States had received over one million people from the former Indochina.

Who were these Asian refugees to America, and how did they fare in their new land? In the first wave, arriving in 1975, many were urban, well educated, knew English, and had formed close ties with U.S. efforts in South Vietnam by working with American armed forces or for American corporations. Some had been officials or military officers in the South Vietnamese government. Among the second wave, coming as part of the large exodus from Indochina in 1978 through the early 1980s, were ethnic Chinese who frequently owned small businesses in the cities. These middle-class people often settled in America's Chinatowns rather than near other East Asians. Included too in this influx were Vietnamese businesspeople and those who had worked for the United States and the government of South Vietnam before 1975. Although a predicted bloodbath did not take place when the communists took over, these people were harassed by the new regime and their old ways of livelihood destroyed. Others in this wave were a large number of desperate people from Laos and Cambodia, many peasants uprooted by the constant fighting. Hmong tribesmen frequently were illiterate farmers who lacked urban skills and experience.

Regardless of their backgrounds, all Vietnamese refugees faced problems in their new land, including racism that erupted into public hostility and even violence. In Philadelphia, Denver, New Orleans, New York, and Seadrift, Texas, refugees encountered chilly receptions. The most newsworthy violent episode pitted Vietnamese fishermen against white Texans. Some refugees who entered in 1975 settled along the Texas Gulf Coast to engage in shellfishing. Unfamiliar with American regulations and customs about fishing for shrimp and crabs, immigrants used smaller boats than did Americans and did not always follow established rules and procedures. Tempers flared as prices for shrimp and crabs remained low and fuel prices were high in 1978 and 1979. One American complained, "There's too many gooks and too few blue crabs. The government gives them loans and houses but doesn't care about us. Who's gonna protect our rights? The Vietnamese are gonna take over, it just isn't right." In the summer of 1979, an American trapper was killed during a fight between native whites and refugees. Although the Vietnamese were arrested and indicted, tensions remained high when they were acquitted of murder charges.

While the rapid growth of racial violence was troubling, most refugees did not experience it. Their most acute problems included lack of English, lack of familiarity with American ways, and little or no capital. Federal government programs, along with aid from church and community groups, helped many of the newcomers become self-sufficient, and by the 2000s some of the first wave of refugees was on the way to becoming successful in the new land. In Chicago, Vietnamese immigrants revived the once economically depressed Argyle Street. Within ten years of their arrival they operated fifty shops in this "Little Saigon." A city alderman remarked of their success, "The change has been astronomical. No one used to dare go there after 5 P.M. and now there is a real night life."

For the boat people and others who arrived in the 1980s the picture was not as bright. Many had survived horrendous conditions at sea and malnutrition in refugee camps. Moreover, many were poorly educated; some of the Laotians were not even literate in their own language. Uprooted by constant fighting and emotionally drained by refugee camp living, they lacked the knowledge and means to adapt readily to American ways. The cultural gap was deep. An official working with the Hmong people relocated in Montana observed that they had never encountered freeways, food stamps, checkbooks, or birth control pills. He explained, "This is like Disneyland to them. It's like us going to Mars and starting over again."

Although most refugees came as families or were able to reunite with their loved ones within a few years, it was not always possible to do so. One quarter of Cambodian families were headed by women. Their husbands had been killed or had been lost trying to escape to Thailand. For these women, with little education and only an elementary knowledge of English, life was hard. Social workers reported that they had an especially difficult time adjusting to the United States. They knew little English, and they were reluctant to go out. "When I go out," explained one, "some people ask me lots of questions and I can't answer enough." Some had been raped during their escapes, which added to their fears of leaving their apartments. Thus, in addition to the problems they faced economically, many experienced mental health difficulties. Low-paying jobs often lacked health insurance; this made welfare a necessity to keep Medicaid benefits. Because their children were learning English in the schools, women had to rely upon them to interpret and explain American ways. For some, such reliance was a loss in status and proved embarrassing as well when questions were asked about birth control. The jobs they found were low-paying and in the service sector. Cambodians, for example, found a niche in California's Dunkin' Donuts shops, even though few if any had ever heard of doughnuts in Asia. Government officials worried that Cambodians, Hmong, and even some Vietnamese would become a permanent dependent class. Surveys after 1980 reported high rates of welfare, although they also revealed that the longer the refugees remained here the more likely they were to learn English, find jobs, and become self-sufficient. No doubt the first wave, with their higher status, would help the newest Asian immigrants adjust, but only time would tell the final stories of the refugees.

People from India's neighbors, Pakistan and Bangladesh, also looked to the United States as a nation of economic opportunity. Pakistan was given a small quota in the McCarran-Walter Act of 1952, and as a result only a few immigrants entered until the Hart-Celler Act of 1965. Even then, Pakistani immigration remained light until the 1980s. After 1990 approximately 14,000 Pakistanis entered annually, but it remained a fraction of India's flow. In 2005 Pakistan's immigration total was just under 15,000 whereas persons from India numbered 84,000 in that year. At times Indians and Pakistanis found themselves in conflict in the United States. Both groups decided to hold their own independence parade in New York City, but as an Indian put it about the Indian independence parade, Pakistani immigrants "have no business being here," and they also disagreed about the future of Kashmir.

However, there were similarities between the immigrants from these two nations. The first wave of Pakistanis was highly educated and included medical professionals. Two of the most prominent physicians were Adbus Saleem and his wife. They arrived in the United States in 1971. After practicing medicine in several locations, Adbus Saleem became chief of hematology at Methodist Hospital in Dallas and a professor of pathology at the Baylor College of Medicine. While considerably fewer in number compared to Indian doctors, Pakistani physicians organized their own medical society. Other Pakistanis worked in newsstands and drove cabs and struggled to make a living. Cabdrivers on occasion were robbed and even killed. The prospect of running one's own business was also a lure. Like Indians they ran small stores in chains. In Chicago, Pakistanis saved and purchased their own Dunkin' Donuts stores. Pakistani women sometimes found employment as teachers or helped run small ethnic groceries, which catered to both Indians and Pakistanis.

Pakistanis are having an impact of American religion. They added to the growth of Islam as dozens of new mosques were opened in American cities. They were the largest Islamic Asian group, and they have taken the lead in some cases in opening Islamic day schools.

Until Bangladesh's independence from Pakistan in 1971, persons looking to America as a land of opportunity had to come under the Pakistan quota of 20,000, excluding family members of American citizens. However, few arrived until the 1990s. Bangladesh is a poor country, subject to periodic flooding and limited opportunities for professionals. As a result, when knowledge of a much higher standard of living in America spread, many decided to move. With family unification being the heart of the preference system, Bangladeshis had to come under the occupational preferences category, for which there was a wait of several years. However, the diversity visa (DV) program established in 1990 offered a new opportunity because diversity visas were determined by lottery for those nations with little immigration. The word was out and many Bangladeshis won the lottery. One applicant said, "Why should I rot in Bangladesh and starve almost every day if I have a place in America?" As these winners knew, once established in the United States, immigrants and U.S. citizens could then sponsor their relatives. As a result, immigration from Bangladesh began to grow and was over 11,000 in 2005.

Like Indians and Pakistanis, the first immigrants from Bangladesh were often highly skilled. Others took what jobs were available, such as cabdrivers. As the popularity of Indian restaurants grew, these immigrants opened "Indian" restaurants. One owner insisted, "If we called them Bangladeshi only Bangladesh immigrants will come. Americans don't know about our food; they come only to eat Indian food. So we serve them South Asian food and call it Indian."

While the number of East Asians grew substantially after 1965, increases were also recorded from the Middle East. Following the Islamic revolution in Iran in 1979, many fled to the United States, some entering as refugees and others as regular immigrants. A good number of these people were professionals and entrepreneurs who found that their livelihoods were threatened in Iran. Some were Jews who feared persecution. In California and elsewhere Iranians utilized their skills, became self-employed, or worked as professionals. Many were fortunate to know English and were relatively successful. The Iranians of Los Angeles located in Beverly Hills and Brentwood, two of the city's most affluent neighborhoods. This group was active in construction and some, like the Ersa Grae firm, built shopping centers and subdivisions in several states.

The Soviet invasion of Afghanistan in 1980 triggered another wave of refugees. As the war dragged on, thousands of Afghanis fled to neighboring Pakistan; authorities estimated their number to be 3 million. The United States supported those fighting the Soviets and at the same time recognized that assistance would have to be granted to the unfortunate refugees. Those who entered without proper papers had a difficult time convincing the government they were entitled to asylum, but eventually several thousand were admitted annually as refugees in the 1980s. Their numbers began to decline when the Soviets ended the war, and only 616 refugees were accepted in 1995. Afghanis came to a nation that had few of their compatriots, and most who came before 1979 were highly educated. The newest refugees had diverse backgrounds. A few opened restaurants, but they became better known for operating fried chicken stands. "It's like Koreans with markets," remarked one. "When one starts, he gives jobs to friends and they get started in the same business."

Other Middle Eastern immigrants consisted of Armenians, Turks, Palestinians, and Israelis. Their numbers were not large, and they were not increasing at a high rate. Drawing the most notice were Arabs. The Arabs who came around 1900 were Christians and Christians dominated the first flows after 1945. But in recent years Muslims have overtaken Christians in number. The center of Arab population in the United States is Detroit. Some of these people were fleeing the constant violence in the Middle East while others with skills saw a better future in the United States.

A socioeconomic profile of immigrants from Arab nations indicates that this was an elite migration, which was often the case for the first wave of other groups. Their educational levels and income are what one would expect from elite migrants. Arab immigrants also opened many stores catering to their fellow immigrants, but it was claimed that Palestinians were the most important owners of small grocery stores in California. However, by no means were all of the Arab immigrants professionals or successful business men and women. Yemeni immigrants were often working class who had to take jobs in restaurants or open small stores.

The center of Arab life in America was Michigan, especially Detroit and Dearborn. In Dearborn one heard Arabic spoken on the streets and customers could buy things reminiscent of home. Here too mosques and Arab religious life flourished. The relative peace of Arab communities was shattered after 9/11. The government called many Arabs in for questioning, held some for months without charging them with terrorism. The federal government revealed that over 300,000 Middle Easterners were living illegally in the United States, and did manage to deport a few.

The refugees from Afghanistan and Iran were a sign of shifting priorities, away from the strictly anticommunist criteria for the admission of refugees. Among those receiving an increasing number of refugee slots were Africans. Beginning with the acceptance of Ethiopian refugees, there was a steady growth in Africans, until the United States was accepting about 20,000 per year. These refugees, combined with diverse visas after 1990, helped African nations increase their numbers of immigrants to America. Africans were also well educated and some were able to enter under the occupational preferences stipulation. Many had been driven from their homes under dire conditions.

Ethiopians left to escape a Marxist regime in the 1970s, but a dreadful famine in the 1980s prompted many to immigrate if they could obtain a visa. Many who did leave late saw television programs about those left behind. "It's in the back of our minds all the time," said Bishop Paulos Yohannes of the Ethiopian Orthodox Church of the Savior. "Every time you eat, you see them." Another group of refugees were Somalians, arriving in the 1990s. An estimated 20,000 came after 1991, with 12,000 settling in the cold climate of Minneapolis. Many worked in the food-processing jobs that were available. Mostly Muslim, they organized their own mosques, wore traditional clothing, and tried to maintain their culture. They frowned on women working outside the home. If working in the cold climate of Minnesota seemed unusual, so did the fact that other Africans found employment on the ski slopes of Colorado.

The preference for those with occupations in demand required skills and education; as a result African immigrants were among the best educated of the new post-1945 immigration. They did not have the skills of Indians, but they were equal to most Asians and above most Hispanics. Often these newcomers came to study in American colleges and universities, quite commonly the historically black colleges. Some then returned to their native lands and became important political leaders or intellectuals, but some of the Africans found employment in the United States. As was typical with early flows, African immigrants were largely male.

It was also possible to get into the United States and then overstay one's visa. When the Simpson-Rodino Act was passed in 1986, over 30,000 Africans received an amnesty, which was only 1 percent of the total. How many arrived after that and simply stayed and worked is not known, but some experts say that the African undocumented population has grown considerably and plays an important role in the African community. When a Bronx, New York, fire took the lives of one adult and nine children in March 2007, it made front-page news. The family was from Mali, and the father was an undocumented immigrant, afraid to return there to bury his children. He feared that because of his status he would have considerable difficulty getting back to New York. The federal government responded by permitting him to come back to New York after the burial. In this case the government was flexible, but many unauthorized Africans were reluctant to return home, fearing that they would not be able to migrate to America again.

While being refugees and having skills were ways to get to America, another was through the DV program, originally intended for the Irish and some Europeans. Like Bangladesh, African nations were eligible because so few immigrants had arrived before 1990. A rule of thumb was that nations averaging fewer than 10,000 for the past five years would be eligible for a DV, for which all African nations were eligible. Under the program no nation was to have more than 3,850 places. For countries with a weak link to American immigration policy, this was a high figure.

Once established, Africans used the family preferences category to bring their families to the United States. Nigeria, the nation with the largest number of Africans in the United States, sent 10,598 immigrants to America in 2005; of these, 1,393 used the occupational preferences category, and 5,383 were immediate family members of U.S. citizens; 2,379 used the DV program.

How many of the Africans were black? Authorities did not actually know, because some whites left South Africa and newly independent countries because they believed their future as whites in Africa was bleak. As noted earlier, Asians were also included in the flow, and North Africans were classified as "white." In the early years of the growing immigration blacks made up a majority of Africans in America, and their proportion of the newcomers increased after 1990. In the mid-2000s over one million black Africans lived in the United States. New York City, Chicago, Atlanta, and Washington, D.C., had sizable colonies, complete with immigrant organizations. Many of the latest newcomers were Muslims, but Christians were also prominent in those cities.

As noted, African immigrants were well educated, and not surprisingly their incomes were higher than native-born African Americans. However, their incomes were lower than whites with similar educational backgrounds. The most prominent were physicians, business owners, and college professors. Shortages of doctors and nurses in inner city hospitals drew these newcomers. For Africans to take such positions meant that many vacancies existed. But the prospects were so much better in the United States (and in other developed nations). A study completed in 2005, for example, found that Ghana had only 6 doctors for each 100,000 people and that Ghana lost 3 of every 10 doctors it had graduated to the United States and other developed countries. The United States by way of comparison has more than 220 doctors for every 100,000 persons. Africans, in traditional immigrant fashion, sent remittances to their homelands, and these funds were crucial for those left behind.

Of course only a minority of Africans were physicians or college professors. Many, especially those without papers, took whatever jobs they could find. As one African noted, "If you are foreign and black and looking for a job in New York, you will very likely receive low pay." One of the lowest-paid jobs was delivering food from takeout restaurants. Deliverymen relied on tips, and these were not especially generous.

Others, women as well as men, seeking to avoid working for others, opened restaurants, gift shops, import-export houses, and hair salons. The women usually operated the salons. Another outlet for entrepreneurial Africans was street peddling. People from Mali and Senegal, often undocumented immigrants, sold goods on the streets of New York City and other major cities. The *New York Times* noted that Africans appeared on the streets with umbrellas for sale when the "first raindrops fall." The street merchants also took to the road and peddled their wares in cities having special fairs.

Their numbers are sure to grow, at least in the near future. The African-born population was over 1.2 million in the United States, and Africa's 117,000 immigrants recorded in 2006 made up 10 percent of the total, the highest it had ever been since the United States became a nation.

The Balkan violence of the 1990s produced another flow of refugees: Bosnians. Over 150,000 entered after the peace process ended the ethnic wars there. Not all Bosnians arrived as refugees, but they were escaping violence just the same. Over 400 refugee committees aided the Bosnians, and as a result, they were scattered in the United States, with several thousand living in New York City and several thousand in Salt Lake City, Utah. Wherever they located, Bosnians, like most newcomers, found jobs at the bottom of the pay scale and struggled to learn English and accommodate themselves to American culture. For the most part, the refugees stayed within their communities and assisted other refugee Bosnians. Many had been well educated in Bosnia, but found that their particular professions could not be practiced easily, especially if they lacked English. However, survey data indicated that as many were satisfied with their adjustment to the United States as those who found their adjustment to the United States "to be difficult."

Because the overwhelming majority of Bosnians were Muslims, after 9/11 some found themselves under suspicion though they were not Arabs or from Asia. When a young deranged Bosnian youth shot and killed people at a Salt Lake City shopping mall, hate mail poured into the mayor's office. However, city officials pointed out, as did Bosnian community leaders, that the episode was unique.

A bill introduced by Sen. Frank Lautenberg and passed in 1989 permitted 300,000 persons from the former Soviet Union to become refugees. They were mostly Jews, but a number of others also came as well. The migration of these refugees led to further increases in immigration from the former Soviet Union. From 2004 to 2006 over 50,000 persons came from the Ukraine.

Not all refugees or asylum seekers were accepted by the United States. Following the first Gulf War of 1991, several thousand Iraqis immigrated to the United States, some as refugees and others as regular immigrants. But in the second Gulf War, beginning in 2003, the situation was different. Over 2 million had left their homes by 2008, fleeing violence, and they found a temporary place in Jordan, Syria, and other nearby countries. Fewer than 500 were accepted by the United States. Congressional critics assailed the Bush administration for not doing more, and in 2007 the administration agreed to allow entry to several thousand. But the fate of those left behind was left undecided.

6

Close Neighbors

Immigrants from the Western Hemisphere,
World War II to 2008

Since World War II there has been a continuous increase in the Latino presence in the United States. With the bracero movement, begun during the war, Puerto Rican migrations to New York City and other East Coast locales after the war, and the migration from Mexico in the late 1940s and 1950s, Hispanics have carved a niche for themselves that rivals that of the Germans in the nineteenth century. The signs of Latino vitality are evident almost everywhere in America.

More than a hundred television and radio stations broadcast in Spanish. In February 1998, for example, the top-rated television station in Miami, Florida, WLTV, broadcast exclusively in that language. Other major Spanish-speaking television stations thrive in cities like New York, Los Angeles, and Albuquerque, New Mexico. Pacific Telephone puts out a Spanish-language supplement in California; Chicago bus notices and Philadelphia civil service examinations appear in both languages; and shops from California to New York display *Aqui se habla español* placards in their windows. In Miami, shops display Cuban flags and CUBA LIBRE signs. One can walk for blocks in that city hearing only Spanish and stop at cafes that serve rich, dark Cuban coffee. In 1997 a slick magazine catering to upwardly mobile Latinos, called *Hispanic,* celebrated its first decade.

Aware of the growing buying power of the nation's Latinos, the Plaza Fiesta Mall in Atlanta, Georgia, celebrated a Mexican holiday, Cinco de Mayo, in May 2007. Directors of the mall noted that it had become the center of shopping for the more than one half million Hispanics who lived within 10 miles of the plaza. As Dr. Jeffery Humphreys, director of the center, noted: "To survive in retailing, you have to market to Hispanics and Asians. Hispanics are now the nation's largest target market." Dr. Humphreys no doubt had his eye on the fact that in 2007 America's 44.3 million Hispanics constituted nearly 15 percent of the American population.

The 2000 census revealed that nearly 40 million persons spoke a foreign language at home and in most cases it was Spanish. However, most of the nation's second generation also spoke English well or very well. By the third generation more than two thirds spoke only English at home. What made it seem as if so many Hispanics did not know English was the fact that many newcomers from Latino countries, many of whom spoke English poorly, continued to arrive in substantial numbers after the 1950s.

By 1970 Spanish had replaced Italian as the nation's most frequently spoken foreign language. The changes were reflected in the nation's schools. Beginning with the arrival of Cubans in the 1960s, Miami's schools developed bilingual programs. In 1967 the federal government passed a bilingual education act that provided support for such schools; buttressed by a Supreme Court decision in 1974, that said that children must be taught in a language they can understand, bilingual programs expanded. The vast bulk of the classes were held for Spanish-speaking children. The *Mariachi Hunachi* (Spanish spelling for "Wenatchee") band was reportedly the most popular school marching band in the central part of Washington State in the late 1990s, and rapid growth of the Latino population in that community, which accounted for about one quarter of the city's students, forced the Wenatchee board of education to scramble for Spanish-speaking teachers. The state's bilingual education director reported, "It's taking school districts by surprise. It's a situation we're not ready for."

It is important to keep in mind that Latinos represent many different countries and cultures. Most Latinos speak Spanish, but Brazilians speak Portuguese. In the 1990s Mexicans of Indian heritage, mostly Mextecs, moved across the border to work in California's agricultural fields. Although these "Latinos" were from a Latino or Hispanic nation, many did not speak Spanish; they only spoke their Indian dialects. A 1993 survey of California's Mexican farm workers in labor camps in north San Diego found that 40 percent spoke indigenous Indian languages rather than Spanish. Twelve languages turned up, including Cakchiquel, Chatmo, Kanjobal (Q'anjob'al), Nahuatl, Otomi, Tlapaneco, Trique, Zapoteco, and Mexteco. The new wave of Latinos has included economically successful immigrants and those who are very poor. Cubans and many Central Americans are refugees who have foreign policy issues on their minds, but most Latinos pay little attention to foreign affairs and are simply fleeing poverty or seeking their fortunes in the United States.

Just as new immigrants from Europe, Africa, and the Middle East scattered, so did the nation's Latinos. In 2007 the Census Bureau reported that 300 counties had populations that were 50 percent minority with Hispanics making the largest number of minorities. In 2007, largely fueled by Hispanic children, the nation's public schools reported that minority students accounted for 42 percent of the enrollment in 2007. The 2000 census revealed that New York City, not especially known for its Mexican population, had nearly 200,000 Mexicans. And that number grew in the first decade of the 21st century. In May 2007, Mexico opened its forty-seventh consulate, in Little Rock, Arkansas.

In view of the deportations of the 1930s and the bigotry that Mexicans faced in America, many Mexicans were reluctant to try their hand in the United States. But wages were always higher than those in Mexico. Later, disappointing profits from oil, a high birth rate, and the crisis of the peso in the 1990s were inducements to leave. Then came the results of the North American Free Trade Agreement (NAFTA), implemented in 1994. After 2000, Mexican farmers had to compete with more profitable American ones. As a result many Mexican farmers were forced to leave the land and seek other employment. But Mexican cities had high rates of unemployment; hence, Mexicans took the next step and went to the United States.

Aware of the cheap labor to the south, the United States began to cease deporting Mexicans and encouraged their immigration again during World War II. The United States and Mexico cautiously inaugurated an entirely new program: the importation of contract laborers, known as *braceros*, to work in the fields and on the railroads. According to the bracero agreement, Mexicans came into the United States for temporary seasonal jobs, then returned home when their tasks were completed. Begun in 1942, the initial program ended in 1947; while it lasted, the United States received about 220,000 braceros. The U.S. Department of Agriculture

[TABLE 6.1]

Top Five Countries of Origin of the Foreign-Born Population
Living in the United States in 2005*

COUNTRIES OF BIRTH	NUMBER	PERCENT OF TOTAL FOREIGN-BORN POPULATION
Mexico	10,969,941	30.7
Philippines	1,593,421	4.5
India	1,422,492	4.0
China (excluding Taiwan & Hong Kong)	1,208,905	4.4
Vietnam	1,066,055	3.0
All other countries	16,260,844	45.6
TOTAL	35,689,467	100.0

Note: *Estimates are limited to the household population and exclude the population living in group quarters such as college dormitories and institutions. The term *foreign-born* refers to people residing in the United States who were not United States citizens at birth. According to estimates from the 2005 American Community Survey, the foreign-born represented 12.4 percent (35,689,467) of the total population of the United States in 2005.

Source: U.S. Census Bureau, 2005 American Community Survey.

administered the program and the agreement stipulated that there would be a guaranteed minimum number of working days, adequate wages, and suitable living accommodations. Braceros worked in 21 states, with more than half of them going to California. The Mexican government would not allow any of its nationals to work in Texas because of intense discrimination in the Lone Star State.

Although protective provisions had been written into the law, many observers were later appalled to find braceros living in converted chicken coops, abandoned railroad cars, and rickety wooden structures that were on the verge of collapse. The braceros themselves, however, were attracted by the wages and kept returning whenever they could. In *The Bracero Program,* published in 1971, Richard B. Craig explained why these people accepted conditions that others would find deplorable and degrading. The Mexican laborer, Craig noted, is "accustomed to living, and indeed thriving, in a virtual state of physical and mental peonage. The Mexican ... bracero or wetback* probably found little except language (and not always that) to distinguish between the *patron* and the strawboss. It would appear, in sum, that the sociopsychological milieu in which the average Mexican peasant was reared prepared him ideally for his role as the servile, hard-working, seldom complaining, perpetually polite bracero."

Although the original bracero program ended in 1947, there were temporary extensions until 1951 when the clamorings from southwestern growers and the impact of the Korean War combined to induce Congress to reestablish it. The new law lasted until 1964. Table 6.2 shows the numbers of braceros entering the United States during the 22-year program. The apparently bottomless reservoir of cheap labor from south of the border helped build up the multibillion-dollar agricultural concerns from California through Texas, which, unlike during the war years, were now included in the revised program. One appreciative and callous grower acknowledged: "We used to own slaves but now we rent them from the government."

In the 1950s braceros earned 50 cents an hour (30 cents for cotton chopping in Arkansas) and upset American laborers. The Mexican Americans in the Southwest were particularly resentful. They did the same work as the braceros, often side by side, but for lower wages, worse housing and facilities, and no transportation. The humiliation and bitterness that these citizens felt when they compared their situation to that of the imported foreign laborers eventually reached the ears of liberal politicians in Congress and prominent labor officials. Both groups protested the continuation of the bracero program, but they lacked the numbers or the influence to prevail in the 1950s. In the 1960s the Democratic administrations proved more sympathetic and helped bring the program to a close. Yet before the termination of the program, Mexican laborers had sent $200 million home

[TABLE 6.2]

Braceros Entering the United States Under Contract, 1942–1964

1942	4,203	1950	67,500	1958	432,857
1943	52,098	1951	192,000	1959	437,643
1944	62,170	1952	197,100	1960	315,846
1945	49,454	1953	201,388	1961	291,420
1946	32,043	1954	309,033	1962	194,978
1947	19,632	1955	398,650	1963	186,865
1948	35,345	1956	445,197	1964	177,736
1949	107,000	1957	436,049		

Source: U.S. Congress, Senate Committee on the Judiciary, *Temporary Worker Programs: Background and Issues,* 96th Congress, 1st Session (1980).

in remittances, and in addition they had learned about employment in the United States.

With wages so low in Mexico, many Mexicans who were unable to secure a bracero agreement or a green card decided to try their luck anyway in the United States. Most of them resembled braceros. They willingly crossed the border without proper immigration papers to labor in American agricultural fields. The growers, of course, found them ideal laborers, just as reliable as braceros. The conditions these aliens were willing to accept in the United States—wages of 20 to 30 cents an hour, housing without plumbing or electricity, washing in irrigation ditches—hint at what life must have been like in Mexico. Fearing disclosure of their illegal status, the Mexicans performed their tasks well. Some unscrupulous southwestern grower entrepreneurs even turned these undocumented aliens in to immigration officials before payday, thereby saving themselves the cost of the workers' meager wages. Between 1947 and 1954 the Immigration and Naturalization Service (INS) found and deported over 4 million unauthorized Mexicans. In 1954, alarmed by the growth of undocumented farm workers, the INS carried out "Operation Wetback," an intense effort to plug the border separating the two nations. "Operation Wetback" was a temporary success, partly because the United States doubled the number of braceros in the late 1950s. In one of the most laughable statements ever written by a governmental agency, the INS declared in 1955, "The so-called 'Wetback' problem no longer exists. ... The border has been secured." For a few years not many Mexicans without green cards tried to head north.

The number of persons caught trying to enter the United States without papers remained low for a decade. But then the ending of the bracero program in 1965, coupled with a ceiling on Western Hemispheric immigration, led to a growing number trying to cross the border illegally. Congress then enacted the Simpson-Rodino Act of 1986 (also the Immigration Reform and Control Act, or IRCA), which legalized nearly 3 million undocumented workers, over one half of whom were Mexicans. In the mid-1990s the undocumented population rose again; experts estimated that 11 million unauthorized persons lived in the United States in 2008. Again over one half were from Mexico.

At the same time, the number of Mexicans who had green cards also increased. In the 1950s, 299,811 Mexican immigrants were recorded and in the 1960s, 453,937. In the 1990s over 2.5 million entered and immigration from Mexico was running well over 150,000 annually in the first decade of the 21st century. By then approximately one third of the foreign-born population hailed from Mexico.

Most Mexicans, legal or illegal, found employment in low-paying jobs. In the barrios, they learned of day labor jobs, secured standing on street corners waiting for someone willing to hire them for a day. They also worked in service jobs in hotels, restaurants, motels, or as janitors in office buildings. Still others labored in expanding chicken-processing plants located along was often called "the chicken trail."

The "chicken trail" developed in many communities where few immigrants had settled before the 1980s. Chicken-processing plants appeared in Storm Lake, Iowa: Milan, Missouri; and Siler City, North Carolina. Noel, Missouri, had a population of only 1,300 in 1990 before the Hudson Foods poultry plant opened its plant along "the chicken trail." Within a few years the plant alone employed 1,400 workers, most of whom were Hispanic. Tyson Foods, Inc., the nation's largest chicken processor, operated in several nearby towns. Conditions in these plants were poor to say the least and paid only a few dollars above the minimum. Needless to add, the labor turnover was high. Yet one woman employed in Noel claimed, "Here, I am working."

In other towns, this time in the suburbs, Mexican men stood on street corners hoping to find someone who desired their labor. Of course these jobs, painting and repairing houses, mowing yards and doing a variety of menial tasks, were not unionized or protected by labor laws. On occasion, Mexican men found decent-paying jobs. "It's strange, but man, the money is here. I never dreamed about $100 [a day]," one remarked. One study of day laborers, published in 2006, found low wages and many workers who lacked immigration papers. However, such workers were family men, and their families living in Mexico depended upon the remittances from America. In 2007 about $25 billion were sent back to Mexico.

Just how important remittances were to local communities was revealed in a 2005 study of the villages in Oaxaca. Roughly half of those surveyed indicated that they had a family member who had gone to the United States to earn money. The vast majority were men who headed for southern California. About 60 percent of the remittances they sent home were used for household (including construction) expenses. The remittances amounted to $700 every two months, which was a tidy sum for these villages. One man who had returned to Mexico reported in a 2001 interview, "Look at this kitchen. We finished it with the money we saved from my time in the

U.S. And now we have a nice bathroom with a shower too." The downside of the migration north meant with that many women were left behind to manage household affairs, without a father present.

In addition to being day laborers and getting jobs along the chicken trail, the new immigrants found employment in agriculture, where some had worked as braceros before or had labored as undocumented migrants. The number of jobs in farming declined after the 1950s and fewer Mexicans sought employment there after the 1980s, but there still existed a demand for workers picking fruit and vegetables. Growers constantly complained that they could not find enough help and that American-born hands were unreliable. One labor recruiter insisted, "We're serving a need" because American workers would not do the bend-and-stoop work. "You'd look out on the fields and they'd be leaning on their hoes." But his Mexican workers were "a machine in the fields." Moreover, Americans had to be paid more than immigrants and had to be provided with housing and transportation. The growers insisted that new braceros were required, but they could not convince the federal government to reenact a large-scale bracero-type program. Growers said they had no hesitation about hiring undocumented Mexicans, estimated to be half the farming labor supply in the first decade of the 21st century.

For Mexican men, employment in construction usually paid better than jobs along the "chicken trail," and lasted longer than work in landscaping. But without knowledge of English and with little education in Mexico, they had few options when it came to finding high-paid employment. Most newcomers lacked a high school education, and the jobs available were entry-level low-paying positions. The gender difference was also marked. Whereas a study reported that 38 percent of the men took home less than $300 per week, 75 percent of the women made less than that amount.

While undocumented aliens from Mexico had previously been single males with few skills and little education, the situation in Mexico deteriorated so drastically in the 1980s that border agents reported catching new types of illegal entrants: skilled workers and highly educated professionals. An immigration official in Washington, D.C., observed, "There is a perception on the border that there are more people with higher-level skills coming in. We seem to be running into more middle-class people and family units than we did be fore the big influx at ... the start of their economic crisis."

The reference to family migration meant that more women were crossing the border. Mexico, unlike most other nations after World War II, sent more men than women to the United States, but by the 1990s the gender totals were about even. Some women followed or accompanied their husbands, but others came on their own. Like male undocumented aliens, women knew of opportunities north of the border, and they wanted to help their families. "My heart broke, my heart broke," said one. "But I had to give them [her children] a better life. I told them I would go and work, and we could buy a small plot of land and build a little house and have a dog," she concluded. Like the men, Mexican women knew of the ethnic networks that led to housing and jobs. For the women this often meant work as domestics or in the garment shops of California.

Once in the United States Mexican parents recognized how important speaking English and having a good education were. And there were gains in education, but mostly by the second and third generations, who had higher levels of education and greater incomes than the immigrant generation, and many of these generations had achieved middle-class status in terms of income and employment by the early 21st century. The children and grandchildren of the immigrants were the ones with incomes that enabled them to move from the barrios. Moreover, they were more apt to marry persons other than those of Mexican descent. However, the continued high rates of immigration drew the figures downward. The 2000 census revealed that Mexican immigrants had completed only 8.5 years of schooling on average, and scarcely one half had completed high school, compared to 88.4 percent of all Americans. However, U.S.-born Mexicans had an average of 12.2 years of schooling. Even so, Mexican-origin persons lagged behind non-Hispanic whites in educational achievement and incomes. In view of these figures it is no surprise that Mexicans had much higher rates of persons (roughly 25 percent) living below the poverty line. Overall, Mexican incomes were only 60 percent of white non-Hispanics.

The new immigrants were certainly aware of the importance of education and speaking English. Huge conflicts and debates over the best way for Mexican children to learn English should not lead the reader to the conclusion that Mexican immigrants wanted to remain apart from American society, speaking only Spanish and living in the barrio with its many organizations supporting Mexican culture. To be sure, the immigrants wanted their children to know of their own culture and background, but education and speaking English were high priorities. One early 21st century survey found that 97 percent of immigrant parents wanted their children to master English.

Moreover, there is evidence that Mexican immigrants are doing some-what better in recent years. A study of Mexicans arriving between 1995 and 2005 revealed that they had higher levels of education, were older, and had more work experience than those coming before 1995. As a result these latest immigrants found better-paying employment and were less apt to labor in the bottom of the income pile.

In spite of the handicap of the immigrants, there were individual success stories. Maria Elbo Molina immigrated with her family to Arizona when she was 8 years old. Through education and hard work she became a vice president of Home Federal Savings and Loan in Tucson. Still dissatisfied, however, she began her own company, the J. Elba Corp. Inc., to sell products in the Hispanic community. "I decided I would incorporate my own firm, do what I had always wanted, which was to be on my own; I would try it," she recalled. She successfully sold not only to small clients but also to television stations and banking institutions.

Individual Mexican Americans have been successful in various areas of American life, winning the admiration of other Americans. In 1997 the magazine *Hispanic* singled out "Movers and Shakers," the 25 most "powerful Hispanics in Washington, D.C." They included Maria Echaveste, an assistant to President Bill Clinton; Xavier Becerra, chair of the Congressional Hispanic Caucus; Raul Yzaguirre, head of the National Council of La Raza; Aida Alvarez, head of the Small Business Administration; Anita Perez Ferguson, head of the National Women's Political Caucus; and Antonia Hernandez, president of the Mexican American Legal Defense and Educational Fund.

In 2005 *Hispanic* magazine profiled outstanding Hispanics, including Mexicanos. They included Dennis Pastdrana, president and CEO of Goodwill Industries of South Florida, TransAtlantic Bank president Miriam Lopez and retired Major General Felix A. Santoni. On the staff of First Lady Laura Bush was Sonya E. Medina. In television and movies, derogatory images began to give way to more favorable ones as Hispanic stars moved to the forefront.

A truly remarkable story is that of Dr. Alberto Quinones-Hinojosa. He was born in Mexico, and left at age 19 because he saw little future there and wanted an education. Crossing illegally (literally hopping over the fence), he worked as a farm laborer (sun up, sun down) in California. Dr. Quinones-Hinojosa also worked as a common laborer, before entering a community college at night. A mentor aided him, and after finishing his undergraduate education he attended Harvard University's medical school. By 2008 he had become a prominent neurosurgeon at Johns Hopkins.

Perhaps the most notable persons in the public eye were the many Latinos playing professional baseball. In 2006 roughly 25 percent of all players were Hispanics. Teams began to hire teachers for their Spanish players to enable them to speak English. One of the first prominent Mexican players was Fernando Valenzuela, a star pitcher for the Los Angeles Dodgers. He was the youngest of 12 children of a Mexican farm family. According to one reporter, "He galvanized LA's Mexican-American community with a deep sense of pride and a newfound feeling of participation in the American experience." Other Mexicans followed the path of Valenzuela and, by 2004, of the 195 players from Spanish-speaking nations, 19 were from Mexico, but the major source for Hispanic players was the Dominican Republic. In the first decade of the 21st century, Albert Pujos of the St. Louis Cardinals was probably the best player in the National League. Pujos joined the Cardinals in 2001 and batted over .300 in his first eight seasons. The Dominican-born Pujos became an American citizen in 2007.

Some Mexicans turned to unions to win better wages and benefits. In areas where Hispanics, and especially Mexicans, provided the bulk of the workers, such as hospitals employees, janitors, and domestics, unions achieved limited victories. In 1999 California's Justice for Janitors won a 3-year contract for some Los Angeles janitors, complete with a 24 percent increase in wages. Seven years later, Houston's Service Employees International Union won an increase in wages after a month-long strike. For Mercedes Herrera from Mexico this meant a two-dollar-an-hour raise over a 2-year period. Her $5.65 hourly pay went to $6.25 in January 2007. "It's going to be a big difference in my personal finances," she said. However, her new wages still left her below $13,000 per year.

In addition to unions, Mexican Americans adopted new forms of protest. During the 1960s three prominent leaders—Reies López Tijerina, Rudolpho (Corky) Gonzalez, and José Angel Guitierrez—applied different strategies, all directed to securing justice for Mexicans. Other organizations became active in the 1960s. The League of United Latin American Citizens was formed in the 1920s in Texas. But as its title indicates it was devoted to improving the lives of Latino immigrants who were naturalized or who were the second generation, who by birth were American citizens. Its membership was not large but the League expanded its efforts after World War II to aid all Mexicanos. The GI Forum, organized after World

War II, concentrated its efforts on making sure that Mexicanos who were veterans received their fair share of veteran benefits. It too branched out after the 1960s. Perhaps the most well-known Mexican leader was César Chávez, who headed the United Farm Workers Union, even though the union lost most of its members after the 1970s.

Since the 1950s many new organizations and groups have developed: the Brown Berets, the Mexican American Youth Organization (MAYO), the Mexican American Legal Defense and Educational Fund (MALDEF, largely funded by the Ford Foundation), and a Congress of Mexican American Unity representing 200 Chicano organizations, all dedicated to fostering the goals that leaders articulated so well. These groups are now sophisticated in using their political influence. One of the most important is a coalition of 26 Hispanic organizations founded in 1968 as the Southwest Council of La Raza and renamed the National Council of La Raza in 1973. The council's move to Washington, D.C., in 1970 reflected its national orientation.

These rising leaders attested to growing Latino influence. In the late 1960s, when African Americans and American Indians were protesting, the Chicano movement took shape. The Chicanos wanted to retain their ethnic identity while raising the standard of living of all Mexican Americans. Although they cherished the traditional values of their culture, including respect and affection for the family, the cult of masculinity (*machismo*), and sense of obligation to others in the community, their demands for equal education, training, and job opportunities awakened state and federal legislatures to problems that needed attention.

Mexican American women were also an integral part of the protests. Women active in labor and civil rights groups participated in campus activism that emphasized Latino and women's studies programs in college and university curricula. In 1971 they held the first national Chicana conference, which put forth a feminist platform. At times they criticized Mexican American men for their attitudes and neglect of women's issues. Vilma Martinez assumed the presidency of MALDEF in 1973 and became the first woman to head a Hispanic civil rights group. In 2000 when the AFof L-CIO decided to organize all workers, regardless of their immigrant status, it selected Linda Chavez-Thompson to head the project. Women also became active at the national stage of politics. In 2008 five women were among the Hispanic Caucus. Mexican-born Ester Aguilera was executive director of the Caucus, and Grace F. Napolitano of California was the legislative whip.

In the 1960 election Latinos, chiefly Mexicans, organized Viva Kennedy clubs to rally Hispanics to support candidate John F. Kennedy in his bid for the presidency. The election produced few gains for Mexicanos, but it demonstrated to leaders the importance of voting. Henry B. Gonzalez had been the first Mexican American from Texas to be elected to Congress. On his retirement in 1996, when he looked back he could see signs of Mexican Americans' growing political power. He helped organize the Hispanic Caucus in 1976, which had only 5 members at that time. It grew to 21 by 1998, and after the 2006 election it claimed 24 members in the House of Representatives and two United States senators. The figures fell short of the Black Caucus's 43 in 2007, even though Hispanics had surpassed African Americans as the nation's largest minority. Cubans in Florida were strongly Republican, but most Hispanics were Democrats. A Cuban American, Robert Menendez, was elected as a Democratic senator in New Jersey in 2006. The caucus had several agendas, and the ones related to immigration were especially important; the group worked with liberals to ensure that IRCA had a generous amnesty for undocumented aliens.

Politicians have responded to the growing power of Hispanics. Whereas Richard Nixon appointed fewer than 10 Hispanics to presidential and policy positions in the federal government and Gerald Ford fewer than 25, by mid-1979 Jimmy Carter had appointed nearly 200 Latinos to important managerial and judicial posts. Presidents Ronald Reagan and George H. W. Bush, and the Republican Party generally, paid little attention to Latino concerns despite the 1988 appointment of Lauro F. Cavazos, the first Hispanic ever to serve in a president's cabinet, as Secretary of Education; but the administration of Bill Clinton was aware that Mexican Americans voted for his party, and he appointed several Latinos to cabinet and other important positions. Henry Cisneros became head of the Department of Housing and Urban Development; Bill Richardson (whose mother was Latino), UN ambassador; and Federico Peña, head of the Department of Transportation and later the Department of Energy.

George W. Bush, the son of George H. W. Bush, was also aware of the Hispanic vote, and many Hispanic leaders praised him for appointing many Latinos to office. In 2001 he selected Mel Martinez as secretary of the Department of Housing and Urban Development. President Bush's most prominent appointment was of Alberto Gonzales, who grew up in Texas as the son of migrant workers. He served as general counsel under then Governor George Bush of Texas. When Bush was elected president,

Gonzales followed him to Washington, D.C. As one of the authors of the Patriot Act of 2001, he became visible at the national level. In 2005 President Bush appointed him as the first Hispanic U.S. Attorney General, but in 2007 he resigned in controversy.

Below these national positions, a number of Latinos began to win election to state, county, and local offices as well as to Congress. At the local level in 2007 Antonio R. Villaraigo was elected to become mayor of LosAngeles, the nation's second-largest city. Yet they remained underrepresented; in 1999, for example, in California where Latinos were 31 percent of the population, they held only 17 of the 80 seats in the state assembly and 7 of the 40 senatorial seats. In 1986 the National Association of Latino Elected and Appointed Officials reported that 3,202 Latinos were serving in public office. By 2008 the figure had increased to over 5,000. While this growth was impressive, as in California, Hispanics were underrepresented. In 2008 they made up only about 1 percent of the nation's elected officials.

The most prominent Mexican-origin elected official was Governor Bill Richardson of New Mexico. He was born in California but was raised in Mexico City until age 16; his mother was Mexican. After graduating from Tufts University, he worked as a staff member of the Senate Foreign Relations committee. In addition he served in the Department of State and the United Nations before his election to the House of Representatives from New Mexico. He was a member of the House for 14 years before becoming governor of New Mexico in 2002. In 2008 he made a brief run for the Democratic nomination as President.

Both political parties sought out the Latino voter in 2000, and candidate Al Gore won that effort with 62 percent of these voters. George W. Bush did only slightly better than his father, George H. W. Bush. In 2002, Hispanics gave Republicans a greater percentage of their votes, but in 2006 Democrats won 77 percent of the Latino vote. Passage of Proposition 187 to cut benefits to undocumented immigrants (later declared unconstitutional) in the California election of 1994, along with cuts in welfare programs for immigrants, stimulated many Latinos to become citizens. Congressional debates of 2006 and 2007 over immigration prompted another surge of citizenship applications. The Republican tone of the debates had angered many Hispanics. Democratic candidates for the 2008 presidential nomination made special efforts to win Hispanic votes. But neither political party could afford to neglect these voters in the future.

A key issue for Mexicans is naturalization. Both Bill Richardson and Alberto Gonzales were American-born U.S. citizens. Naturalization drives from the mid-1990s and into the 2000s substantially increased the Latino vote. The Pew Hispanic Center estimated that 17 million Hispanics were eligible voters in the 2006 election, which was 8.6 percent of the electorate; it had been 7.4 percent in the 2000 election. A huge surge in applications by Hispanics for naturalization in 2008 was a sign that this demographic growth was becoming more important in American politics.

Mexicans comprised over 60 percent of the nation's Hispanics, but other groups also increased their migration to the United States. Puerto Ricans are not immigrants. They were granted citizenship in 1917, but they are often thought to be immigrants because they come from a Spanish-speaking culture and shared many of the hardships that immigrants have. Some migrated during the 1920s but jobs dried up during the Great Depression. Then came the great migration. After World War II ended in 1945 the American economy exploded and swelled Puerto Rican migration to the mainland.

Relatively cheap air transportation and an abundance of skilled and semiskilled jobs in New York City served as the magnets. As late as 1940 New York City had slightly more than 60,000 Puerto Ricans; in a decade the figure had quadrupled. Today there are over 2 million Puerto Ricans scattered throughout the continental United States, with a third in the New York City area. In 1998, the other major centers for Puerto Ricans were Chicago with a colony of about 100,000 and Philadelphia with more than 30,000, but the official figures probably underestimate the actual totals. There were also Puerto Rican communities in Bridgeport, Connecticut; Rochester, New York; Dayton, Ohio; Boston, Massachusetts; Miami, Florida; Milwaukee, Wisconsin; and numerous cities in New Jersey.

By the mid-1970s the exodus from Puerto Rico had slowed and it appeared that the number of Puerto Ricans leaving the mainland was greater than those arriving. No one knew the exact figures but some experts suggested that the net flow back to Puerto Rico was around 200,000. The severe recession and inflation of that period accounted for much of the trend. Some Puerto Ricans found that the skills they picked up in New York City, Chicago, and other cities, including mastery of English, enabled them to get ahead in Puerto Rico. But those returning were not always welcome and were sometimes derided as "Newyoricans," a pejorative term meaning pushy, aggressive, and out of touch with life in Puerto Rico.

The Puerto Rican experience in New York and other major cities on the continent is probably closer to that of the European immigrants who landed on the East Coast and settled in urban areas than to that of the Mexicans in the West. Although there are Puerto Rican migrant workers who move up and down the East Coast according to the seasons, essentially they are an urban people with the problems of the city's poor.

In New York they replaced the European immigrants in lower-level factory jobs—especially the Jews and Italians in the garment district—and in the city's worst slums. Like the Europeans, they spoke a foreign language, but unlike them, they encountered a color problem. Many Puerto Ricans are the products of centuries of racial mixing between the island's white and black populations. Although higher status is accorded those of lighter complexions, darker skin does not have quite the impact in Puerto Rico that it has in the United States. On the mainland, though, Puerto Ricans learned that the darker their skin, the greater the difficulty in gaining acceptance and adjusting to the dominant culture. One social worker reported that in her dealings with Puerto Rican drug addicts, inevitably the darkest member of the family was the one affected. Piri Thomas, in his moving *Down These Mean Streets,* an autobiographical account of growing up in New York City's East Harlem ghetto, recalled his own difficulties as the darkest member of his family and how bitter he felt toward his father for passing along such pigmentation to him.

To read the social and economic statistics of Puerto Ricans in New York City and elsewhere is to recall the plight of minorities in the past. Although they gained in real incomes during the 1980s, the 1990 census revealed that 38 percent of their families, and more than half of the children, lived in poverty, double the rate for the city as a whole. A distressing number of families were headed by women. Many did not work but lived on welfare, which did not provide a decent standard of living. The proportion reporting a high school diploma had increased since 1980, but still lagged behind the general average. Twenty-three percent of New Yorkers had college degrees, but only 6 percent of Puerto Ricans. Conditions improved over the next 25 years. By then 15 percent of Puerto Rican men and 18 percent of women had college degrees. They still remained below the graduation rates of most of the city's groups.

In addition Puerto Ricans had a higher incidence of juvenile delinquency and drug addiction, and were particularly susceptible to ailments like tuberculosis and venereal diseases. There were also greater incidents of police brutality toward them. In a word, they have been plagued with the disabilities historically associated with lower-class, poorly educated immigrants.

Dominicans also settled in New York City. Some came as tourists and then stayed to become illegal immigrants. As a result their exact numbers are not known. The immigration authorities recorded approximately one million by 2008. Nearly three quarters claimed the New York area as their home.

In 1990 they constituted the largest foreign-born group in New York City. On the Upper West Side of Manhattan their community was known as the second largest "Dominican" city in the world. Because many were undocumented their employment opportunities were limited. Yet even among the legal immigrants, many lacked skills and education, and few spoke English fluently. For those coming from a rural background, the adjustments were especially difficult. Restaurants, hotels, and nonunion construction jobs provided their main employment. Some Dominican families had small grocery stores (*bodegas*). One Dominican noted that his store carried special products for customers; however, running such stores did not mean high profits, and several *bodega* owners were killed or badly injured when their businesses were robbed.

Scholars find that Dominican women favor America's more liberal society compared to the one at home where their roles are clearly proscribed. As wage earners for their families, they have a definite say in household issues, and they are less likely to return home. But life has not been kind to Dominican women in the United States. They find themselves employed in the garment shops and low-paid manual jobs, and almost half of Dominican households are headed by women. In addition to public aid and what they earn, they are assisted by groups such as the Union of Dominicans, an organization of professionals. Dominicans and Puerto Ricans are the poorest ethnic groups in New York City. Some second-generation Dominicans have improved their lot, and as they have naturalized they have become more politically sophisticated. They are now using their growing power to better their communities.

The third Latino group that has had a major impact on the East Coast, and the first immigrant group to change the complexion of a southern city in the twentieth century, is the Cubans, whose experience has been quite different from those of Puerto Ricans and Dominicans. Cubans came in several waves. The first began in 1959 and lasted until the Cuban Missile Crisis of 1962 brought it to a halt. Another exodus began in the fall of 1965 and lasted into the early 1970s. The third migration came in 1980 when over 120,000 landed in Key West, Florida. As a group the Cubans are considerably different from most other immigrants into this country. First, the bulk of them were political refugees who left their homes because of the policies inaugurated by Fidel Castro after he led a successful revolution against the regime of Fulgencio Batista in 1958. Second, many Cuban refugees came from the elite of their society. According to one study, in the first wave about 70 percent were professional, skilled, or white-collar workers; almost 40 percent had some college education; and 80 percent had yearly incomes above those earned by the average Cuban.

The exodus of 1980 was somewhat different. Social and economic problems in Cuba and the reports coming from the United States by visiting Cuban Americans in the late 1970s set the stage for the dramatic exodus. When Castro decided to permit the dissatisfied to leave, a vast flotilla of ships, large and small, set sail from Florida to pick up refugees in Cuba. Relatives and friends of the Cubans and those eager to make money out of providing transportation were involved in the movement, as were nonprofit agencies helping the newcomers settle. The Carter administration was uncertain how to handle the situation, but for the most part permitted hundreds of boats to land their passengers. Using the camps inhabited by the Vietnamese refugees in the mid-1970s, the immigration authorities worked with private and governmental agencies to settle the Cubans and reunite them with their families in the United States.

Another, somewhat smaller, Cuban exodus occurred in 1994 when a growing number of persons traveled on rafts to the United States. Fearful that the "rafters" might lead to another uncontrolled immigration such as that of the Marielitos, the Clinton administration negotiated an agreement with the government of Cuban to regularize the flow. Castro promised to halt the exodus and the United States agreed to bring persons, usually relatives of Cuban Americans, directly from Cuba. While this agreement seemed to repeal the Cuban Adjustment Act of 1966, a few Cubans managed to flee from Cuba to reach American soil by going to Mexico first and then crossing to American soil where they claimed to be refugees entitled to remain in the United States.

Miami is the closest to Havana in both distance and culture; most Cuban refugees went there. They have made an impressive impact in the city since they left Cuba a generation or more ago and have moved up the economic ladder to achieve middle-class and upper-middle-class status in this country faster than any other ethnic group since the Huguenots of colonial times.

The 900,000 or so Cubans in fact revitalized a sleepy southern town and transformed it into a major international hub. Miami is now regarded as the capital of Latin America because it attracts businesspeople and financiers from the entire Western Hemisphere. Argentine ranchers, Ecuadoran manufacturers, and Colombian drug peddlers find the city enticing and exciting. Nightclubs, resorts, and hotels abound. It is perhaps the most comfortable place in the country for Latin Americans because both Spanish and English are the languages of communication. Businesspeople who speak English only are at a severe competitive disadvantage. Enterprising Cubans have taken over or established thousands of businesses. Whereas in 1970 there were fewer than 1,000 establishments owned by Cubans, a decade later the figure hovered around 10,000—banks, construction companies, radio and television stations, and so forth. No significant area of business has been immune to the Hispanic presence. Miami now has more international and out-of-state banks than any other city in the country save New York. These banks and financial institutions attract money from every Latin American nation. In addition, an enterprising Cuban thought up the now established Trade Fair of the Americas, an annual event in which practically all Latin American nations participate.

Individual success stories about Cubans abound. Carlos Arboleya was chief auditor of Cuba's largest bank when he fled his native land. Beginning anew with little money, he worked as a clerk in a shoe factory before finding his place in banking again. By 1968 he had become president of the Fidelity Bank and a U.S. citizen. He later assumed the vice chairmanship of the Barnett Bank of South Florida, which had assets of $3.5 billion. While banking was attractive to Cubans, so was Miami's garment industry, formerly run by Italians and Jews. "The Cubans really put some zing into this industry. Almost 100 percent of the small manufacturers are Cuban, almost 100 percent of the contractors, big and small, are Cuban and almost all the top management is Cuban," noted one businessman.

Another Cuban immigrant, Yvonne Santa Maria, had never held a job before leaving for Miami in 1963. She arrived with no funds. "No money. No jewels. We were not even allowed to take out phone numbers," she recalled. She worked in several of the city's banks, and at age 57 was president of the Ponce de Leon Federal Savings and Loan Association in Coral Gables, Florida. But no Cuban was as successful as Roberto Goizueta, who until his death in 1997 headed the Coca-Cola Company. Educated at Yale University, he began to work for the corporation in Havana in 1954. When he fled Cuba he had to start over, but rose rapidly to become the company's billionaire chairman and chief executive.

Many Cubans at first did not think of themselves as Americans, but looked instead to the day when Fidel Castro's government would be overthrown and they could return home. Some did return in the 1990s, but only as visitors. To be sure, some still agitated for strong American action to bring down Castro, and were angry when the Clinton administration moved in 1994 to head off another boat exodus from Cuba to the United States. But they subsequently made rapid economic progress, became American citizens, and began to be involved in American politics. In 1985, Miami elected Harvard-educated lawyer Xavier Suarez as its first Cuban American mayor. He defeated another Cuban, Raul Masvidal; both men were born in Cuba and had come to America 25 years earlier. The following year, Richard Martinez, another Cuban, won the governorship of Florida. As noted, President George W. Bush appointed him to be Secretary of the Department of Housing and Urban Development, a position he gave up in 2003 to make a race for senator for Florida. He was successful and in 2004 he joined Ken Salazar of Colorado as the first Hispanic senators since the 1970s. In 1988 Ileana Ros-Lehten became the first Cuban American woman elected to Congress, and a second Cuban American joined the Congressional Hispanic Caucus a few years later. As the older exiles died, the younger Cubans looked more to America and less to Cuba.

Refugees from Central America found themselves treated quite differently. Like Cubans, Central Americans from Nicaragua, Guatemala, and El Salvador were fleeing political turmoil and violence. The civil wars in those nations prompted many to leave. Many claimed asylum, but only a few were successful. The anticommunist Nicaraguans fared a little better, but the U.S. government did not wish to give asylum because it supported right-wing governments in both Guatemala and El Salvador. To grant asylum would be an admission that the United States supported governments that abused their citizens. Those who arrived before 1982 were covered by the Simpson-Rodino Act of 1986, but they continued to migrate to the United States after that law was passed.

Central Americans generally settled in areas that already housed other Latinos. The largest Nicaraguan community developed in the Miami area, the center of a growing population from South and Central America. In

1970 Cubans constituted 91 percent of the Latinos there, and even though their population grew, the figure had dropped to only 59 percent by 1990. Moreover, 200,000 new immigrants settled in Dade County (Miami) between 1990 and 1996. Nicaraguans joined not only Cubans but also people from Honduras, Peru, and Colombia. The parish of St. John Bosco Church was founded in 1963 to tend to the religious needs of Cuban Catholics, but in 1997 over two thirds of its members were Nicaraguans. The first Nicaraguans to come to the Miami area were the wealthy, who fled a left-wing government that took power in 1979. However, as conditions deteriorated in their homeland the middle and working classes also left. Like so many other Latino women, the Nicaraguan women became domestics or found employment in garment factories, replacing Cubans who found better opportunities elsewhere. The men worked in construction or at manual labor. Miami's Latinos did not always get along with one another. The latest newcomers were not as well off as the Cubans, who generally voted Republican and were strongly anti-Castro. In Little Havana in 1996 the banning from the Calle Ocho festival of a Puerto Rican singer suspected of communist sympathies angered Puerto Ricans. And when the president of the Latin Chamber of Commerce blamed newcomers for trash piling up in Little Havana, he drew protests from Nicaraguan groups.

Guatemalans and Salvadorans located in cities such as Miami, San Antonio, Chicago, San Diego, Houston, and San Francisco. Washington, D.C., also became a center for their settlement. Others could be found in smaller communities on Long Island or in Spring Valley, New York, doing a variety of manual jobs. Their major settlement was in southern California, especially Los Angeles.

While they had political motives for immigration, Central Americans closely resembled Mexicans in socioeconomic status. According to the 1990 census, only 3 percent of Salvadorans and 4 percent of Guatemalans had a college degree. The vast majority had not graduated from high school. Central American women were usually working for money, but in low-paid occupations. In Los Angeles over 80 percent of working Salvadoran and Guatemalan women were maids. The men also took low-paid jobs, and even though a high proportion of the women worked, two-earner families struggled to get ahead. One fourth of these families lived below the poverty line.

The situation was similar elsewhere. East of New York City, a network of Salvadorans helped their countrymen find jobs and housing. They cleaned houses, cut and trimmed lawns, or did other casual day labor. Men without their families shared housing and even beds with other Salvadorans. While they made little, they hoped to learn English and find better jobs. In the meantime, they provided a cheap labor force for other residents and still managed to send money home. Like Mexicans, in some communities they congregated at particular street corners to offer their labor for a day.

Central Americans were not without friends. Lawsuits and a congressional law, the Nicaraguan Adjustment and Central American Relief Act of 1997, forced immigration authorities to hear their cases under improved and proper procedures. While this was not a blanket amnesty, a number of Central Americans managed to receive a green card. From 2004 to 2006 over 80,000 Salvadorans and nearly 60,000 Guatemalans became immigrants.

South America is much larger in land mass and population than Central America, and even Central America combined with Mexico. But South Americans did come to the United States with the same urgency as their neighbors to the north. Actually, nations such as Argentina and Brazil had long histories of being receiving nations. Yet South Americans had reasons to look elsewhere for opportunities. In general, South American immigrants resemble Cubans in social characteristics more than they do Central Americans. Overall, they are better educated, and well off compared to other Latinos. In the United States, fewer live below the poverty line and they have higher incomes than their neighbors just to the north.

While better off than Central Americans and faced with less hostility in some cases, many South Americans were still willing to try their luck in the United States. Colombia sent the largest number of South Americans to America. Many were middle class, but because of the turmoil involving insurgency and drug wars, Colombia was unsafe, even for the privileged. As one woman put it, "My husband was killed over a business deal because people can just get away with that sort of thing." Facing such violence, Colombians applied for asylum and a few thousand were able to obtain it. However, the U.S. government was unwilling to grant many asylum visas. The United States was also unwilling to give many tourist visas to Colombia because officials believed that visitors would use their visas as a way to live in the United States illegally. An unstable economy added to the nation's woes. While many were able to obtain green cards, those who could not entered on visitors' visas and then stayed on, so that the exact population of Colombians in the United States is unknown. The major pockets of Colombian settlement are New York City, Florida, and California. Colombian migration to New York peaked in the 1990s and then they headed to suburban areas and other states. Indicative of the change was Manuel Miranda. When Colombians first moved into the Queens borough of New York City, Colombian-born Miranda opened a shop with 16 employees producing 10 million arepas (a popular corn-based bread) a year. As Colombians moved to the surrounding suburbs, he set his eye on a national market. The expansion would be like bagels he said and "you're going to have arepas in every store."

Other migration streams included Ecuadorians, Argentineans, and Peruvians. These migrants faced unstable economic conditions, including high inflation and slow economic growth, so that many were willing to head north. Argentina, for example, had relatively high unemployment combined with inflation in the 1990s and experienced further discontent during the early 21st century when the government could not make its foreign debt payments. For many Jews, the anti-Semitism of the past prompted migration to Israel, but some also came to the United States. Most of those who left were middle class, many of whom were professionals. And not a few were undocumented immigrants.

Brazil was not a Hispanic nation, but Portuguese-speaking Brazilians faced many of the same economic problems as other South Americans. Yet most of the Brazilians who left were middle class. One survey indicated that over 30 percent were college graduates and were disproportionately white. When in the United States, they were often able to find only working-class jobs. Remarked one, "When you come to this country, you know what kind of job you will find—because you don't have language, you don't have papers." But these jobs paid more than they could earn at home, and another concluded, "When you get a taste of the good life, it's hard to go back to what you had before." Of course, many of the immigrants, living in various ethnic communities such as Newark's Ironbound district, found social and institutional support for their cultures. And, too, like so many Latino immigrants, they sent remittances home. In 2008 a number of Brazilians were beginning to return to Brazil. Faced with a weak American economy and a housing crisis, many became uneasy about their future. The failure of Congress to grant an amnesty was the deciding factor for some of these immigrants. "You can't spend your entire life waiting to be legal" was the way one immigrant stated it.

English-speaking West Indians also added a new dimension to black America. As before World War II, immigrants from the Bahamas went to Florida, and Jamaicans and Guyanese settled in New York City. Other cities that received these immigrants were Philadelphia, Hartford, and Washington, D.C. The Hartford community was originally formed by farm workers who picked apples and tobacco in the Connecticut River Valley. Immigration laws made it possible for West Indian women to take the lead in moving to the United States. Using the occupational preferences category, they came as nurses and as childcare workers. Some were single but others, once established, petitioned to have their families join them. West Indian women had one of the highest labor force participation rates of all the ethnic groups. Their fluency in English also made it possible for many to find white-collar clerical work in American cities. The men had a reputation for running their own small-scale businesses, such as shops catering to the immigrants or livery services, which in New York City took subway tokens as payment. Most of the men and women were not entrepreneurs. Still some were successful in turning their hands to business. Lowell Hawthorne, who was Jamaican-born, opened his first bakery in the Bronx, New York City, in 1989. By 2007 he had parlayed his first enterprise into a national chain of 100 restaurants, specializing in both Jamaican food and dishes "with a crossover appeal."

Because of the existence of so many two-wage families, they had incomes above those of native-born black Americans. Yet they still encountered the same racism. Many people believe that white Americans favor West Indians because of their reputation as hard workers. As a result some West Indians did not wish to be identified with African Americans, or as one said, "Since I have been here, I have always recognized that this is a racist country and I have made every effort not to lose my accent."

These new immigrants often returned home periodically or permanently. But as so many settled in the United States they formed organizations built around their economic needs and culture. Cricket was played in places where West Indians congregated, and shops sold food such as curried goat. Each island differed, and West Indians did not necessarily believe that they were part of a larger West Indian culture. Although these immigrants spoke English, newspapers such as the New York Carib News, dedicated to their particular needs, began publication. In Brooklyn in the late 1940s West Indians began holding a parade that celebrated their traditions. Repeated every Labor Day, by the 1990s it had become the largest ethnic parade in the nation, drawing over one million people to see the pageantry, hear West Indian music, and eat ethnic food. Like an earlier generation of West Indians, the latest newcomers began to naturalize and move into politics. By the 1980s they were electing their fellow countrymen to political office in New York City. The prospects for influence in New York were relatively good, for foreign-born blacks made up over one quarter of the city's black population of 2 million.

French and Creole speakers from Martinique, Guadeloupe, and Haiti joined the Caribbean flow. The largest group by far was from Haiti but their reception in the United States was considerably different from that of Jamaicans, Guyanese, or Barbadians. These mostly Creole-speaking migrants fled the dictatorial regime of the Duvalier family and a wretched economy, which made Haiti the poorest country in the Caribbean. The elite left first, but by the 1970s desperate Haitians unable to obtain immigrant visas were boarding rickety boats and heading for Florida. Once in the United States they took any jobs they could find. In Miami, where many of them settled, they were often scorned as another poor immigrant group. If caught they could be deported as illegal aliens. Haitians and their supporters among civil rights and religious groups insisted that they were refugees and entitled to asylum, much like Cubans. The Simpson-Rodino Act of 1986 granted asylum to those who arrived before 1982, but before that act passed the U.S. government rejected their contention that they were refugees and, beginning during the Reagan administration, intercepted Haitian boats at sea and returned them to Haiti.

While Bill Clinton criticized Reagan's policy, as president Clinton followed Reagan's path of trying to halt another arrival of "boat people." Clinton also intervened in Haiti's affairs in 1994 with military force to enforce democracy, but the intervention was partially meant to halt the Haitian exodus to the United States. According to Clinton, "Today more than 14,000 refugees are living at our naval base in Guantanamo. Three hundred thousand more Haitians—more than five percent of their entire population—are in hiding in their own country. If we don't act, they could be the next wave of refugees at our door." Congress finally passed a bill in 1998 to provide for hearings for those Haitians who were desperate to go to the United States. Some Haitians were able to win green cards. Yet conditions did not improve in Haiti, and Haitians were still willing to take a risky sea voyage in hopes of gaining asylum in the United States. Some sailed in unsafe boats that sank and sent their passengers to their graves.

The plight of Haitians drowning at sea presented a graphic view of the dilemmas of immigration. There are 15 million refugees in the world, with the largest number in Africa. Just how many should the United States accept? Should refugee policy be tied only to foreign policy or should other humanitarian considerations be the criteria? And what of the 2 million Iraqis now living outside their homeland, for which the U.S. invasion of Iraq in 2003 was largely responsible. What does the United States owe to them?

Refugees are only part of the story. With so many poor people in Latin America, what standards should the United States use to admit these people, especially when their labor seems needed? And how should the United States deal with the existence of 11 million undocumented immigrants? There is also the question of the highly skilled who have contributed to the American economy. There are currently over one million skilled persons waiting for a green card to the United States. Obviously these issues are serious. Given the continuing lure of America and the desire of so many who would like to become immigrants, the making of a policy deciding who becomes a green card holder will be a contested issue for many years.

* The term "wetback" (*mojado*), which designates an illegal immigrant, originated because many Mexicans swam across the Rio Grande River, which separates Mexico from Texas, and waded across during relatively dry periods when the water was shallow.

[7]

Confronting Immigration

Following the election of George W. Bush as president in 2000, he met with President Vicente Fox of Mexico to discuss immigration issues between the United States and Mexico and suggested that a temporary workers program might be a possibility. Then came the attack and demise of the World Trade Center in New York City on September 11, 2001. After that, all immigration issues were placed on the back burner. Concern about security along the borders of the United States made any suggestions about an increase in immigration and a temporary workers program a dead issue for several years. But by 2009 Congress was willing to consider immigration reform.

Security was not the only issue. Beginning in the mid-1990s the number of undocumented immigrants increased, and by 2008 officials and scholars estimated that 11 million persons lived in America without proper papers. The majority of these individuals were from Mexico and the overwhelming numbers were Hispanic. As a result attention was focused on Mexico and the border between the United States and Mexico. Almost half of the members of the U.S. House of Representatives represent congressional districts where significant numbers of constituents oppose all immigration, but particularly immigration of foreigners without appropriate entry documents. Moreover, these opponents of immigration believe that the newcomers have inferior cultures and would pollute American society. In 2006, therefore, the House of Representatives passed a bill that provided for the building of 700 miles of new fences between the United States and Mexico and tighter enforcement of laws controlling undocumented immigration. It did not provide for increases in immigration and was opposed to any type of amnesty or legalization for over 11 million undocumented aliens.

When the Senate took up immigration, it passed a different bill. It, too, provided for a larger number of border enforcers as well as increases in inspections of employers suspected of hiring undocumented immigrants. While the two proposals differed in some particulars about bringing undocumented immigration under control, the big difference was over legalization or an amnesty for illegal immigrants. The Senate passed its bill by a vote of 62 to 36, drawing support from both Democrats and Republicans. However, there was no chance that the House would accept the Senate's version.

In 2007 the Senate once again took up immigration and voted on a bill with similar provisions. But there was a new twist. The Senate proposal added a provision about legal immigration. It called for downplaying family unification and replacing much of it with a point system (such as Canada's) giving more spots to those with skills needed in the United States. This addition alarmed many groups who utilized family unification and stirred opposition to the measure and made its passage more difficult.

The big issues were legalization and temporary workers. Heated discussions and intensified lobbying led to the defeat of the Bush-backed proposal. Undocumented immigrants staged large demonstrations, but they were without influence in Congress. Looming over the debates was the Simpson-Rodino Act of 1986. It had given an amnesty to approximately 3 million unauthorized persons, but the provisions outlawing the known employment (employer sanctions) of such persons had become a dead letter. Moreover, outside groups barraged Congress with telegrams and visits. Some senators claimed that the tone of some of their emails, telegrams, and letters were nasty and racist, especially about Hispanics. As one Wisconsin resident put it, "If I come from Mexico, I can jump the fence and get all those American benefits. ... It's outrageous."

The Federation for American Immigration Reform (FAIR) was one group urging opposition. In addition to FAIR was Numbers USA, which orchestrated opposition to the Senate bill. This "grass-root army," which claimed to have 447,000 members, worked intensively against an amnesty of any kind. Some business-oriented senators favored temporary workers and some type of amnesty, but others did not. Some liberal Democrats worried about a temporary workers program. The bracero program of the 1940s and 1950s had few provisions protecting the workers, and some of the ongoing temporary workers programs were not well supervised. In the end the Senate killed the proposal, but a bill with legalization would have never been accepted in the House because too many Congressmen and Congresswomen opposed any legalization program. Several months later a more modest proposal to give undocumented aliens an amnesty if they completed two years of college or service in the military was rejected by the Senate.

Even before the failure of immigration reform, President Bush and Congress had been beefing up the southern border of the United States. From 1990 to 2008 the number of agents stationed in the border patrol had quadrupled. Moreover, additional funds had been made available for new equipment and technology. Then in February 2007 the president requested $13 billion for 2008 immigration affairs, an increase of $3 billion from the year before. In addition to providing for additional border agents, funds were also to be given for internal enforcement to remove undocumented aliens. Members of the border patrol noted that much more supervision was needed to halt the flow of undocumented aliens trying to cross into the United States. However, in 2007 officials also believed that the number of Mexicans trying to enter the United States had declined.

Yet problems remained. Once crossing had been made more difficult in one place, persons determined to get to the United States tried other locations. Central Americans entering who were called "other than Mexicans" (OTM) were placed in detention centers to await a hearing about their status. Because the federal government lacked enough beds, OTMs were often released and given a date for a hearing. Most simply did not show up for the hearing. Cubans had discovered that the 1994 agreement between the United States and Cuba to regularize immigration from Cuba to the United States had made it difficult to reach America directly on their own. As a result, a growing number of Cubans went to Mexico first and then crossed into the United States. Once their feet were placed on American soil they had the right to request refugee status under the terms of the Cuban Adjustment Act of 1966.

There also remained the cars and trucks crossing the border (many under the 1994 North American Free Trade Agreement), which were growing in number and difficult to inspect. Moreover, several hundred thousand persons who lived in Mexico had American green cards or American citizenship and were legally allowed to live in Mexico and cross daily into the United States for employment. Another several million persons held a "border crossing card" (later changed to a laser card) that allowed them to enter the United States and shop and visit for a period of three days. Of course once in the United States they could work without government approval. As a result, tens of thousands of persons crossed into the United States daily and the border guards did not have enough time for close supervision.

If the border remained somewhat porous, there was still the issue of "visa abusers," persons who entered with a legal visa and simply remained when the date of their visit ended. The Immigration and Naturalization Service and the new Immigration and Customs Enforcement estimated that 40 percent of all undocumented persons entered in this manner. If they were working illegally the federal government needed to improve enforcement of that part of the Immigration Reform and Control Act of 1986 that called for employer sanctions. Following the failure of his immigration proposals, President Bush pledged a "crackdown" on unauthorized immigrants. The President said that construction of fences along key crossing areas would be speeded up. He also indicated that additional inspection of those employers suspected of hiring unauthorized immigrants was in the wind. Several businesses were raided by immigration officials, and employees found without appropriate papers were deported. Overall, the number of persons deported from the United States grew in 2006 and 2007. How effective future inspections might be could not be predicted in the summer of 2008.

The debates of 2006 and 2007 were part of a long history of hostility and ambivalence about immigration. Whether it was in the colonial period, when Benjamin Franklin feared that the Germans in Philadelphia might overwhelm those of British heritage, or the late nineteenth century when "blue bloods" of every ethnic background hailed their long-standing status as "real and better Americans," or in our own day when so many believe that "illegal aliens," especially Hispanics, are "invading" our country, a negative attitude toward immigrants has always existed. Alongside this feeling there has always been a desire, as well, to bring in more people to meet the economic needs of an expanding society and/or to demonstrate that America can offer asylum to those fleeing persecution. Such conflicting views have generally caused tensions between and among different Americans. The charges against many of the immigrants include the fallacious beliefs that members of the new groups would not blend well with Americans who were already here. As we have made abundantly clear, when the hostility was bedded in racism, it was especially harsh against Asians, Latin Americans, Africans, and Middle Easterners, whose presence, it was claimed, would overwhelm and pollute American society. In the past some Europeans were also seen as members of different races who were not quite "white." As one Lebanese American observed, "ethnic stereotypes and caricatures corrupt the imagination, narrow our vision and blur reality." These negative impressions, attitudes, and feelings toward foreigners exist among many Americans, and over half of those answering recent polls believe that not only is the United States accepting too many immigrants but that granting a blanket amnesty to more than 11 million undocumented individuals already in this country is wrong.

Despite such attitudes, our Fourth of July speeches have always glorified the immigrants of yesteryear whose hard work and contributions to society have made the United States the great country that it is. President Ronald Reagan, for example, saw immigrants seeking to live among us as people with "a special kind of courage that enabled them to leave their own land, leave their friends and their countrymen, come to this new and strange land," and make better lives for themselves and for the Americans already here.

What does the past tell us about the experience of immigrants? Does it indicate that the charges of immigrants not becoming Americans have validity? A striking factor of American history is that the vast majority of the descendants of European immigrants has blended in with other citizens and over the course of decades has moved up socially and economically in what has generally been a fluid and open society. Such was the experience of the colonial Scots-Irish, Scots, and Germans, among others, and their descendants (with perhaps the exception of the Amish), who have moved into the mainstream. It would be difficult to distinguish them from other Americans because in every succeeding generation fewer members of any ethnic group choose marital partners similar to those that their parents and grandparents had chosen. Thus most European-origin immigrants of the colonial era have descendants whose ethnic heritage does not mirror their own. To be sure, there are scions of old Southern, New England, and other East Coast Americans who still proudly inform others that their forebears hark back to the Revolutionary era (one cannot become a member of the Daughters of the American Revolution unless one can trace an ancestor from eighteenth-century colonial America), but few of them can claim pure-bred ancestry.

Similarly, descendants of members of the major immigrant groups of the nineteenth century, the Germans and the Irish, who settled in every part of our country, are difficult to single out even though aspects of their Old World cultures can still be seen, sometimes only as tourist attractions. Scandinavians, too, have been part of the integration of America, but there are still indications of their heritage in the upper Midwest. Before the 1960s, children and grandchildren of most ethnic groups publicized how quickly they embraced American culture and how they contributed to the development of the United States. Since the revival of ethnicity in the 1970s, however, any number of groups has held annual events to commemorate their ethnic heritage. Octoberfests and St. Patrick's Day celebrations when so many wear green (whether or not they have any Irish ancestors) may be the best known, but there are also Italian, Greek, Polish, and other Old World peoples who recall their heritage in a variety of festivals throughout the year in different parts of the United States. Of the more recent immigrants, in New York City the West Indian parade on Labor Day attracts over one million persons to celebrate Caribbean nations. Many cities have Chinese New Year celebrations in January while in the West, and other places where large numbers of Mexicans live, Cinco de Mayo events overshadow all other ethnic occasions.

To be sure, not all European immigrants and their descendants moved up the socioeconomic ladder quickly or have chosen to honor their heritage with public events. In fact, so many different variables came into play— one's religious and family values, kinship networks, organizational associations, adventuresome spirit, quickness to learn the English language, adaptation to the existing culture, choice of vocation, entrepreneurial skills, area of settlement, existing prejudices and legal restrictions, among other attributes—that to single out any one factor affecting behavior and/or the pace of mobility is risky. But some generalizations may be made. White males have had the greatest opportunities to determine the course of their lives. After the colonial era, as church and state became separate from one another, and property rights for voting were lifted, there were no legal barriers that prevented their movement. Of course during the post-Revolutionary era prejudice against Catholics and Jews was common. After World War II religious bigotry declined significantly. Legal restrictions and economic opportunities affected women more than men, for women's status was often tied to that of their fathers or husbands, while racism in the form of customs and laws established barriers for blacks, Asians, and Hispanics that remained common well into the twentieth century.

Moreover, hard work, entrepreneurial skills, luck, and educational opportunities propelled the pace of mobility for most while the religious beliefs of some groups often retarded it. For Protestants and Jews (and for Asians and Middle Easterners after World War II), who valued education, mobility came more quickly. For Roman Catholics whose prime values included devotion to the Church and whose discretionary funds often went to church coffers rather than toward their children's education, mobility was slower.

There is no way to negate the grim living conditions faced by different waves of immigrants, which also affected their children and often their grandchildren as well. Beginning in the mid-nineteenth century with the arrival of the Irish, generations of urban newcomers, and to a lesser extent those who settled in rural areas, faced harsh realities in a bruising society. By the early 1890s only a minority of all the people in America lived above what today we would call the "poverty line." In urban areas where people worked 10- or 12-hour days (in the Pennsylvania steel industry the schedule was 12 hours on and 12 hours off, with a double shift every other Sunday and a day off every other Sunday), they nonetheless persevered. The price of the crops of farmers was almost totally dependent on weather and international agricultural conditions, so their incomes were often uncertain, but nineteenth-century German and Norwegian agriculturists, in particular, fared better than most.

For example, we can look at the Irish, who, after the Chinese, stood out as the most despised and hated group arriving in the nineteenth century. They had the misfortune of being both poor and Catholic and were rarely received with open arms except when the American economy needed their labor. In many parts of the country individual groups were associated with particular occupations, and it is within these enclaves that mobility often began. Irish saloon owners dominated the pubs in their neighborhoods, and this entrepreneurial activity fit well in the system of American capitalism and politics. Irish men also went into the Church in such large numbers that they controlled the hierarchy throughout the United States well into the twentieth century. Similarly, they exerted strong political influence, dominated the police and fire departments in the largest American cities, and were heavily represented in New York City's powerful Transportation

Workers Union. By the 1930s, for example, the Irish constituted 76 percent of New York's fire department workers, half of the city's police, and an overwhelming majority of the city's transit system workers. Some, but only a few, of the Irish men benefited from their political associations and became contractors and builders. They had been informed ahead of time when and where city governments expected their territories to expand or their transportation systems to move. Such advice from insiders allowed these men to purchase strategically located land ahead of public announcements.

For Irish women, domestic service in well-to-do homes provided them the opportunity to wear clean clothes and have a place to eat and sleep. Because of their circumstances they also saved some money and sent some of it to relatives in Ireland. Later, positions as clerks in telephone and insurance companies, waitresses in some of the nicer middle-class restaurants, and professional opportunities in teaching and nursing also paved their way to a better life.

The Great Depression of the 1930s interrupted economic progress and delayed new opportunities for the Irish and most other ethnic Americans. The onset of World War II once again stimulated economic development while the government's generous GI Bill offered educational opportunities for veterans afterwards. At that point the Irish and others began moving into the middle class and out to the suburbs in large numbers. By 2007, persons of Irish descent worked as executives in banks, insurance companies, and large industries while at the same time they had no difficulty in becoming lawyers, doctors, and engineers. In 1960, as another sign of declining prejudice, John F. Kennedy, an Irish Roman Catholic, was elected president. While most of the Irish never achieved the status of the most famous Irish family in the country, the Kennedys, today they occupy a central place in the middle and upper middle class of our country. Being Catholic is no longer a barrier to mobility, even to the presidency.

Descendants of nineteenth-century German and other European ancestry have also done well, even when cultural shock became dramatic. World War I was a setback to German Americans, who found themselves persecuted and their language decried. Some changed their names (e.g., from Schmidt to Smith), and today while one might identify many people of partial German ancestry by their surnames, in reality, like the colonial Germans, integration with others has occurred, and politicians no longer feel a need to appeal to any German ethnic group when running for office.

There are many other groups of immigrants, including Jews (the rise of the East European Jewish immigrants' children and grandchildren has been characterized as "nothing short of meteoric" by historian Kenneth A. Scherzer), Greeks, and Armenians, whose descendants have done quite well economically. Italians were perhaps slower to head for advanced educations, better jobs, and moves to the suburbs, but increasing numbers of them did so in the 1950s and 1960s.

Non-Europeans were not so fortunate. West Indians, Mexicans, and Asians were regarded as inferiors by their Caucasian neighbors, bullied and attacked more frequently than were those of European ancestry, and even manhandled and manipulated by those who saw themselves as superior to members of these groups, even to people who were born in the United States. Nonetheless, while custom and legislation held Latinos, Asians, and African Americans in low regard, several generations later their status and accomplishments in American society are now far beyond what anyone three or more generations ago would have considered possible.

It is hard to see Africans as immigrants because they were brought to the British colonies, and then to the United States, as slaves. Slavery was a brutal system; while white indentured servants were kept in bondage for only a limited time, Africans who arrived in the 1660s and afterwards were slaves for life. Not until the American Revolution did the northern colonies begin to end slavery, and it took the Civil War to end the institution in the South. Yet within a few years southern whites built a new system of oppression: Jim Crow, which placed blacks in a virtual caste system. When black immigration began again in the twentieth century, the newcomers settled in the north where conditions were somewhat better.

Yet conditions after 1945 radically improved the chances for many new immigrants (if not, then for their children and grandchildren). Many of the new immigrants from Asia needed only equal opportunities, and when given them they succeeded to a much greater degree than did most other Americans. Over one million refugees from South East Asia fled to the United States after 1975. With governmental help and much effort, most of the Vietnamese and/or their children prospered. Many of the first group were well educated and spoke English because they had worked for the United States in Vietnam.

Post–World War II Asian immigrants were better educated than most Americans. Forty-four percent of recent Asian immigrants (compared to 25 percent of the general population) were college graduates, and as a result they entered various scientific and technical industries where their skills reward them with high remuneration. Especially long days of labor also characterized some Asian immigrants. Korean household incomes fell within the range of the middle class because so many of them operated family-run businesses where husbands, wives, and even children labored long hours to improve their lives and status.

The key to much of the Asian success in the United States was not only declining prejudice but also education. Asian children were drilled about its value. As one Vietnamese parent in the United States explained, "My children knew that if they become doctors or become engineers, I share it with them, and our friends and neighbors share it. But if they fail, we all fail!" In 2007 Bobby Jindal became the first Asian of Indian background elected to a governorship (Louisiana). Reflecting on his upbringing as the son of two highly educated Indian immigrants, he said that he was not expected to come home from school with anything "less than 100 on tests." In many communities special private "after school" programs have provided the children of Asians, as well as youngsters of other ethnic groups, with an enriched knowledge of their cultural backgrounds and preparation for college entrance examinations.

Yet there remained the other half of Asians, including Chinese, Cambodians, and Laotians, with little knowledge of English and few skills, who had a difficult time and who often depended on governmental aid. These people did not have much education, knew little English, and could only find poorly paid jobs in the garment shops and restaurants in American cities. Some scholars have suggested that Chinese immigration is bipolar, with the highly educated and well off at the top and the very poor at the bottom, with few in between.

To see how things have changed in the United States, one need only contrast the experiences of the Chinese in the nineteenth century with those in the late twentieth and early 21st centuries. For the most part, Chinese "coolies" first settled in the West and, aside from the American Indians, were the most detested and abused group in the region. They were mocked, harassed, and victimized by attacks. They were the first group of people excluded from the immigration rolls in the nineteenth century and, together with all other Asians, were practically barred from American shores in the 1920s.

With the repeal of the Chinese Exclusion acts in 1943 and with passage of the 1965 immigration act, Chinese and other Asians found new opportunities and millions migrated to America to seek better lives. Whereas in 1960 there were barely a quarter of a million Chinese in this country, that figure increased to 1.6 million in 1990 and over 3 million in our own day. The 2000 census recorded over 12 million Asians in the United States, about 5 percent of the population, the majority of whom are immigrants and their children. The largest Chinese-American community is now in the New York City area although most of them still dwell in the West. In the early 21st century, not only were Chinese immigrants and people of Asian background among the best-educated and highest-paid workers in the United States, but in some places they constituted one of the elite groups in society. Chinese immigrants along with Asian Indians founded 30 percent of the high-tech firms in California's Silicon Valley.

Some have forsaken their religious heritage and have joined evangelical churches. Moreover, in the post-1970 era, more than 30 percent of all the Chinese in the United States marry someone of a non-Asian background, which seems to follow the marital paths of those of European backgrounds.

This pattern is not unique. One half of Japanese Americans marry outside their group. The figure for Koreans is 19 percent. Among Hispanic groups 29 percent of Puerto Ricans, 37 percent of Dominicans, and 63 percent of Cubans chose partners from another group. These figures mask differences among generations. Among first-generation Hispanics in 2000, 8 percent married outside their group, but the figure for the second generation was 32 percent and was 57 percent of the third generation. The same pattern holds true for Asians. Among religious groups, intermarriage is also common, with about half of Jewish Americans marrying non-Jews. Moreover, young adults were more likely to approve of mixed marriages than did their parents and grandparents. Among blacks, marriage to whites is much less common, but here too intermarriage has increased in the last 20 years.

Similarly, like the Chinese, Asian Indians and Filipinos in the United States, and other groups dismissed before World War II as inferior peoples, possess strong family values and a high regard for education. The more than 2 million Asian Indians in this country, 82 percent of whom arrived after 1980, are among the fastest-growing group in the United States today. They constitute a variety of cultures and habits and are mostly Hindu, but some are Islamic, Sikh, or Christian. Over half have degrees beyond college. They speak English, are well paid, and can be found in many white-collar and professional positions. Many of the Indians have chosen science,

education, and medicine as their fields of endeavor. In 2000, census takers found that 20 percent of all physicians practicing in this country were
foreign-born, and Indians alone constituted over 35,000 of them. Similarly,
Filipinos, many of whom have also chosen to work in the medical field, are
highly valued, especially in a society with a shortage of nurses, which seems
to characterize most parts of our country. A unique aspect of Filipino immigration is that often the women came first and after settling sent money
back home to bring over their husbands and children. This, of course, con-
trasted with the experiences of most of the nineteenth- and early twentieth-
century immigrants where the males usually arrived first.

As for black immigrants, the civil rights movement of the 1960s changed
the legal system of oppression just as a growing number of blacks migrated to the United States from Africa and the Caribbean. Clearly the changes
begun in the 1960s altered race relations in America, but it is also appar-
ent that racial equality was by no means achieved by the first decade of the
21st century. New West Indians and Africans, coming from backgrounds
where blacks were in a majority, immediately noticed the role of racism in
American society.

Another indication that immigrants of our era fit in and achieve success
is that because men are successful professionals and/or managers, they
do not constitute a burden on society. One need only look at the status of
some immigrant women. Many Israeli and Iranian women do not choose
to work outside of the home because their families do not need their incomes. However, those who do seek outside employment, mostly professionals, have no difficulty finding well-paying jobs. Russian women also
have several options when they seek employment. One source noted that
occupying highly technical and skilled jobs was "especially true of Soviet
women." Of course many other immigrants, men and women, are gain-
fully employed. In 2005, 84 percent of immigrant males were in the paid
working force, a figure higher than that for the native-born. Immigrants,
both men and women, come to the United States to work and achieve better lives than they could have had in their native countries. Despite one
popular misconception, they are not here to seek welfare. While immigrants comprise 12.5 percent of the population in 2008, they constitute 15
percent of the workforce.

What of the Hispanics, and especially Mexicans, the largest group of
immigrants in recent decades? In 2006 they stood out as the largest minority in 27 states and accounted for about one third of all immigrants

arriving in the late twentieth and early 21st centuries. (In 1900, we recall, Germans were the largest minority in 31 states but were not even ranked as a minority group in 2001.) Most Mexicans have entered the United States with appropriate documents allowing them to reside in this country; but beginning in the late 1990s, a majority of the newcomers came without legal documentation.

Mexicans who arrived before the major civil rights changes of the 1960s were not offered many opportunities. Nonetheless, since the 1960s they have been the recipients of greater assistance from governmental agencies and private foundations to help them succeed in American society. They have now moved into regions and industries that they had not even thought of 40 years ago. New York City and manufacturing establishments in several of the southern states are examples of the places that have attracted them. For example, in Tar Heel, North Carolina, home of the world's largest hog-butchering plant, low-wage Hispanics, mostly Mexicans and Central Americans, labored in brutal and unsafe areas. These conditions no doubt explain the plant's high turnover. After a federal government raid on the plant to remove undocumented Latinos in 2007, many native-born Americans were offered employment. Their labor turnover quickly surpassed that of the immigrants.

Yet there are signs of progress of mobility and assimilation among Hispanics. From 1994 to 2006, for example, the percentage of Hispanic immigrants (Mexicans and others from Central and South America) in production, craft, and repair occupations rose from 11 percent to 25 percent. They have close families (88.6 percent of Mexicans live with relatives compared to 69.5 percent of non-Hispanic whites and 68.3 percent of African Americans), a strong work ethic, and, since the 1990s, a larger number (about 25 percent) of their young adults have started attending college. Whereas 30.7 percent of the Mexicans lived in poverty in 1994, the figure totaled only 20 percent in 2006, a sure sign of new opportunities and economic success. Moreover, with their improved circumstances, about 70 percent of all Hispanics sent a total of $35 billion back to their relatives in the countries from which they came. This indicated not only their devotion to family members but also that they possessed some discretionary funds. Thus to judge all Mexicans and Central Americans only by the numbers of their fellow ethnics standing on street corners waiting to be hired as day laborers is to ignore the experiences of the vast majority who have steady work elsewhere.

The United States has always prided itself on the diversity, and then integration, of its European-origin population. In every era people from different countries have pioneered here, spoken their own languages, fought with one another, got on with one another, but eventually integrated so that ethnic divisions began to diminish as children and grandchildren learned English, acculturated, and ultimately assimilated. By the 1940s there were still strong pockets of ethnic groups in every major city in this country, but after World War II major divisions started to focus on race and class rather than religion and nationality. In 1999, Pyong Gap Min, a professor of sociology at Queens College in New York City, wrote, "color and educational level are the two most significant determinants of socioeconomic status in the United States."

In recent years much lip service has been given to diversity as a positive value. While not all Americans approve of the new diversity, it is happening nonetheless. And in some ways the changes are truly remarkable and highly related to immigration. In 1900, 80 percent of Americans were Protestants, but in 2007 the figure dropped below 50 percent for the first time in American history. And within the major religious groups demographic changes have also occurred. Among Protestants, Korean-language congregations are thriving, while among Catholics approximately 40 percent of the membership is Hispanic. As for the relative decline of Protestants, intermarriage with Jews and Catholics account for some of the change, but Muslims, Hindus, and Buddhists have also become part of the religious mosaic. This trend will continue unless immigration is drastically changed simply because immigration is largely responsible for the changing characteristics of people in the United States.

At the end of World War II, 88 percent of Americans were "white," but in 2007 the figure dropped to 68 percent. Given this decline and the high rates of intermarriage, one can only conclude that the old division of America into different black and white categories (which meant that whites treated blacks as inferior people) is no longer accurate. Somewhat ironically these changes in the American population were made by presidents and members of Congress, who until the 1970s were overwhelmingly white men.

Hispanics are nearly half of the foreign-born and account for much of the change. Yet, as noted, Asians have grown rapidly in the last decades. What are the prospects for assimilation? Because of the global influence of American culture (food, movies, television, fashion, and contact with

American servicemen), foreigners have a much better understanding of what it means to be an American and how Americans are expected to behave in different situations. Moreover, today's immigrants, such as Asian Indians, Jamaicans, and other West Indians and Filipinos, speak English before they arrive. Among the elite, many studied in American colleges and universities before becoming immigrants. In recent years a majority of persons receiving green cards are already in the United States. While many immigrants say they want to return home, and about 20 percent do so, the vast majority remain in the United States.

With all of the technological and educational advances of the twentieth and 21st centuries, both acculturation and assimilation are faster now than they had been in the days when there was much less intermingling of groups and relatively primitive means of mass communication. Immigrants at the turn of the twentieth century usually did not speak English, and had difficulty learning it. Their children became bilingual, and their grandchildren, for the most part, knew only English. This pattern is repeating itself today, but some scholars believe it is taking less than three generations to become fully Anglophone, and there is a shortage of English classes for today's immigrant generation.

One cannot deny, of course, that there are millions of people who find members of different ethnic groups repellent. However, as in the past, immigrant labor is needed. To paraphrase the words of a former U.S. Secretary of Labor, Linda Chavez, if Americans would pick their own fruit, tidy up their own homes and hotel rooms, bus their own dishes when they went out to eat, cut their own lawns, and take care of their own children, we probably would have no need for illegal workers willing to break their backs for tasks and wages which other Americans turn their noses up at. In cities near the southern border of the United States, housework is largely done by Hispanics.

In the past immigrants, both documented and undocumented, contributed to the growth of the American economy and they are still an important part of our workforce today. They constitute about half the labor in farming, fishing, and forestry; one third of the employees in building cleaning and maintenance; a quarter of construction workers; and one out of every five health care workers. Immigrants running small businesses often employ other people, and they provide services for their communities. But even those workers are not enough. American employers cannot fill all of their job openings. There is also a real need for legal and highly skilled newcomers. Our country cannot compete in the world's economy without importing some of the most talented scientific and technological individuals from other nations

Thomas Donohue, president and chief executive officer of the U.S. Chamber of Commerce, told an audience hosted by the Arizona Chamber of Commerce and Industry in October 2007 that this nation needs a rational immigration policy that will bring more and better-educated people to our shores. Immigrant labor propels the economy, he pointedly told his listeners. "A fundamental purpose in creating an effective, rational, and national immigration system," he continued, "should not be to stop the flow of immigrants to our country but rather to expand it because we're going to need more and more workers as our economy grows and grows." Moreover, according to the Pew Center for Hispanic Studies, there is no correlation between opportunities available for American workers and the number of new immigrants in any particular area. Donohue favors some way to legalize the undocumented workers and "give them an opportunity to come out of the shadows." For those who favor rounding up unauthorized persons living in the United States and sending them back to where they came from, Donohue responds, "Stop and think what would happen to key industries if we rounded up and sent home 12 million undocumented workers that are in this country today."

In the United States today, knowledgeable politicians, businessmen, and many others recognize the importance of admitting immigrants into the United States. Many who have studied immigration history also know how valuable foreigners (as well as their descendants) have been and how, for the most part, second and third generations of these people blended in with other Americans. It seems that a greater knowledge of economics would enhance all Americans' understanding of why immigrants have been so important to the development of the United States and why more of them are needed for this country to maintain its place in the world.

It is well to remember also that it has only been in the last 65 years that the United States has attempted to end racial, ethnic, and religious prejudice. And that task is not yet completed, as the hostility toward suspected Muslims, including hate crimes, after the bombing of the World Trade Center towers on September 11, 2001, demonstrates. Ethnics are only one of the targeted groups. Others include nontraditional women and gays. Recent debates in Congress also reveal much anger toward Middle Easterners and Mexicans. And of course prejudice against African Americans remains. After a period of desegregation, American public schools are becoming more racially segregated, and most housing remains segregated. In 1995 L. Edward Purcell concluded his study of foreigners in the United States with the words, "it is abundantly clear that immigration has been the lifeblood of the American experience and that no matter what problems arise—usually the same ones over again in slightly different forms—the nation will find ways to channel the energy of immigration into positive pathways for the future." In the process immigrants and their offspring have become Americans, and this has made the United States a more diverse and enriched society, hence a better place for all of us to live.

Bibliographic Essay

The first point of departure for those interested in reading further should be Stephan Thernstrom, ed., *Harvard Encyclopedia of American Ethnic Groups* (Cambridge: Harvard University Press, 1980), which contains entries for over 100 groups. It has been brought up to date in Mary C. Waters and Reed Ueda, eds., with Helen B. Marrow, *The New Americans: A Guide to Immigration Since 1965* (Cambridge: Harvard University Press, 2007). Another very useful book is Elliott Robert Barkan, ed., *A Nation of Peoples: A Sourcebook on America's Multicultural Heritage* (Westport, Conn.: Greenwood, 1999). It includes 27 original essays on different ethnic groups in the United States and reflects the latest scholarship on immigrants.

For general views Maldwyn Allen Jones, *American Immigration* (2d ed.; Chicago: University of Chicago Press, 1990), is good through the nineteenth century. Roger Daniels, *Coming to America* 2d ed.; New York: HarperCollins, 2002), is broader in scope and extremely sympathetic in its treatment of immigrants. Readable and filled with insights is Ronald Takaki, *A Different Mirror: A History of Multicultural America* (Boston: Little Brown, 1993). See also Donna Gabaccia, *Immigration and American Diversity: A Social and Cultural History* (Maiden, Mass.: Blackwell, 2002). A controversial book is Paul Spicard, *Almost All Aliens: Immigration, Race, and Colonialism in American History and Identity* (New York: Routledge, 2007). On urban immigrants, see John Bodnar, *The Transplanted: A History of Immigrants in Urban America* (Bloomington: Indiana University Press, 1985); Nancy Foner, *From Ellis Island to JFK: New York's Two Great Waves of Immigration* (New Haven: Yale University Press, 2000); and for the West, see the rich account in Elliott Robert Barkan, *From All Points: America's Immigrant West, 1870s to 1952* (Bloomington: Indiana University Press, 2007).

Several books with a social science approach are Reed Ueda, ed., *A Companion to American Immigration* (Maiden, Mass: Blackwell, 2006); Frank Bean and Gillian Stevens, *America's Newcomers and the Dynamics of Diversity* (New York: Russell Sage, 2003); Richard Alba and Victor Nee, *Remaking the American Mainstream: Assimilation and Contemporary Immigration* (Cambridge: Harvard University Press, 2003); and Alejandro Portes and Ruben G. Rumbaut, *Immigrant America: A Portrait* (3d ed., Berkeley: University of California Press, 2006). The literature on immigrant women has flourished in recent years, but the reader should begin with Donna Gabaccia, *From the Other Side: Women, Gender, and Immigrant Life in the United States* (Bloomington: Indiana University Press, 1994); and Evelyn Nakano Glenn, *Unequal Freedom: How Race and Gender Shaped American Citizenship and Labor* (Cambridge: Harvard University Press, 2002). Other treatments are indicated under the topics for various immigrant groups.

For the colonial era the reader might start with Bernard Bailyn's *Voyages to the West* (New York: Knopf, 1986). Another rich account of the British migration is David Fischer, *Albion's Seed: Four British Folkways in America* (New York: Oxford University Press, 1989). For the Scots-Irish see Patrick Griffen, *The People with No Name: Ireland's Ulster Scots, America's Scots Irish and the Creation of a British Atlantic World, 1689–1764* (Princeton: Princeton University Press, 2001). For the Scots, see Ray Celeste, *Highland Heritage: Scottish Americans in the American South* (Chapel Hill: University of North Carolina Press, 2001).

For colonial Germans see Aaron Spencer Fogelman, *Hopeful Journeys: German Immigration: Settlement and Political Culture in Colonial America, 1717–1775* (Philadelphia: University of Pennsylvania Press, 1996); Marianne S. Wokeck, *Trade in Strangers: The Beginnings of Mass Migration to North America* (University Park: Pennsylvania State University Press, 1999); and Steven M. Holt, *Foreigners in Their Own Land: Pennsylvania Germans in the Early Republic* (University Park: Pennsylvania State University Press, 2002). For the early Dutch, consult Jaap Jacobs, *New Netherlands: A Dutch Colony in Seventeenth-Century America* (Leiden: Brill, 2005). For the Acadians, see John Mack Faragher, *A Great and Nobel Scheme: The Tragic Expulsion of the French Acadians from Their American Homeland* (New York: Norton, 2005). On slavery read Ira Berlin, *Many Thousands Gone: The First Two Centuries of Slavery in North America* (Cambridge: Harvard University Press,

1998); and David Brion Davis, *Inhuman Bondage: The Rise and Fall of Slavery in the New World* (New York: Oxford University Press, 2006).

Additional information for the Germans after 1789 can be found in Russell A. Kazal, *Becoming Old Stock: The Paradox of German-American Identity* (Princeton: Princeton University Press, 2004); Peter Conolly-Smith, *Translating America: An Immigrant Press Visualizes American Popular Culture, 1855–1918* (Washington, D.C.: Smithsonian Books, 2004); and Thomas Jaehn, *Germans in the Southwest, 1850–1920* (Albuquerque: University of New Mexico Press, 2005). See also Stanley Nadel, *Little Germany: Ethnicity, Religion, and Class in New York City* (Urbana: University of Illinois Press, 1994); Dorothee Schneider, *Trade Unions and Community: The German Working Class in New York City* (Urbana: University of Illinois Press, 1992); and Kathleen Neils Conzen, *Immigrant Milwaukee, 1836–1860: Accommodation and Community in a Frontier City* (Cambridge: Harvard University Press, 1976). For German women see Linda S. Pickle, *Contented Among Strangers: Rural German-Speaking Women and Their Families in the Nineteenth-Century Midwest* (Urbana: University of Illinois Press, 1996). For the crisis of German Americans during World War I, Frederick Luebke's *Bonds of Loyalty: German Americans and World War I* (De Kalb: Northern Illinois University Press, 1974) is still the best book.

An excellent collection of essays on the Irish is J. J. Lee and Marion R. Casey, eds., *Making the Irish American: History and Heritage of the Irish in the United States* (New York: New York University Press, 2006). An overview is Kevin Kenny, *The American Irish* (New York: Longman, 2000). Two other outstanding books on the Irish in America are Kerby A. Miller, *Emigrants and Exiles: Ireland and the Irish Exodus to North America* (New York: Oxford University Press, 1985); and Hasia Diner, *Erin's Daughters in America* (Baltimore: Johns Hopkins University Press, 1981). A good local study of Irish immigrants is David M. Emmons, *The Butte Irish: Class and Ethnicity in an American Mining Town, 1875–1925* (Urbana: University of Illinois Press, 1989). For New York see Mary C. Kelly, *The Shamrock and the Lily: The New York Irish and the Creation of a Transatlantic Identity, 1845–1921* (New York: Lang, 2005); and for post-1945 see Linda Dowling Almeida, *Irish Immigrants in New York City, 1945–1995* (Bloomington: Indiana University Press, 2001).

For Norwegians see Theodore Blegen, *Norwegian Migration to America* (Northfield, Minn.: Norwegian American History Association, 1940); and Jon Gjerde, *From Peasants to Farmers: The Migration from Balestrand, Norway, to the Upper Middle West* (Cambridge: Cambridge University Press, 1985). Gerjde has written another fine book, *The Minds of the West: Ethnocultural Evolution in the*

Rural Middle West, 1830–1917 (Chapel Hill: University of North Carolina Press, 1997). For a book on urban Norwegians see Odd S. Lovoll, *A Century of Urban Life: The Norwegians in Chicago Before 1998* (Urbana: University of Illinois Press and The Norwegian American Historical Society, 1998). David Mauk, *The Colony That Rose from the Sea* (Urbana: University of Illinois Press and the Norwegian American Historical Society, 1997), deals with Norwegians in Brooklyn, New York. For Swedes see Robert C. Ostergren, *A Community Transplanted: The Trans-Atlantic Experience of a Swedish Immigrant Settlement in the Upper Middle West, 1835–1915* (Madison: University of Wisconsin Press, 1988).

Since the 1960s Italians have benefited from renewed historical interest. Useful is John W. Briggs, *An Italian Passage: Immigrants to Three American Cities, 1890–1930* (New Haven: Yale University Press, 1978). See also Dino Cinel, *From Italy to San Francisco* (Stanford: Stanford University Press, 1982); and Gary R. Mormino and George E. Pozzetta, *The Immigrant World of Ybor City: Italians and Their Neighbors in Tampa* (Urbana: University of Illinois Press, 1987). Virginia Yans McLaughlin, *Family and Community: Italian Immigrants in Buffalo* (Ithaca: Cornell University Press, 1977), pays particular attention to women and family life. For other studies dealing with gender, see Miriam Cohen, *From Workshop to Office: Two Generations of Italian Women in New York City, 1900–1950* (Ithaca: Cornell University Press, 1993); and Dianne C. Vecchio, *Merchants, Midwives, and Laboring Women: Italian Migrants in Urban America* (Urbana: University of Illinois Press, 2006). Other works are Thomas A. Gugilielmo, *White on Arrival: Italians, Race, Color, and Power in Chicago, 1890–1945* (New York: Oxford University Press, 2003); Donna Gabaccia, *Italy's Many Diasporas* (Seattle: University of Washington Press, 2000); and Christopher M. Sterba, *Good Americans: Italian and Jewish Immigrants During the First World War* (New York: Oxford University Press, 2003).

There is an excellent five-volume history of American Jews edited by Henry A. Feingold and published by Johns Hopkins University Press in 1992. The volumes are Eli Faber, *A Time for Planting: The First Migration, 1624–1829*; Hasia Diner, *A Time for Gathering: The Second Migration, 1820–1880*; Gerald Sorin, *A Time for Building: The Third Migration, 1880–1920*; Henry L. Feingold, *A Time for Searching, 1920–1945*; and Edward S. Shapiro, *A Time for Healing: American Jewry Since World War II*. Howard M. Sachar's *A History of the Jews in America* (New York: Knopf, 1992) is a seminal history. For an excellent study of Jews in a small town see Ewa Morawska, *Insecure Prosperity: Small-Town Jews in Industrial America, 1890–1940* (Princeton: Princeton University Press, 1996). For New York City see Daniel Soyer, *Jewish Immigrant Associations and American Identity in New York, 1880–1939* (Cambridge: Harvard University Press, 1997). One history of anti-Semitism is Leonard Dinnerstein, *Antisemitism in America* (New York: Oxford University Press, 1994). For Jewish women see Susan A. Glenn, *Daughters of the Shtetl: Life and Labor in the Immigrant Generation* (Ithaca: Cornell University Press, 1990).

The east central Europeans have found a brilliant historian to analyze their experiences in Johnstown, Pennsylvania; see Eva Morawska, *For Bread with Butter* (Cambridge: Cambridge University Press, 1985). For other books on immigrants from central and eastern Europe, see John Bukowczyk, *And My Children Did Not Know Me: A History of Polish-Americans* (Bloomington: Indiana University Press, 1987); and Dominic A. Pacyga, *Polish Immigrants and Industrial Chicago: Workers on the South Side, 1880–1922* (Columbus: Ohio State University Press, 1991); Helena Lopata, *Polish Americans: Status Competition in an Ethnic Community* (Englewood Cliffs: Prentice Hall, 1976). For Greeks see Theodore Saloutos, *The Greeks in the United States* (Cambridge: Harvard University Press, 1965). Additional works covering eastern Europeans are June Alexander, *The Immigrant Church and Community: Pittsburgh's Slovak Catholics and Lutherans, 1880–1915* (Pittsburgh: University of Pittsburgh Press, 1987), and *Ethnic Pride, American Patriotism: Slovaks and Other New Immigrants in the Interwar Era* (Philadelphia: Temple University Press, 2004); and also John Bodnar's excellent *Immigration and Industrialization: Ethnicity in an American Mill Town, 1870–1940* (Pittsburgh: University of Pittsburgh Press, 1977). For a firsthand look at immigrant steel workers, see Thomas Bell, *Out of This Furnace* (Boston: Little Brown, 1941).

Treatments of other groups include William A. Douglass and John Bilbao, *Amerikanauk: The Basques in the New World* (Reno: University of Nevada Press, 1975); Alix Naff, *Becoming American: The Early Arab Immigrant Experience* (Carbondale: Southern Illinois University Press, 1985); and Gregory Orfalea, *The Arab Americans: A History* (Northampton, Mass: Olive Branch Press, 2005). Muslim women are treated in Shahnz Khan, *Muslim Women: Crafting a North American Identity* (Gainesville: University of Florida Press, 2000). See also Yvonne Yazbeck, Jane I. Smith, and Kathleen Moore, *Muslim Women in America: The Challenge of Islamic Identity Today*. For the Dutch see Robert Swierenga, *Faith and Family: Dutch Immigration and Settlement in the United States* (New York: Holmes and Meier, 2000). For Canadians consult Bruno Ramirez, *Crossing the 49th Parallel: Migration from Canada to the United States, 1900–1930* (Ithaca: Cornell University Press, 2001).

Black immigrants have been receiving increasing attention. For Africans see John A. Arthur, *Invisible Sojourners: African Immigrant Diaspora in the Unit-*

ed States (Westport, Conn.: Praeger, 2000); Paul Stoller, *Money Has No Smell: The Africanization of New York City* (Chicago: Chicago University Press, 2002); and Jon D. Holtzman, *Nuer Journeys, Nuer Lives: Sudanese Refugees in Minnesota* (Boston: Allyn and Bacon, 2000). Black immigrants from the Caribbean are the subject of Mary Waters, *Black Identities: West Indian Immigrant Dreams and American Realities* (Cambridge: Harvard University Press, 1999); Irma Watkins-Owens, *Blood Relations: Caribbean Immigrants and the Harlem Community, 1900–1930* (Bloomington: Indiana University Press, 1996); Winston James, *Holding Aloft the Banner of Ethiopia: Caribbean Radicalism in Early Twentieth-Century America* (London: Verso, 1998); and Philip Kasinitz, *Caribbean New York: Black Immigrants and the Politics of Race* (Ithaca: Cornell University Press, 1992). African immigrants are also the subject of Marilyn Halter, *Between Race and Ethnicity: Cape Verdean American Immigrants, 1860–1965* (Urbana: University of Illinois Press, 1993).

The easiest introduction to Mexican American history is Manuel G. Gonzales, *Mexicanos: A History of Mexicans in the United States* (Bloomington: Indiana University Press, 1999). Important monographs are Abraham Hoffman, *Unwanted Mexican Americans in the Great Depression: Repatriation Pressures, 1929–1939* (Tucson: University of Arizona Press, 1974); Albert Camarillo, *Chicanos in a Changing Society: From Mexican Pueblos to American Barrios in Santa Barbara and Southern California, 1848–1930* (Cambridge: Harvard University Press, 1979); and Juan Ramon Garcia, *Operation Wetback* (Westport, Conn.: Greenwood Press, 1980). Garcia's most recent book is *Mexicans in the Midwest* (Tucson: University of Arizona Press, 1996). Silvia Pedraza-Bailey, *Political and Economic Migrants in America* (Austin: University of Texas Press, 1985), discusses Mexicans and Cubans in the United States. Additional works on Mexicans are George Sanchez, *Becoming Mexican American: Ethnicity, Culture, and Identity in Chicago and Los Angeles, 1900–1945* (New York: Oxford University Press, 1993); Douglas Monroy, *Thrown Among Strangers: The Making of Mexican Culture in Frontier California* (Berkeley: University of California Press, 1991); and David G. Gutierrez, *Walls and Mirrors: Mexican Americans, Mexican Immigrants, and the Politics of Ethnicity* (Berkeley: University of California Press, 1995). Robert Smith deals with New York City in *Mexican New York: Transnational Lives of New Immigrants* (Berkeley: University of California Press, 2006). Two books dealing with the border are Oscar J. Martinez, *Troublesome Border* (Tucson: University of Arizona Press, 2006); and Douglas Massey, Jorge Durand, and Noland J. Malone, *Beyond Smoke and Mirrors: Mexican Immigration in an Era of Economic Integration* (New York: Russell Sage, 2002).

For Mexican American women see Vicki Ruiz, *Cannery Women, Cannery Lives: Mexican American Women, Unionization, and the California Food Processing Industry, 1939–1950* (Albuquerque: University of New Mexico Press, 1987), and *From Out of the Shadows: Mexican Women in Twentieth-Century America* (New York: Oxford University Press, 1997).

For Cubans see Maria Cristina Garcia, *Havana USA: Cuban Exiles and Cuban Americans in South Florida, 1959–1994* (Berkeley: University of California Press, 1996); and Robert Masud-Piloto, *From Welcomed Exiles to Illegal Immigrants: Cuban Migration to the United States, 1959–1995* (Lanham, Md.: Rowman and Littlefield, 1996). Cubans and other Hispanics in Miami are covered in Alejandro Portes and Alex Stepick, *City on the Edge: The Transformation of Miami* (Berkeley: University of California Press, 1993). For Dominicans consult Sherri Grasmuck and Patricia Pessar, *Between Two Islands: Dominican International Migration* (Berkeley: University of California Press, 1991). Another good book is Jesse Hoffnung-Garskof, *A Tale of Two Cities: Santo Domingo and New York After 1950* (Princeton: Princeton University Press, 2008).

For Central Americans see Leon Fink, *The Maya of Morgantown: Work and Community in the Nuevo New South* (Chapel Hill: University of North Carolina Press, 2003); Cecila Menjivar, *Fragmented Ties: Salvadoran Immigrant Networks in America* (Berkeley: University of California Press, 2000); and Nora Hamilton and Norma Stoltz, *Seeking Community in a Global City: Guatemalans and Salvadorans in Los Angeles* (Philadelphia: Temple University Press, 2001). Brazilians are the subject of Maxine L. Margolis, *Little Brazil: An Ethnography of Brazilian Immigrants in New York City* (Princeton: Princeton University Press, 1994). Three books dealing with Latinos generally are David Badillo, *Latinos and the New Immigrant Church* (Baltimore: Johns Hopkins University Press, 2006); Victor Valle and Rodolfo Torres, *Latino Metropolis* (Minneapolis: University of Minnesota Press, 2000); and Arlene Davila, *Latinos Inc: The Marketing and Making of a People* (Berkeley; University of California Press, 2001).

The number of works about Asian Americans has been growing in recent years. The most readable book is Ronald Takaki, *Strangers from a Different Shore: A History of Asian Americans* (Boston: Little, Brown, 1998), but see also Sucheng Chan, *Asian Americans: An Interpretive History* (Boston: Twayne, 1991); and Roger Daniels, *Asian American: Chinese and Japanese in the United States Since 1850* (Seattle: University of Washington Press, 1988).

An overall view of the Chinese is Peter Wrong and Dusanka Miscevic, *Chinese America: A History in the Making* (New York: The New Press, 2005). A penetrating study of a suburban Chinese community is John Horton, *The Politics of Diversity: Immigration, Resistance, and Change in Monterey Park, California* (Philadelphia: Temple University Press, 1995). Urban Chinese are discussed in *Chinatown No More: Taiwan Immigrants in Contemporary New York* (Ithaca: Cornell University Press, 1992). For Chinese laundrymen see Renqui Yu, *To Save China, to Save Ourselves: The Chinese Hand Laundry Alliance of New York* (Philadelphia: Temple University Press, 1993). For undocumented Chinese immigrants, see Peter Kwong, *Forbidden Workers: Illegal Chinese Immigrants and American Labor* (New York: The New Press, 1997).

Newer works covering the exclusion era are Yong Chen, *Chinese San Francisco, 1850–1943* (Stanford: Stanford University Press, 2000); and especially Erika Lee, *At America's Gates: Chinese Immigration During the Exclusion Era, 1882–1943* (Chapel Hill: North Carolina University Press, 2003). See also Scott K. Wong, *Americans First: Chinese Americans and the Second World War* (Cambridge: Harvard University Press, 2005); Madeline Yuan-yin Hsu, *Dreaming of Gold, Dreaming of Home: Transnationalism and Migration Between the United States and China, 1883–1924* (Stanford: Stanford University Press, 2000); and Xialian Zhao, *Remaking Chinese America: Immigration, Family, and Community* (New Brunswick: Rutgers University Press, 2002).

Chinese women are treated in Xiaolan Bao, *Holding Up More Than Half the Sky: Chinese Women Garment Workers in New York City, 1948–1992* (Urbana: Illinois University Press, 2001); Judy Yung, *Unbound Feet: A Social History of Chinese Women in San Francisco* (Berkeley: University of California Press, 1995); and Huping Ling, *Surviving on the Gold Mountain: A History of Chinese American Women and Their Lives* (New York: State University Press of New York, 1998).

For the Japanese see John Model, *The Economics and Politics of Racial Accommodation: The Japanese of Los Angeles* (Urbana: University of Illinois Press, 1977); and Paul Spicard, *Japanese Americans: The Formation and Transformation of an Ethnic Group* (New York: Twayne, 1996). For anti-Japanese sentiment see two books by Roger Daniels, *The Politics of Prejudice* (New York: Atheneum, 1968), and *Prisoners Without Trial: Japanese Americans in World War II* (New York: Hill and Wang, 1993). In addition, consult Tetsuden Kashima, *Judgment Without Trial: Japanese American Imprisonment During World War II* (Seattle: University of Washington Press, 2003). For Japanese women see Nancy Brown Diggs, *Steel Butterflies: Japanese Women and the American Experience* (New York: State University Press of New York, 1998); and Evelyn Glenn, *Issei, Nisei, War Bride: Three Generations of Japanese American Women in Domestic Service* (Philadelphia: Temple University Press, 1986).

The literature for other Asian immigrants has also been growing. For Asian Indians see Mitra S. Kalita, *Suburban Sahibs: Three Immigrant Families and Their Passage from India to America* (New Brunswick: Rutgers University Press, 2003); Madhulika S. Khandelwal, *Becoming American, Being Indian: An Immigrant Community in New York City* (Ithaca: Cornell University Press, 2002); and Joan Jensen, *Passage from India: Asian Indian Immigrants in North America* (New Haven: Yale University Press, 1988). For Koreans see Wayne Patterson, *Ilse: First Generation Korean Immigrants in Hawaii, 1903–1973* (Honolulu: University of Hawaii Press, 2001); Illsoo Kim, *New Urban Immigrants: The Korean Community in New York City* (Princeton: Princeton University Press, 1981); Nancy Abelman and John Lie, *Blue Dreams: Korean Americans and the Los Angeles Riots* (Cambridge: Harvard University Press, 1995); and Kyeyoung Park, *The Korean Dream: Immigrants and Small Business in New York City* (Ithaca: Cornell University Press, 1997). For Filipinos see Juanita Tamayo Lott, *Common Destiny: Filipino Generations* (New York: Rowman and Littlefield, 2006); and Yen Le Espiritu, *Home Bound: Filipino Americans Living across Cultures, Communities, and Countries* (Berkeley: University of California Press, 2003).

For refugees from South Asia, see Paul James Rutledge, *The Vietnamese Experience in America* (Bloomington: Indiana University Press, 1992); and Min Zhou and Carl Bankston, *Growing Up American: How Vietnamese Children Adapt to Life in the United States* (New York: Russell Sage, 1998). For other Indochinese refugees see Sucheng Chan, *Survivors: Cambodian Refugees in the United States* (Urbana: Illinois University Press, 2004); and Nancy D. Donnelly, *Changing Lives of Refugee Hmong Women* (Seattle: University of Washington Press, 1994).

For nativism and immigration John Higham's *Strangers in the Land: Patterns of American Nativism, 1860–1925* (New Brunswick: Rutgers University Press, 1988), is a classic, but the best overall treatment is Aristide R. Zolberg's *A Nation by Design: Immigration Policy in the Fashioning of America* (Cambridge: Harvard University Press, 2006). Another excellent overall view is Daniel J. Tichenor, *Dividing Lines: The Politics of Immigration Control in America* (Princeton: Princeton University Press, 2002). Attitudes about immigrants and disease are covered in Alan Kraut, *Silent Travelers: Germs, Genes, and the "Immigrant Menace"* (New York: Basic Books, 1994). For views of the Irish in the nineteenth century see Dale T. Knobel, *"America for the Americans": The Nativist Movement in the United States* (New York: Twayne, 1996). Also for the early nineteenth century, see Ray A. Billington, *The Protestant Crusade. 1800–1860* (Chicago: Quadrangle Press, 1964). For the early twentieth century see Robert Zeidel, *The Dillingham Commission* (De Kalb: Northern Illinois University Press, 2004); Desmond

King, *Making Americans: Immigration, Race, and the Origins of Diverse Democracy* (Cambridge: Harvard University Press, 2000); Mae M. Ngai, *Impossible Subjects: "Illegal Aliens" and the Making of Modern America* (Princeton: Princeton University Press, 2004). For the field of 'whiteness" see Matthew Frye Jacobson, *Whiteness of a Different Color: European Immigrants and the Alchemy of Race* (Cambridge: Harvard University Press, 1998); David R. Roediger, *Working Toward Whiteness: How America's Immigrants Became White. The Strange Journey from Ellis Island to the Suburbs* (New York: Basic Books, 2005); and Eric L. Goldstein, *The Price of Whiteness: Jews, Race, and American Identity* (Princeton: Princeton University Press, 2006).

For the post-1924 era, see Robert Divine, *American Immigration Policy, 1924– 1952* (New Haven: Yale University Press, 1957), but his analysis of the displaced persons acts is contradicted by Leonard Dinnerstein, *America and the Survivors of the Holocaust: The Evolution of a United States Displaced Persons Policy, 1945– 1950* (New York: Columbia University Press, 1982). See also Gil Loescher and John A. Scanlan, *Calculated Kindness: Refugees and America's Half-Open Door, 1945–Present* (New York: The Free Press, 1986); and David Reimers, *Still the Golden Door: The Third World Comes to America* (2d ed.; New York: Columbia University Press, 1992).

The latest movement to restrict immigration has drawn the attention of scholars. See Philip G. Schrag, *A Well-Founded Fear: The Congressional Battle to Save Political Asylum in America* (New York: Routledge, 2000); Roger Daniels, *Guarding the Golden Door: American Immigration Policy and Immigrants Since 1882* (New York: Hill and Wang, 2003); and Carolyn Wong, *Lobbying for Inclusion: Rights, Politics, and the Making of Immigration Policy* (Stanford: Stanford University Press, 2006).

There are a number of useful sources on the Internet. The Center for Immigration Studies (cis.org) has considerable information about books, articles, reports, and governmental conferences. It also has a huge collection of newspaper sources, but its own reports generally favor substantial reductions in immigration. The Pew Hispanic Center (pewhispanic.org) has information about Hispanics while official government data can be obtained by looking at the Department of Homeland Security's Web page (immigrationstatistics.gov) and the Bureau of the Census (census.gov). Also very useful are the many short reports of the Migration Information Source (migrationinformation.org). For the nineteenth century see the Harvard Collections Program, Immigration to the United States, 1789–1930, at http://ocp.hul.harvard.edu/immigration/.

Immigration by Region and Selected Country of Last Residence, 1820 to 2006

(Continued on next page)

REGION AND COUNTRY OF LAST RESIDENCE	1820 TO 1829	1830 TO 1839	1840 TO 1849	1850 TO 1859	1860 TO 1869	1870 TO 1879	1880 TO 1889	1890 TO 1899
Total	128,502	538,381	1,427,337	2,814,554	2,081,261	2,742,137	5,248,568	3,694,294
Europe	99,272	422,771	1,369,259	2,619,680	1,877,726	2,251,878	4,638,677	3,576,411
Austria-Hungary	—	—	—	—	3,375	60,127	314,787	534,059
Austria	—	—	—	—	2,700	54,529	204,805	268,218
Hungary	—	—	—	—	483	5,598	109,982	203,350
Belgium	28	20	3,996	5,765	5,785	6,991	18,738	19,642
Bulgaria	—	—	—	—	—	—	—	52
Czechoslovakia	—	—	—	—	—	—	—	—
Denmark	173	927	671	3,227	13,553	29,278	85,342	56,671
Finland	—	—	—	—	—	—	—	—
France	7,694	39,330	75,300	81,778	35,938	71,901	48,193	35,616
Germany	5,753	124,726	385,434	976,072	723,734	751,769	1,445,181	579,072
Greece	17	49	17	32	51	209	1,807	12,732
Ireland	51,617	170,672	656,145	1,029,486	427,419	422,264	674,061	405,710
Italy	430	2,225	1,476	8,643	9,853	46,296	267,660	603,761
Netherlands	1,105	1,377	7,624	11,122	8,387	14,267	52,715	29,349
Norway-Sweden	91	1,149	12,389	22,202	82,937	178,823	586,441	334,058
Norway	—	—	—	—	16,068	88,644	185,111	96,810
Sweden	—	—	—	—	24,224	90,179	401,330	237,248
Poland	19	366	105	1,087	1,886	11,016	42,910	107,793
Portugal	177	820	196	1,299	2,083	13,971	15,186	25,874
Romania	—	—	—	—	—	—	5,842	6,808
Russia	86	280	520	423	1,670	35,177	182,698	450,101

REGION AND COUNTRY OF LAST RESIDENCE	1820 TO 1829	1830 TO 1839	1840 TO 1849	1850 TO 1859	1860 TO 1869	1870 TO 1879	1880 TO 1889	1890 TO 1899
Spain	2,595	2,010	1,916	8,795	6,966	5,540	3,995	9,189
Switzerland	3,148	4,430	4,819	24,423	21,124	25,212	81,151	37,020
United Kingdom	26,336	74,350	218,572	445,322	532,956	578,447	810,900	328,759
Yugoslavia	—	—	—	—	—	—	—	—
Other Europe	3	40	79	4	9	590	1,070	145
Asia	34	55	121	36,080	54,408	134,128	71,151	61,285
China	3	8	32	35,933	54,028	133,139	65,797	15,268
HongKong	—	—	—	—	—	—	—	—
India	9	38	33	42	50	166	247	102
Iran	—	—	—	—	—	—	—	—
Israel	—	—	—	—	—	—	—	—
Japan	—	—	—	—	138	193	1,583	13,998
Jordan	—	—	—	—	—	—	—	—
Korea	—	—	—	—	—	—	—	—
Philippines	—	—	—	—	—	—	—	—
Syria	—	—	—	—	—	—	—	—
Taiwan	—	—	—	—	—	—	—	—
Turkey	19	8	45	94	129	382	2,478	27,510
Vietnam	—	—	—	—	—	—	—	—
Other Asia	3	1	11	11	63	248	1,046	4,407
America	9,655	31,905	50,516	84,145	130,292	345,010	524,826	37,350
Canada and Newfoundland	2,297	11,875	34,285	64,171	117,978	324,310	492,865	3,098
Mexico	3,835	7,187	3,069	3,446	1,957	5,133	2,405	734

REGION AND COUNTRY OF LAST RESIDENCE	1820 TO 1829	1830 TO 1839	1840 TO 1849	1850 TO 1859	1860 TO 1869	1870 TO 1879	1880 TO 1889	1890 TO 1899
Mexico	3,835	7,187	3,069	3,446	1,957	5,133	2,405	734
Caribbean	3,061	11,792	11,803	12,447	8,751	14,285	27,323	31,480
Cuba	—	—	—	—	—	—	—	—
Dominican Republic	—	—	—	—	—	—	—	—
Haiti	—	—	—	—	—	—	—	—
Jamaica	—	—	—	—	—	—	—	—
Other Caribbean	3,061	11,792	11,803	12,447	8,751	14,285	27,323	31,480
CentralAmerica	57	94	297	512	70	173	279	649
Belize	—	—	—	—	—	—	—	—
Costa Rica	—	—	—	—	—	—	—	—
El Salvador	—	—	—	—	—	—	—	—
Guatemala	—	—	—	—	—	—	—	—
Honduras	—	—	—	—	—	—	—	—
Nicaragua	—	—	—	—	—	—	—	—
Panama	—	—	—	—	—	—	—	—
Other Central America	57	94	297	512	70	173	279	649
SouthAmerica	405	957	1,062	3,569	1,536	1,109	1,954	1,389
Argentina	—	—	—	—	—	—	—	—
Bolivia	—	—	—	—	—	—	—	—
Brazil	—	—	—	—	—	—	—	—
Chile	—	—	—	—	—	—	—	—
Colombia	—	—	—	—	—	—	—	—
Ecuador	—	—	—	—	—	—	—	—

REGION AND COUNTRY OF LAST RESIDENCE	1820 TO 1829	1830 TO 1839	1840 TO 1849	1850 TO 1859	1860 TO 1869	1870 TO 1879	1880 TO 1889	1890 TO 1899
Guyana	—	—	—	—	—	—	—	—
Paraguay	—	—	—	—	—	—	—	—
Peru	—	—	—	—	—	—	—	—
Suriname	—	—	—	—	—	—	—	—
Uruguay	—	—	—	—	—	—	—	—
Venezuela	—	—	—	—	—	—	—	—
Other South America	405	957	1,062	3,569	1,536	1,109	1,954	1,389
Other America	—	—	—	—	—	—	—	—
Africa	15	50	61	84	407	371	763	432
Egypt	—	—	—	—	4	29	145	51
Ethiopia	—	—	—	—	—	—	—	—
Liberia	1	8	5	7	43	52	21	9
Morocco	—	—	—	—	—	—	—	—
South Africa	—	—	—	—	35	48	23	9
Other Africa	14	42	56	77	325	242	574	363
Oceania	3	7	14	166	187	9,996	12,361	4,704
Australia	2	1	2	15	—	8,930	7,250	3,098
New Zealand	—	—	—	—	—	39	21	12
Other Oceania	1	6	12	151	187	1,027	5,090	1,594
Not Specified	19,523	83,593	7,366	74,399	18,241	754	790	14,112

REGION AND COUNTRY OF LAST RESIDENCE	1900 TO 1909	1910 TO 1919	1920 TO 1929	1930 TO 1939	1940 TO 1949	1950 TO 1959	1960 TO 1969	1970 TO 1979
Total	8,202,388	6,347,380	4,295,510	699,375	856,608	2,499,268	3,213,749	4,248,203
Europe	7,572,569	4,985,411	2,560,340	444,399	472,524	1,404,973	1,133,443	825,590
Austria-Hungary	2,001,376	1,154,727	60,891	12,531	13,574	113,015	27,590	20,387
Austria	532,416	589,174	31,392	5,307	8,393	81,354	17,571	14,239
Hungary	685,567	565,553	29,499	7,224	5,181	31,661	10,019	6,148
Belgium	37,429	32,574	21,511	4,013	12,473	18,885	9,647	5,413
Bulgaria	34,651	27,180	2,824	1,062	449	97	598	1,011
Czechoslovakia	—	—	101,182	17,757	8,475	1,624	2,758	5,654
Denmark	61,227	45,830	34,406	3,470	4,549	10,918	9,797	4,405
Finland	—	—	16,922	2,438	2,230	4,923	4,310	2,829
France	67,735	60,335	54,842	13,761	36,954	50,113	46,975	26,281
Germany	328,722	174,227	386,634	119,107	119,506	576,905	209,616	77,142
Greece	145,402	198,108	60,774	10,599	8,605	45,153	74,173	102,370
Ireland	344,940	166,445	202,854	28,195	15,701	47,189	37,788	11,461
Italy	1,930,475	1,229,916	528,133	85,053	50,509	184,576	200,111	150,031
Netherlands	42,463	46,065	29,397	7,791	13,877	46,703	37,918	10,373
Norway-Sweden	426,981	192,445	170,329	13,452	17,326	44,224	36,150	10,298
Norway	182,542	79,488	70,327	6,901	8,326	22,806	17,371	3,927
Sweden	244,439	112,957	100,002	6,551	9,000	21,418	18,779	6,371
Poland	—	—	223,316	25,555	7,577	6,465	55,742	33,696
Portugal	65,154	82,489	44,829	3,518	6,765	13,928	70,568	104,754
Romania	57,322	13,566	67,810	5,264	1,254	914	2,339	10,774

REGION AND COUNTRY OF LAST RESIDENCE	1900 TO 1909	1910 TO 1919	1920 TO 1929	1930 TO 1939	1940 TO 1949	1950 TO 1959	1960 TO 1969	1970 TO 1979
Russia	1,501,301	1,106,998	61,604	2,463	605	453	2,329	28,132
Spain	24,818	53,262	47,109	3,669	2,774	6,880	40,793	41,718
Switzerland	32,541	22,839	31,772	5,990	9,904	17,577	19,193	8,536
United Kingdom	469,518	371,878	341,552	61,813	131,794	195,709	220,213	133,218
Yugoslavia	—	—	49,215	6,920	2,039	6,966	17,990	31,862
Other Europe	514	6,527	22,434	9,978	5,584	11,756	6,845	5,245
Asia	299,836	269,736	126,740	19,231	34,532	135,844	358,605	1,406,544
China	19,884	20,916	30,648	5,874	16,072	8,836	14,060	17,627
Hong Kong	—	—	—	—	—	13,781	67,047	117,350
India	3,026	3,478	2,076	554	1,692	1,850	18,638	147,997
Iran	—	—	208	198	1,144	3,195	9,059	33,763
Israel	—	—	—	—	98	21,376	30,911	36,306
Japan	139,712	77,125	42,057	2,683	1,557	40,651	40,956	49,392
Jordan	—	—	—	—	—	4,899	9,230	25,541
Korea	—	—	—	—	83	4,845	27,048	241,192
Philippines	—	—	—	391	4,099	17,245	70,660	337,726
Syria	—	—	5,307	2,188	1,179	1,091	2,432	8,086
Taiwan	—	—	—	—	—	721	15,657	83,155
Turkey	127,999	160,717	40,450	1,327	754	2,980	9,464	12,209
Vietnam	—	—	—	—	—	290	2,949	121,716
Other Asia	9,215	7,500	5,994	6,016	7,854	14,084	40,494	174,484
America	277,809	1,070,539	1,591,278	230,319	328,435	921,610	1,674,172	1,904,355
Canada and Newfoundland	123,067	708,715	949,286	162,703	160,911	353,169	433,128	179,267

REGION AND COUNTRY OF LAST RESIDENCE	1900 TO 1909	1910 TO 1919	1920 TO 1929	1930 TO 1939	1940 TO 1949	1950 TO 1959	1960 TO 1969	1970 TO 1979
Mexico	31,188	185,334	498,945	32,709	56,158	273,847	441,824	621,218
Caribbean	100,960	120,860	83,482	18,052	46,194	115,661	427,235	708,850
Cuba	—	—	12,769	10,641	25,976	73,221	202,030	256,497
Dominican Republic	—	—	—	1,026	4,802	10,219	83,552	139,249
Haiti	—	—	—	156	823	3,787	28,992	55,166
Jamaica	—	—	—	—	—	7,397	62,218	130,226
Other Caribbean	100,960	120,860	70,713	6,229	14,593	21,037	50,443	127,712
Central America	7,341	15,692	16,511	6,840	20,135	40,201	98,560	120,374
Belize	77	40	285	193	433	1,133	4,185	6,747
Costa Rica	—	—	—	431	1,965	4,044	17,975	12,405
El Salvador	—	—	—	597	4,885	5,094	14,405	29,428
Guatemala	—	—	—	423	1,303	4,197	14,357	23,837
Honduras	—	—	—	679	1,874	5,320	15,078	15,651
Nicaragua	—	—	—	405	4,393	7,812	10,383	10,911
Panama	—	—	—	1,452	5,282	12,601	22,177	21,395
Other Central America	7,264	15,652	16,226	2,660	—	—	—	—
South America	15,253	39,938	43,025	9,990	19,662	78,418	250,754	273,608
Argentina	—	—	—	1,067	3,108	16,346	49,384	30,303
Bolivia	—	—	—	50	893	2,759	6,205	5,635
Brazil	—	—	4,627	1,468	3,653	11,547	29,238	18,600
Chile	—	—	—	347	1,320	4,669	12,384	15,032
Colombia	—	—	—	1,027	3,454	15,567	68,371	71,265
Ecuador	—	—	—	244	2,207	8,574	34,107	47,464

REGION AND COUNTRY OF LAST RESIDENCE	1900 TO 1909	1910 TO 1919	1920 TO 1929	1930 TO 1939	1940 TO 1949	1950 TO 1959	1960 TO 1969	1970 TO 1979
Guyana	—	—	—	131	596	1,131	4,546	38,278
Paraguay	—	—	—	33	85	576	1,249	1,486
Peru	—	—	—	321	1,273	5,980	19,783	25,311
Suriname	—	—	—	25	130	299	612	714
Uruguay	—	—	—	112	754	1,026	4,089	8,416
Venezuela	—	—	—	1,155	2,182	9,927	20,758	11,007
Other South America	15,253	39,938	38,398	4,010	7	17	28	97
Other America	—	—	29	25	25,375	60,314	22,671	1,038
Africa	6,326	8,867	6,362	2,120	6,720	13,016	23,780	71,408
Egypt	—	—	1,063	781	1,613	1,996	5,581	23,543
Ethiopia	—	—	—	10	28	302	804	2,588
Liberia	—	—	—	35	37	289	841	2,391
Morocco	—	—	—	73	879	2,703	2,880	1,967
SouthAfrica	—	—	—	312	1,022	2,278	4,360	10,002
Other Africa	6,326	8,867	5,299	909	3,141	5,448	9,314	30,917
Oceania	12,355	12,339	9,860	3,306	14,262	11,353	23,630	39,980
Australia	11,191	11,280	8,404	2,260	11,201	8,275	14,986	18,708
New Zealand	—	—	935	790	2,351	1,799	3,775	5,018
Other Oceania	1,164	1,059	521	256	710	1,279	4,869	16,254
Not Specified	33,493	488	930	—	135	12,472	119	326

REGION AND COUNTRY OF LAST RESIDENCE	1980 TO 1989	1990 TO 1999	2000	2001	2002	2003	2004	2005	2006
Total	6,244,379	9,775,398	841,002	1,058,902	1,059,356	703,542	957,883	1,122,373	1,266,264
Europe	668,866	1,348,612	131,920	176,892	177,059	102,546	135,663	180,449	169,197
Austria-Hungary	20,437	27,529	2,009	2,303	4,004	2,176	3,689	4,569	2,991
Austria	15,374	18,234	986	996	2,650	1,160	2,442	3,002	1,301
Hungary	5,063	9,295	1,023	1,307	1,354	1,016	1,247	1,567	1,690
Belgium	7,028	7,077	817	997	834	515	746	1,031	891
Bulgaria	1,124	16,948	4,779	4,273	3,476	3,706	4,042	5,451	4,690
Czechoslovakia	5,678	8,970	1,407	1,911	1,854	1,472	1,871	2,182	2,844
Denmark	4,847	6,189	549	732	651	435	568	714	738
Finland	2,569	3,970	377	497	365	230	346	549	513
France	32,066	35,945	4,063	5,379	4,567	2,926	4,209	5,035	4,945
Germany	85,752	92,207	12,230	21,992	20,977	8,061	10,270	12,864	10,271
Greece	37,729	25,403	5,113	1,941	1,486	900	1,213	1,473	1,544
Ireland	22,210	65,384	1,264	1,531	1,400	1,002	1,518	2,083	2,038
Italy	55,562	75,992	2,652	3,332	2,812	1,890	2,495	3,179	3,406
Netherlands	11,234	13,345	1,455	1,888	2,296	1,321	1,713	2,150	1,928
Norway-Sweden	13,941	17,825	1,967	2,544	2,082	1,516	2,011	2,264	2,111
Norway	3,835	5,211	508	582	460	385	457	472	532
Sweden	10,106	12,614	1,459	1,962	1,622	1,131	1,554	1,792	1,579
Poland	63,483	172,249	9,750	12,308	13,274	11,004	14,048	14,837	16,705
Portugal	42,685	25,497	1,373	1,611	1,301	808	1,062	1,084	1,439
Romania	24,753	48,136	6,506	6,206	4,515	3,305	4,078	6,431	6,753
Russia	33,311	433,427	43,156	54,838	55,370	33,513	41,959	60,395	59,760

REGION AND COUNTRY OF LAST RESIDENCE	1980 TO 1989	1990 TO 1999	2000	2001	2002	2003	2004	2005	2006
Spain	22,783	18,443	1,390	1,875	1,588	1,102	1,453	2,002	2,387
Switzerland	8,316	11,768	1,339	1,786	1,493	862	1,193	1,465	1,199
United Kingdom	153,644	156,182	14,427	20,118	17,940	11,155	16,680	21,956	19,984
Yugoslavia	16,267	57,039	11,960	21,854	28,051	8,270	13,213	19,249	11,066
Other Europe	3,447	29,087	3,337	6,976	6,723	6,377	7,286	9,486	10,994
Asia	2,391,356	2,859,899	254,932	336,112	325,749	235,339	319,025	382,744	411,795
China	170,897	342,058	41,804	50,677	55,901	37,342	50,280	64,921	83,628
Hong Kong	112,132	116,894	7,181	10,282	7,938	5,015	5,421	5,004	4,514
India	231,649	352,528	38,938	65,673	66,644	47,032	65,507	79,140	58,072
Iran	98,141	76,899	6,481	8,003	7,684	4,696	5,898	7,306	9,829
Israel	43,669	41,340	3,871	4,892	4,907	3,686	5,206	6,963	6,667
Japan	44,150	66,582	7,688	10,424	9,106	6,702	8,655	9,929	9,107
Jordan	28,928	42,755	4,476	5,106	4,774	4,008	5,186	5,430	5,512
Korea	322,708	179,770	15,107	19,728	19,917	12,076	19,441	26,002	24,472
Philippines	502,056	534,338	40,465	50,644	48,493	43,133	54,651	57,656	71,134
Syria	14,534	22,906	2,255	3,542	3,350	2,046	2,549	3,350	3,080
Taiwan	119,051	132,647	9,457	12,457	9,932	7,168	9,314	9,389	8,546
Turkey	19,208	38,687	2,702	3,463	3,914	3,318	4,491	6,449	6,433
Vietnam	200,632	275,379	25,159	34,537	32,372	21,227	30,074	30,832	29,705
Other Asia	483,601	637,116	49,348	56,684	50,817	37,890	52,352	70,373	91,096
America	2,695,329	5,137,743	392,461	470,794	477,363	305,936	408,972	432,748	548,848
Canada and Newfoundland	156,313	194,788	21,289	29,991	27,142	16,447	22,439	29,930	23,913
Mexico	1,009,586	2,757,418	171,445	204,032	216,924	114,758	173,711	157,992	170,046

REGION AND COUNTRY OF LAST RESIDENCE	1980 TO 1989	1990 TO 1999	2000	2001	2002	2003	2004	2005	2006
Caribbean	790,109	1,004,687	84,250	96,384	93,914	67,498	82,116	91,378	144,480
Cuba	132,552	159,037	17,897	25,832	27,435	8,685	15,385	20,651	44,248
Dominican Republic	221,552	359,818	17,373	21,139	22,386	26,112	30,063	27,366	37,997
Haiti	121,406	177,446	21,977	22,470	19,151	11,924	13,695	13,496	21,628
Jamaica	193,874	177,143	15,603	15,031	14,507	13,045	13,581	17,775	24,538
Other Caribbean	120,725	131,243	11,400	11,912	10,435	7,732	9,392	12,090	16,069
CentralAmerica	339,376	610,189	60,331	72,504	66,298	53,283	61,253	52,636	74,258
Belize	14,964	12,600	774	982	983	616	888	901	1,263
CostaRica	25,017	17,054	1,390	1,863	1,686	1,322	1,811	2,479	3,459
El Salvador	137,418	273,017	22,301	30,876	30,472	27,854	29,297	20,891	31,259
Guatemala	58,847	126,043	9,861	13,399	15,870	14,195	18,655	16,475	23,687
Honduras	39,071	72,880	5,851	6,546	6,355	4,582	5,339	6,825	8,036
Nicaragua	31,102	80,446	18,258	16,908	9,171	3,503	3,842	3,196	4,035
Panama	32,957	28,149	1,896	1,930	1,761	1,211	1,421	1,869	2,519
Other Central America	—	—	—	—	—	—	—	—	—
South America	399,862	570,624	55,143	67,880	73,082	53,946	69,452	100,811	136,149
Argentina	23,442	30,065	2,472	3,426	3,791	3,193	4,672	6,945	7,239
Bolivia	9,798	18,111	1,744	1,804	1,660	1,365	1,719	2,164	4,000
Brazil	22,944	50,744	6,767	9,391	9,034	6,108	10,247	16,331	17,748
Chile	19,749	18,200	1,660	1,881	1,766	1,255	1,719	2,354	2,727
Colombia	105,494	137,985	14,125	16,234	18,409	14,400	18,055	24,710	42,024
Ecuador	48,015	81,358	7,624	9,654	10,524	7,022	8,366	11,528	17,625
Guyana	85,886	74,407	5,255	7,835	9,492	6,373	5,721	8,772	9,010

REGION AND COUNTRY OF LAST RESIDENCE	1980 TO 1989	1990 TO 1999	2000	2001	2002	2003	2004	2005	2006
Paraguay	3,518	6,082	394	464	413	222	324	523	725
Peru	49,958	110,117	9,361	10,838	11,737	9,169	11,369	15,205	21,300
Suriname	1,357	2,285	281	254	223	175	170	287	341
Uruguay	7,235	6,062	396	516	499	470	750	1,110	1,639
Venezuela	22,405	35,180	5,052	5,576	5,529	4,190	6,335	10,870	11,758
Other South America	61	28	12	7	5	4	5	12	13
OtherAmerica	83	37	3	3	3	4	1	1	2
Africa	141,990	346,416	40,790	50,009	56,002	45,559	62,623	79,701	112,108
Egypt	26,744	44,604	4,323	5,333	6,215	3,928	6,590	10,296	13,163
Ethiopia	12,927	40,097	3,645	4,620	6,308	5,969	7,180	8,380	13,395
Liberia	6,420	13,587	1,225	1,477	1,467	1,081	1,540	1,846	3,736
Morocco	3,471	15,768	3,423	4,752	3,188	2,969	3,910	4,165	4,704
South Africa	15,505	21,964	2,814	4,046	3,685	2,088	3,335	4,425	3,173"
Other Africa	76,923	210,396	25,360	29,781	35,139	29,524	40,068	50,589	73,937
Oceania	41,432	56,800	5,928	7,201	6,495	5,076	6,954	7,432	8,001
Australia	16,901	24,288	2,694	3,714	3,420	2,488	3,397	4,090	3,770
New Zealand	6,129	8,600	1,080	1,347	1,364	1,030	1,420	1,457	1,344
Other Oceania	18,402	23,912	2,154	2,140	1,711	1,558	2,137	1,885	2,887
Not Specified	305,406	25,928	14,971	17,894	16,688	9,086	24,646	39,299	16,315

Provisions of the Major United States Immigration Laws and Programs

1819	The federal government requires numeration of immigrants.
1864	Congress passes a law facilitating the importation of contract laborers.
1875	Congress passes the first federal restriction of immigration, prohibiting the importation of prostitutes and alien convicts.
1882	The Chinese Exclusion Act curbs the immigration of the Chinese.
1882	Congress excludes convicts, lunatics, idiots, and people likely to become public charges, and places a head tax on immigrants.
1885	The contract labor laws end.
1891	The federal government assumes the supervision of immigration and the next year opens Ellis Island.
1903	Congress expands the list of excluded immigrants to include polygamists, anarchists, and other radicals.
1907	Congress raises the head tax on immigrants and adds to the excluded list people with physical or mental defects that might affect their ability to earn a living, those with tuberculosis, and children unaccompanied by their parents.
1907	The United States and Japan make the Gentlemen's Agreement restricting immigration from Japan.
1917	Congress codifies previously excluded classes and includes a literacy test banning those over sixteen who cannot read some language. People escaping from religious persecution are exempt from the literacy test. The law also bans virtually all immigration from Asia.

1921	Congress sets a limit on European immigration of approximately 358,000. National quotas are instituted and based on a formula allowing each nation 3 percent of the foreign-born population of that nationality who lived here in 1910.
1924	Congress enacts the Johnson-Reed Act, setting the annual quota of each nationality at 2 percent of the number of foreign-born of that nationality resident in the United States according to the 1890 census. This quota is replaced in 1927 with the national origins provision, basing each nationality's quota on its proportion of the population according to the 1920 census. Proportions are based on a figure of 153,714 annually from Europe.
1924	The Oriental Exclusion Act bans immigration from Asia.
1930	President Herbert Hoover directs consuls to enforce strictly the provisions of the immigration acts barring "those likely to become a public charge."
1942	The United States and Mexico agree to the bracero program permitting temporary foreign laborers to work in the United States.
1943	Congress repeals the ban on Chinese immigration.
1945	Congress passes the War Brides Act facilitating the entry of alien wives, husbands, and children of members of the U.S. armed forces.
1948	Congress enacts the Displaced Persons Act allowing the entrance of 205,000 displaced persons in addition to those admitted under the annual quotas.
1950	Congress amends the Displaced Persons Act and adds to the numbers that may be admitted under its provisions.
1952	Congress passes the McCarran-Walter Immigration and Naturalization Act, which —eliminates race as a bar to immigration and naturalization; —reaffirms the national origins system but gives every nation a quota; —provides for a more thorough screening of immigrants; —establishes preferences for those with relatives in America or those with skills.
1953	Congress enacts the Refugee Relief Act authorizing the admission of special nonquota refugees.
1957	Congress passes the Refugee Escape Act liberalizing the McCarran-Walter Act and allowing more nonquota immigrants to enter.
1960	Congress passes the World Refugee Year Law permitting the entrance of additional refugees.
1962	Congress enacts the Migration and Refugee Assistance Act facilitating the admission of refugees.
1964	The United States and Mexico terminate the bracero program.
1965	Congress passes the Immigration Act of 1965, which —abolishes the national origins system;

—establishes a limit of 170,000 from outside the Western Hemisphere and a limit of 20,000 from any one country;

—admits immigrants on a first-come, first-qualified basis;

—establishes preferences for close relatives as well as refugees and those with occupational skills needed in the United States;

—places a ceiling of 120,000 on immigration from the Western Hemisphere.

1976 Congress extends the 20,000 limit per country to the Western Hemisphere and establishes a modified preference system for the hemisphere.

1978 Congress establishes a single worldwide ceiling of 290,000 for the admission of immigrants and a uniform preference system.

1978 Congress creates a Select Commission on Immigration and Refugee Policy to study and evaluate existing immigration policy.

1980 Congress passes the Refugee Act of 1980, which

—increases the total annual immigration to 320,000;

—increases the number of refugees from 17,400 to 50,000 annually;

—defines "refugee" to include people from any part of the world, not just the Middle East or communist countries;

—creates the office of U.S. Coordinator for Refugee Affairs.

1986 Congress passes the Immigration Reform and Control Act, which

—prohibits employers from knowingly employing undocumented aliens;

—grants an amnesty to those who came illegally to the United States before 1982 and makes it possible for them to become resident aliens and U.S. citizens;

—provides for the admission of temporary farm workers.

1990 Congress passes the Immigration Act of 1990, which

—increases immigration (excluding refugees) to 700,000 until 1995 when it becomes 675,000. The limit can be exceeded;

—increases employment visas to 140,000 from 54,000;

—creates a new category for "diversity visas." Beginning in 1995 it provides for 55,000 visas annually.

1992 Congress passes the Chinese Student Protection Act, which permits Chinese students in the United States from June 1989 to April 1990 to adjust their status to become immigrants.

1996 Congress passes a new welfare law that limits some federal benefits for immigrants.

1996 Congress passes the Illegal Immigration Reform and Immigrant Responsibility Act, which

—authorizes new border fences and increases size of INS;

—tightens restrictions on illegal immigrants to make it easier to deport them;

—tightens procedures for asylum seekers;

—institutes pilot programs for verification of immigration status for those seeking employment;

—makes sponsors of new immigrants more responsible for their welfare.

1997   Congress passes the Nicaraguan Adjustment and Central American Relief Act. Grants an amnesty to some Central Americans

2001   USA Patriot Act. Tightens rules for entrance to the United States, especially for males from the Middle East.

2003   Reorganization of the Immigration and Naturalization Service (and other agencies) into the Department of Homeland Security. Border enforcement now under Immigration and Customs Enforcement (ICE).

2002–2007   Increased funding for ICE and border agents

2005   National Guard sent to Mexican-American border for aiding ICE to halt the flow of undocumented aliens.

2007   Increased enforcement of Employers' Sanctions enacted in 1986

Sources: Edward P. Hutchinson, *Legislative History of American Immigration Policy, 1798–1965* (Philadelphia: University of Pennsylvania Press, 1981); U.S. Congress, Senate Committee on the Judiciary, *U.S. Immigration Law and Policy, 1952–1979*, report prepared by the Congressional Research Service, 96th Congress, 1st sess.; *Congressional Quarterly* (1980, 1986); annual reports of INS for 1990–2001; and Office of Immigration Statistics, 2002–2006.

Index